How to Tune and Modify
Motorcycle Engine
Management Systems

By Tracy Martin

Dedication

To Leslie and Tristan for all their help and support.

ISBN-13: 978-0-7603-4073-8

Editor: Steve Curnow and Darwin Holmstrom
Creative Director: Michele Lanci
Design Manager: Kim Winscher
Layout by: Danielle Smith

Printed in China

10 9 8 7 6 5 4 3 2

Contents

Preface

Hanging out with motorcycle enthusiasts and debating engine upgrades, the subject inevitably turns to adapting fuel systems to match the modifications under contemplation. As enthusiasts, we used to focus on carburetor adjustments and jet kits for this conversation, but electronic controllers have slowly taken over the discussion. This is because electronic fuel injection (EFI) systems now control the air-fuel ratios in virtually all new motorcycle engines.

Early on, there was not much common knowledge in the powersports industry regarding EFI operation, much less how to modify the systems. Many home technicians, and even some professionals, viewed EFI and their mysterious black boxes as just more stuff to go wrong and stuck to working with what they knew best: carburetors. Carburetors and EFI systems are, of course, very different tools used to accomplish the same goal—delivering air-fuel mixtures to engine combustion chambers—but they do share things in common. Because many riders feel more comfortable around carburetor technology, this book will use carburetor operation as a means to explain how EFI operates, noting similarities between modifying the two systems.

Motorcycles have traditionally been behind the electronic fuel-injection technology curve, only in recent years catching up with their automotive counterparts. Nevertheless, the widespread use of EFI systems in motorcycles and many other types of powersports vehicles is now upon us, and understanding this technology—and, especially, how to modify it—will help enthusiasts get more out of their motorcycle do-it-yourself experience.

Here is a little background on how I managed to learn about electronic fuel injection systems and dynamometers. In the early 1980s, I worked as a lab technician at Garrett AirResearch, a large turbocharger manufacturer in southern California. This company was a pioneering innovator in design and construction of turbochargers for the diesel truck and automotive markets. It also had the largest engine dynamometer facility on the West Coast, with 24 dynamometer rooms and cells that housed dynos of all types. I was fortunate enough to see new and developing automotive technology years prior to its incorporation into production vehicles. In this environment, I received my introduction to some of the earliest electronic engine-management systems, their modes of operation, and their teething problems.

My fellow technicians and I performed dynamometer tests on a variety of gasoline and diesel engines at Garrett. Many times, as testing progressed, computer-controlled fuel injection systems would fail and have to be diagnosed and repaired. Since there were no service manuals available (they aren't written for preproduction engines), automotive engineers were the only source of information about how the systems were supposed to work. This is how I started learning about engine-performance and EFI systems.

I have since worked as a consultant for many national corporations, including Sun, Allen, Nissan, and Snap-On Tools, and I have taught a great number of automotive vocational classes, many of which focused on EFI systems. Typically, this instruction occurred in the evening, after technicians had already put in a full day working on cars. Too often, I was faced with a group of students all wishing they were home eating dinner instead of sitting in class listening to me. Keeping them awake, interested, and learning about the intricacies of EFI systems was a challenge, to say the least. Consequently, over the years I gained invaluable experience and developed, out of necessity, innovative ways of imparting information and keeping things moving during class. Many of these techniques have been incorporated into my books.

If all these experiences have taught me anything, it's that the more I know, the more I realize that I don't know much at all. So I'd like to thank some of the people who have helped me write this book, whose knowledge goes far beyond my own:

Dusty Schaller and Nelson Yee of Dynojet Research. Together, they gave me an exclusive look at Dynojet's facilities in Las Vegas and provided much assistance with technical research.

Zipper's Performance Products' Dan Fitzmaurice, Robert Goad, and Rosie Van Schoor. Access to dyno testing at Zipper's, and a look into their ThunderMax controllers, helped make this a better book.

Dobeck Performance's Dallas Fischer, who helped me understand how their controllers interact with stock EFI systems, and Chris Sanders of Battley Cycles, whose knowledge about EFI systems is exceptional. Nathan at Nonlinear Engineering, the company that manufactures the Veypor data logger.

Stephan Thiel of Hexcode, whose GS-911 diagnostic scan tool proved invaluable.

Denis Manning, owner of BUB Enterprises, for information about the first-ever "legal" aftermarket catalyst mufflers.

And four motorcycle dealerships that have helped me with this book, my other books, and numerous motorcycle-magazine articles: Twigg Cycles, Battley Cycles, Bob's BMW, and Harley-Davidson of Frederick.

Additional information about all these companies is listed in the "Sources" section at the back of this book. Thanks to all. Your involvement with this project made this a better book than I could have produced on my own.

And last but by no means least, there is my wife, whose incredible patience, astute editing skills, and sharp-edged advice (*ouch!*) made this a better book. On one of our first dates, she showed up at my door only to find me in a garage full of motorcycles working on my recently acquired 1964 Corvette. She should have taken it as a portent of things to come. Through it all, however, I have always relied on her incredible knowledge of all manner of things in life, her writing and editing skills, her overall genius, her tolerance for my motorcycle interests (including endless treks to motorcycle shows), and her general kickass attitude that always inspires me to reach beyond myself. For all of this and especially for her continuing efforts to pump some life into me and make me funny and accessible to my students and other humans,

I am forever indebted to her. I don't know where I'd be on my own—probably somewhere sucking crankcase oil for life support and wishing I had a wife just like her.

This book will provide the reader with knowledge of how EFI systems and controllers operate. These are electrical systems, so a basic understanding of motorcycle electrical systems will go a long way toward diagnosing and repairing EFI modification problems. My book *Electrical Systems Troubleshooting and Repair*, also published by Motorbooks, is the perfect companion to this book. You can find more information about all my books, and some background about myself, on my website: www.tracyamartin.com. Send me an email me if you want to comment on a book or just to say hello.

—Tracy Martin

Chapter 1
Introduction to Motorcycle Electronic Fuel Injection

This electronic control module (ECU) is from a late-model BMW motorcycle. Government-mandated emission limits have caused motorcycle manufacturers to follow the automotive industry and make the switch from carburetors to electronic fuel-injection systems. Ten years ago, the motorcycle industry was about 20 years behind the automotive EFI technology curve. Today, they are catching up fast and soon will offer virtually the same types of EFI systems as found on current cars and light trucks, including standard onboard diagnostics (OBD) capabilities. *Bob's BMW*

WHAT HAPPENED TO CARBURETORS?

Carburetors have supplied fuel to motorcycle engines since the beginning. Harley-Davidson's first motorcycle used a simple form of carburetor in 1903 and continued to use carburetor technology exclusively on their motorcycles up until 1995—some 92 years later. Other motorcycle manufacturers also used carburetors up until the 1990s. At first glance, one would think that almost a century of use would seem to be a good reason to keep this technology in place, but government standards for emissions have changed considerably in the last 30 years. Thus, motorcycle manufacturers had to change their technology to comply with the times.

In 1974, the Environment Protection Agency (EPA) enacted the first federal emissions requirements for on-highway motorcycles. These were based on emission standards from the state of California, always on the cutting edge of keeping clean the air we breathe. Initially, the EPA wanted to place controls for exhaust and crankcase emissions for some 1978 and 1979 motorcycles and all new motorcycles starting in 1980. Specifically, engine exhaust gases, including hydrocarbons (HC), carbon monoxide (CO), and oxides of nitrogen (NO_x), would be limited. There have never been any federal standards for evaporative emissions (EVAP) from motorcycles, but that was not the case in California, a state that often requires all types of emissions be limited beyond and above federal standards. The 1980 standards finally adopted were more lenient than those that were originally proposed. They remained in effect until 2003, when California opted for a two-tiered approach with new Tier 1 and Tier 2 standards taking effect in 2004 and 2008, respectively.

What were the effects of the 1980 emission standards? For starters, the beginning of the demise of two-stroke powered street (and eventually off-road) motorcycles. While two-stroke engines make more horsepower than an equivalent sized four-stroke design, they don't accomplish this with "clean" combustion. Two-stroke engines use crankcase pressure and reed valves to get air and fuel into the engine. Once the fuel mixture is burned, it is pushed out an exhaust port (basically a hole) by the action of the piston traveling upward inside the cylinder.

Contrasting the two-stroke design with an overhead valve, four-stroke engine, the two-stroke's handling of intake and exhaust cycles is sloppy at best. Four-stroke engines use camshafts to actuate intake and exhaust valves that more precisely meter air-fuel mixtures and exhaust gases. Another problem with two-stroke design is that the crankcase cannot hold engine lubrication oil. In fact, oil for crankshaft and connecting rod lubrication must be injected into the fuel mixture at the intake tract or pre-mixed with the fuel before it goes in the tank. Some of the oil mist for lubrication burns in the combustion process, and enough is pushed out of the exhaust to make it too dirty to meet the 1980 emission standards. The manufacture of two-stroke engines lasted somewhat longer for off-road motorcycles and watercraft, and some models were produced up until 2008.

There is one exception regarding the EPA's purge of two-stroke engines, Evinrude outboard watercraft engines. Carburetors were used on the company's outboards until the late 1990s when they introduced electronic fuel injection (EFI). The early EFI systems did not work well and were replaced with E-TEC EFI systems when Bombardier bought Evinrude in 2003. E-TEC direct injection does not use conventional fuel injectors placed in the intake manifold but instead injects fuel directly into the combustion chamber. These engines use a pinpoint oiling system that directs oil only to the parts that require it. This eliminates the oil-fuel mix that made older two-strokes "dirty" when it came to emissions. The E-TEC technology is 30 to 50 percent cleaner than a modern four-stroke engine. In fact, the design won the EPA's Clean Air Excellence Award in 2004. E-TEC engines

A pair of CV carburetors are shown for a twin-cylinder engine. The black plastic caps on the tops of the carburetors cover the rubber diaphragms that move the jet needles and slides when the throttles are opened. *Twigg Cycles*

The 1971 Suzuki T-500R Titan was originally introduced by Suzuki as the Cobra in 1968. The Titan's two-stroke engine made 47 horsepower at 7,000 rpm and, unlike other two-strokes of the day, had good street manners in that it provided predictable midrange torque. Suzuki manufactured T500 two-stroke models until 1975. Pending federal legislation at the time foretold the demise of street-legal two-stroke engines. *Vintage Japanese Motorcycle Club*

do not require oil changes because there is no crankcase oil. Could the E-TEC EFI technology be applied to a modern two-stroke motorcycle engine? With an outstanding power-to-weight ratio, no valves to adjust, and cleaner exhaust than a four-stroke, it's a question that may be well worth asking.

Another emission system that came about as a result of the 1980 standards is the air injection, or secondary air injection system. On cars, these systems were powered by a belt-driven air pump (aka smog pump). Air injection is achieved on a motorcycle by taking advantage of the negative pressure pulses in the exhaust system when the engine is idling. A reed valve assembly, located near the exhaust port, draws air directly from the air filter. During warm up when the engine is at idle, short negative pressure pulses in the exhaust system draw air through an aspirator valve and into the exhaust stream. This oxygen-rich fresh air helps burn excessive leftover hydrocarbons that remain in the exhaust gases during cold startup.

When catalytic converters were introduced, the function of the air injection system changed slightly. It now operates in basically the same manner, but the extra oxygen assists in raising the temperature of the converter during warm up.

This system is still used on modern motorcycle engines, and one example is Yamaha's AIS (Air Injection System).

Other changes to clean up motorcycle engine exhaust gases include leaner air-fuel mixtures, electronic ignition systems, improvements in engine manufacturing tolerances, and modifications to camshaft profiles, valve timing, and combustion chamber design. While most of these changes caused losses in engine power, not all of them detracted from performance.

In particular, electronic ignition was a significant improvement over the mechanical points-and-condenser ignition systems that have been used since the early 1900s. A more powerful, higher energy spark was required to ignite the lean air-fuel mixtures that emission regulations demanded. Points-type ignition systems could only produce around 20,000 volts, enough energy to jump an external gap of around a quarter of an inch. Early electronic ignition systems could put out 40,000 volts, capable of jumping an air gap of three quarters of an inch. Currently, coil-over-plug ignitions that eliminate the wire from the coil to the spark plug can make upwards of 80,000 volts and can bridge a gap of well over an inch.

Starting in 1980, all street-ridden motorcycles had to vent crankcase fumes and gases into the airbox instead of into the atmosphere. This was accomplished via a positive crankcase venting (PCV) system. Cars and trucks had to have PCV systems in place in 1964, and the new standards of 1980 required motorcycles to do the same. On a motorcycle, the PCV system is simple and consists of a hose from the crankcase to the engine's airbox where the air filter is located. Some of the early PCV systems would contaminate the air filter when the level of crankcase blowby was high. Later systems used various designs of check valves to keep air filters dry. The PCV system is still used today on all street-legal motorcycles.

Prior to 1980, carburetors on motorcycles had adjustable idle mixture screws that were accessible and could be turned in or out to change the idle fuel mixture. A consequence of the 1980 emissions standards, idle mixture screws were blocked off to prevent owners from changing the idle air-fuel ratio. Idle mixture was set at the factory to very lean (more air and less fuel) settings, often not allowing enough fuel into the engine for a smooth idle, or any idle at all. Motorcycle dealers were given a procedure to adjust the idle mixture if a customer complained about poor idle quality. This procedure consisted of removing a steel plug and adjusting the mixture screw out to allow additional fuel into the engine at idle. It didn't take owners long to figure out how to do this adjustment themselves. By drilling a small hole in the plug and using a no. 8 machine screw to pry it out of the carburetor body, the mixture screw could be accessed and adjusted. *Twigg Cycles*

The EVAP, or evaporative emissions system, has been in place on cars and trucks sold in the United States since 1971. While there are no federal standards for motorcycle EVAP systems, California's stricter standards have required them since 1983. Evaporative emissions are created when fuel vapors escape from anywhere within the fuel system. On motorcycles registered in California, fuel vapors that come from the fuel tank are routed though a hose to a canister that contains activated carbon, or charcoal. The vapors are absorbed within the canister. Then, during certain engine operational modes, fresh air is drawn through the canister, pulling the vapor into the engine where it is burned. The EVAP system does not take power from the engine, but it does take up space—a limited commodity on a motorcycle. *Battley Cycles*

Early motorcycle emission controls and designs mirrored those of automobiles and were mostly "add-on" technology. They were crude in design and caused engine-performance problems, motivating many riders to disconnect, bypass, modify, or remove them altogether.

TWO-TIERED FEDERAL EMISSIONS STANDARDS

In late 2003, the EPA announced plans to establish new federal requirements modeled after those implemented by California. The two-tier plan would be two years behind California's, with Tier 1 beginning in 2006 and Tier 2 taking effect in 2010. Each tier would require a reduction in exhaust pipe emissions and the added technology to make these lower levels possible. With this iteration of emission standards, the difference between California's requirements and those of the rest of the nation were eliminated. No longer did manufacturers have to build two versions of the same make and model of motorcycle—California compliant and 49-State compliant.

The two-tiered standards required new technology to clean up all new motorcycle exhaust emissions, and it came in the form of electronic fuel injection and catalytic converters. Catalytic converters, or CATs, are fitted to an engine's exhaust system to reduce or eliminate HC, CO, and NO_x. Converters have been a requirement for all new cars and light trucks sold in California since 1979. Catalytic converters and electronic fuel injection go hand-in-hand because, to date, EFI is the only fuel delivery technology that allows converters to operate effectively.

It is important to note that California and the EPA do not require the use of either EFI or CAT technologies. They are only interested in the volume of harmful exhaust gases emitting from motorcycle exhaust. Some motorcycle manufacturers were able to meet the first-tier standards without using EFI or catalytic converters. This is not the case anymore, however, because Tier 2 standards require much lower emissions than were previously required for Tier 1. Carburetors disappeared from street legal motorcycles in all 50 states in 2010. There may be a few exceptions for small-displacement bikes, but the vast majority will feature EFI systems and catalytic converters. In addition to motorcycles, other powersports applications, including watercraft, ATVs, scooters, and even lawn tractors, are making the change from carburetors to EFI. With motorcycle fuel delivery systems transitioning from mechanical (carburetors) to digital (EFI), the technology used to modify these fuel systems is changing as well.

In the early 1980s, a man named Mark Dobeck started a company called Dynojet that initially sold technology to modify carburetors. At that time, there was an untapped market of riders who wanted to "fix" their poorly running, emission-compliant bikes, and Dynojet carburetor jet kits were the answer. In the late 1990s, Dynojet started making the transition from manufacturing only carburetor jet kits to producing electronic controllers used to modify the then-newly introduced EFI systems. Today, Dynojet still makes jet kits, but its primary focus is on electronics used to modify EFI systems. Chapter 2, Aftermarket EFI Controllers, has more information on Dynojet's history and details of the company's products.

Modifying carburetors and EFI systems provide similar results regarding engine performance, but each takes a different path to get there. EFI system operation vs. the air-fuel circuits used by a carburetor is somewhat analogous to the difference between a windup watch, with hour and minute hands, and a digital watch. Both tell time, but one operates using gears, springs, and a balance wheel while the other relies on a silicone chip, software, and a battery. Having a better understanding of how to modify motorcycle fuel injection systems starts with how EFI operates. But before addressing EFI theory and concepts, let's quickly review how a carburetor supplies air and fuel for various engine-operating conditions. This will provide the basis for understanding EFI operation and modification.

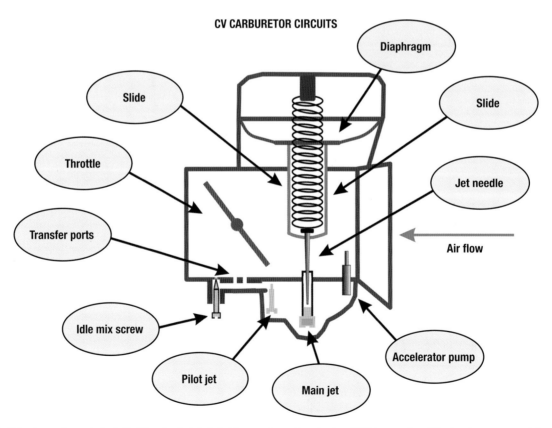

CV CARBURETOR CIRCUITS

FIGURE 1 This cutaway of a constant velocity (CV) carburetor is typical of those used on motorcycles since 1980. In proper tune, CV carburetors can approach the same engine performance regarding fuel delivery as EFI systems.

CARBURETOR OPERATION

To describe how a motorcycle carburetor delivers air and fuel to an engine, we'll use the constant velocity (CV) carburetor as an example because it is the design used on the vast majority of motorcycles manufactured since 1980. A CV carburetor's fuel-delivery system is made up of separate fuel circuits, each with a specific job to perform.

When the engine is cold, a manual choke must be activated. This opens several holes in the carburetor that add extra fuel and air to the engine. The additional fuel provides the engine with the rich air-fuel mixture (more fuel and less air) required for cold starting, and the increased air raises idle speed to keep the engine from stalling. Once the engine is warmed up, the choke is deactivated, closing the choke circuit.

At idle, and at initial throttle opening, the idle mixture and transfer port circuits provide fuel to match the airflow for these operating conditions. As the throttle continues to open, and airflow increases into the engine, a rubber diaphragm starts to move a slide and jet needle upward. The jet needle is tapered, so as it is raised more fuel is added to the air stream going into the engine. The fuel from the jet needle is controlled by the taper of the needle and the size of the main jet located at the bottom of the float bowl. The jet needle and slide control the air and fuel delivery from one-quarter to about three-quarters throttle. At full throttle, the main jet is the primary fuel control.

If the throttle is opened suddenly, the accelerator-pump circuit squirts fuel directly into the intake manifold. This is necessary because air is 400 times lighter than gasoline, and without the accelerator pump the column of moving air would get to the intake valve and into the cylinder ahead of the fuel, causing a flat spot, and possible backfire, during acceleration. The following figures illustrate basic operation of a CV carburetor.

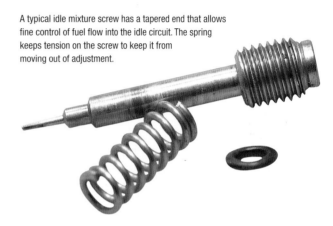

A typical idle mixture screw has a tapered end that allows fine control of fuel flow into the idle circuit. The spring keeps tension on the screw to keep it from moving out of adjustment.

LOW SPEED OPERATION

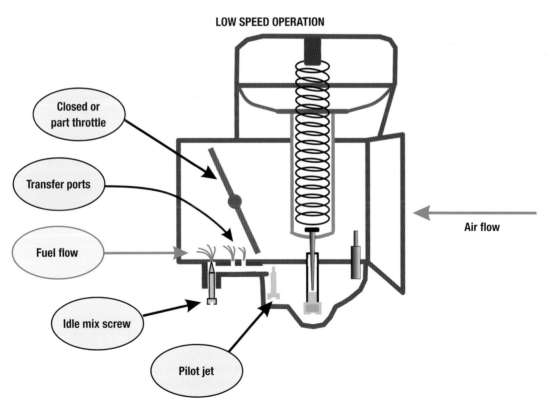

Closed or part throttle

Transfer ports

Fuel flow

Idle mix screw

Pilot jet

Air flow

FIGURE 2 With the throttle closed, fuel is added to the intake manifold via the idle mixture screw. As the throttle plate starts to open, a vacuum is created just above the transfer ports, drawing additional fuel into the air stream. The pilot jet controls the amount of fuel available to the transfer ports.

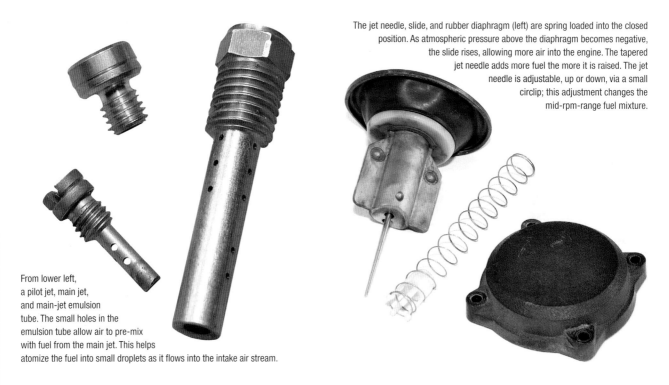

The jet needle, slide, and rubber diaphragm (left) are spring loaded into the closed position. As atmospheric pressure above the diaphragm becomes negative, the slide rises, allowing more air into the engine. The tapered jet needle adds more fuel the more it is raised. The jet needle is adjustable, up or down, via a small circlip; this adjustment changes the mid-rpm-range fuel mixture.

From lower left, a pilot jet, main jet, and main-jet emulsion tube. The small holes in the emulsion tube allow air to pre-mix with fuel from the main jet. This helps atomize the fuel into small droplets as it flows into the intake air stream.

MID-RANGE OPERATION

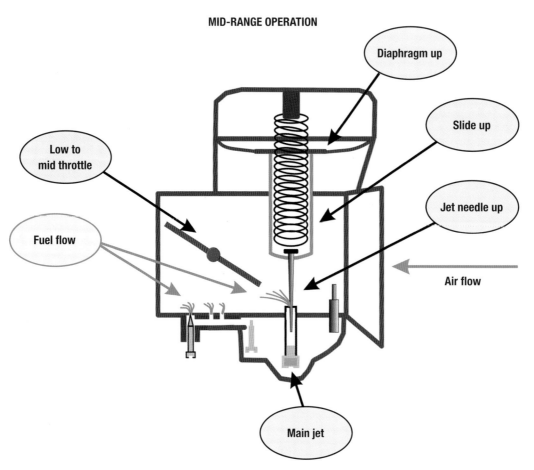

FIGURE 3 At one-quarter to three-quarter throttle opening, air pressure above the diaphragm is less than atmospheric pressure, causing the diaphragm to pull the slide and jet needle upward. This action allows fuel to be drawn out of the main jet and into the incoming air stream. Fuel continues to flow from the idle screw and transfer ports as well.

The slide on the CV carburetor is being pushed up by the screwdriver. The jet needle can be seen between the slide and the lower section of the bore of the carburetor. The slide and jet needle control part-throttle fuel mixture and airflow into the engine. *Twigg Cycles*

Although carburetors have been providing fuel-delivery services for well over a hundred years, and have always worked pretty well, there are some things they just can't handle. A carburetor is basically a hunk of aluminum with a bunch of holes drilled in it. As air pressure within the carburetor changes, fuel and air flow through various holes in the carburetor and into the engine. However, a carburetor is limited in its ability to deal with changes in altitude and engine temperature. Performance issues aside, the real reason carburetors don't have a future with motorcycles is their inability to deal with EPA emission standards. They lack the precise control required for use with catalytic converters. In a word, carburetors are just plain too dumb to continue being able to provide accurate air-fuel mixtures for modern motorcycles. What is needed is a fuel-delivery system with a brain.

FULL THROTTLE OPERATION

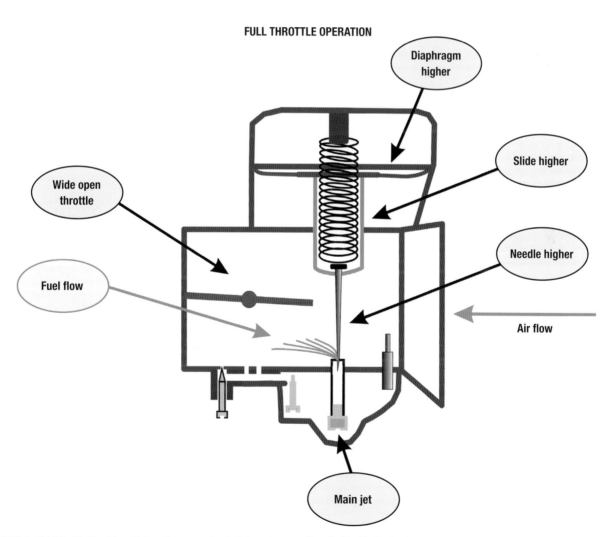

FIGURE 4 At full throttle, the slide and jet needle are moved up to their maximum positions. Fuel is added to the air stream via the main jet. As engine rpm increases, additional airflow pulls more fuel through the main jet. Atmospheric pressure in the float bowl pushes fuel out of the main jet and into the intake manifold. This transfer of fuel from an area of high pressure to an area of lower pressure is caused by a venturi effect that is present in the throttle bore as airflow increases into the engine and is the basic operating principal of all carburetors.

This 2005 Yamaha FJR1300 EFI system provides better performance, more reliability, cleaner emissions, and better fuel mileage than the carburetors of motorcycles past. The fuel injectors (yellow plastic bodies) are located between the fuel rail and the intake ports. *Twigg Cycles*

BRIEF HISTORY OF EFI

Motorcycle technology as a whole has traditionally lagged behind automotive technology, and fuel-delivery systems are not an exception. Driven by ever-tightening federal emissions standards, the widespread use of electronic control of fuel delivery for cars and trucks began in earnest in the early 1980s, but the trend toward using solid-state electronics began with the replacement of mechanical ignition systems (points and condensers) by electronic ignition modules around 1975.

Mechanical, and even a few electronic, fuel injection systems can be found before this, of course. Bosch manufactured fuel injection systems for use on diesel engines as early as the mid-1920s, and the first practical use of fuel-injected, gasoline-powered engines dates to World War II, providing power for military aircraft. For example, the fuel-injected Wright R-3350, an 18-cylinder radial engine, was used in the B-29 Super-fortress bomber.

One of the first commercial gasoline-powered injection systems for automobiles was developed by Bosch and used on the 1955 Mercedes-Benz 300SL. In 1957, Chevrolet introduced a mechanical fuel injection option, made by General Motors' Rochester, New York, division, for its 283 V-8 engine. The Chevrolet fuel injection system used a crude method to measure airflow into the engine via a spoon-shaped plunger, which moved in proportional response to the amount of air entering the engine. The plunger was connected to a fuel metering system that mechanically injected fuel into the cylinders. One of the earliest electronic fuel injection systems intended for mainstream automotive commercial use was developed by Bendix. Called the Electrojector, it was used on the DeSoto Adventure as early as 1958.

During the 1960s, Hilborn mechanical fuel injection systems were widely used in all types of auto racing, but they were designed to yield maximum horsepower, and consequently had relatively bad manners when it came to the more ubiquitous part-throttle driving conditions typically found on America's expanding road networks and developing freeways. Consequently, Hilborn mechanical fuel injection systems were not typically used on street-driven cars, except for the occasional hot-rod.

This automotive-type vane airflow meter (VAF) uses a mechanical door that is pushed open by air flowing into the engine's intake manifold. These sensors were used in early EFI systems by Kawasaki and Suzuki, but proved unreliable when used on vibrating motorcycle engines.

These early fuel injection systems, whether mechanical or electronic, never gained popularity because they were difficult to manufacture, hard to maintain, and did not provide any real benefit to consumers over carburetors. Consequently, American auto manufacturers stuck with the good old carburetor. Then the Environmental Protection Act came along and, by the mid-1980s, the auto manufacturers had started producing EFI systems in large numbers. Carburetors were, for the most part, phased out by 1990. The same evolution occurred in the motorcycle industry, but it started about 20 years after the first automotive EFI applications. The following manufacturers pioneered the use of the EFI system. We will take a quick look at these early attempts at EFI fuel control.

KAWASAKI

Kawasaki was the first manufacturer to make a real commitment to producing EFI systems for motorcycles. The KZ1000, in addition to being featured in the film *Mad Max* and the TV show *CHiPs*, was fitted with fuel injection in 1980, making it the first production bike to be so equipped.

In 1981, the Kawasaki GPz1100 made around 109 horsepower; it too used EFI, although the system was based on automotive designs of the day. It used a mechanical/electric vane airflow (VAF) sensor that had a flapper door that opened based on airflow into the engine. Performance and reliability issues caused most GPz1100 owners to remove the EFI system and replace it with 34-millimeter Keihin CV carburetors. Owners of the 1957 corvette, equipped with mechanical fuel injection, had done the same some 24 years earlier, replacing their fuel injection systems with Holly carburetors.

Early motorcycle EFI systems were also found on most factory turbocharged engines of the day. The Kawasaki GPz750 fuel-injected turbo made 112 horsepower when released in 1984 and ran the quarter mile in 10.71 seconds. The factory claimed it to be "the fastest production motorcycle in the world." Among enthusiasts, it is widely considered to be the "best" factory turbo produced by any of the Japanese manufacturers.

From 1983 to 1988, the Kawasaki Voyager 1300 featured an inline, six-cylinder, water cooled, electronically fuel-injected engine and had shaft drive instead of a chain—all cutting-edge technologies at the time.

The Suzuki XN85 Turbo was born of the 1980s automotive turbocharger era and, just like its automotive counterparts, the turbo system was overly complex and lacked performance when compared to naturally aspirated engines of slightly larger displacement. *Barber Motorsports Museum*

SUZUKI

A Mikuni-Bosch L-Jetronic injection system was featured on Suzuki's 673cc XN85 Turbo motorcycle, released in 1983. This system used the same type of vane airflow sensor as Kawasaki's, and was based on systems used by Volkswagen and other auto manufacturers at that time. Performance was lackluster, as it only ran the quarter mile in 12.30 seconds at 106 miles per hour, according to a *Motorcyclist* magazine test in 1983.

HONDA

Honda was the first manufacturer to produce a turbocharged motorcycle—the CX500 Turbo in 1982. It was equipped with EFI as well as multiple, redundant fail-safe systems that overly complicated the system.

In 1983 the bike was upsized to 650cc, and the EFI system was made more compact and less complex. In fact, the fuel injection used on the 1983 model is the basis for Honda's PGM-FI fuel injection system, which is still in use today. However, the turbo application for this motorcycle suffered from excessive turbo lag, as the engine made the transition from no boost (turbocharger spinning too slowly to have any effect) to on boost (turbocharger spooled up enough to pressurize the engine and make additional power) quite abruptly. This light-switch throttle characteristic was not especially safe when riding through turns. Because of the EFI system's complexity and the turbo lag, the CX650 only saw one year of production.

BMW

BMW's K100 was introduced in 1983 and was unique in that it was an inline four-cylinder that was laid on its side. Bosch L-Jetronic fuel injection was adapted from automotive use for the K100 and was used until the mid-1990s on it and various other models. In 1990, BMW switched to a Bosch Motronic (also originally designed for cars) engine-management system (EMS) that controlled ignition functions as well as fuel delivery. This newer fuel injection system offered better performance and more reliability.

DUCATI

Ducati used its racing experience in the early 1980s to develop its first EFI-equipped production motorcycle: the liquid-cooled, four-valve head, 90-degree V-twin 851. The bike was made available for sale in 1987, with production lasting until 1992.

The 1982 Honda CX500 Turbo was the first factory fuel-injected motorcycle. Honda used technology from its automobile research and development and gave EFI a try on motorcycles. *Courtesy Peter Kroll and the Turbo Motorcycle International Owners Association*

A Harley-Davidson Delphi EFI system's throttle body. The throttle position sensor is located on the lower left, and the idle air controller that regulates idle speed is atop the throttle body. The front- and rear-cylinder injectors are not visible. *Harley-Davidson of Frederick*

Ducati contracted Magneti Marelli to develop the 851's EFI system. Magneti Marelli had previously provided fuel injection systems for Fiat and Ferrari automobiles, and the result was the P7 EFI system. It was a true digital system, completely unlike earlier systems from other motorcycle manufacturers that used analogue designs. In fact, the 851's fuel maps could be modified by plugging a chip into the motherboard of the EFI computer. Thus, Ducati was the first manufacturer to offer alternative fuel-mapping capabilities for motorcycle EFI systems.

TRIUMPH

In 2000, Triumph beat the Japanese to the punch by introducing the first sportbike with EFI—the TT600. Prior to that, the 1997 Triumph Speed Triple had used EFI, but it was considered a naked bike and not a sportbike.

The TT600 used a Sagem MC1000 engine-management system that was quite advanced for its time. The MC1000 featured automatic cold-start compensation and even had self-diagnostic capabilities not seen on other early motorcycle EFI systems. The early Sagem systems were a little rough running, but their fuel maps and engine performance improved over the next several years. These early systems featured an automotive OBDII-style (on-board diagnostics II) data link connector.

YAMAHA

Yamaha introduced its first EFI-equipped sportbike in 2002, the YZF-R1. Its system was a crossover from CV carburetors in that it used a vacuum slide to control airflow into the engine as the throttle was twisted. A lightweight electronic control unit (ECU) used data from various sensors to inject the correct amount of fuel. Based on Yamaha's racing program, the vacuum-controlled intake offered the linear characteristics of a conventional CV carburetor, combined with the stronger low- to mid-range torque levels and improved high-rpm operation associated with fuel injection performance. This hybrid system provided smoother throttle control at low revs, where contemporary EFI designs tended to stumble. One magazine coined the term "carbojectors" to describe it.

HARLEY-DAVIDSON

Harley-Davidson introduced EFI on its Electra Glide touring motorcycles in 1995. Eventually, the Magneti-Marelli system was used on all Harley touring models. It used engine rpm and throttle position to determine engine load. This type of EFI design is called an Alpha-N system.

In 2002, Harley changed to EFI systems manufactured by Delphi. The Delphi EFI system used engine rpm and throttle position sensors, but added one important parameter:

a manifold absolute pressure (MAP) sensor. The MAP sensor uses intake manifold pressure to further determine engine load, and its input makes the Delphi EFI system more accurate in delivering fuel to the engine. It is known as a Speed Density system, where speed is the engine's rpm and density is the intake manifold's pressure (its vacuum level compared to atmospheric pressure).

HOW EFI WORKS

EFI systems do everything carburetors do, and a lot more. In addition to metering fuel and air entering the engine, many EFI systems also control the ignition system, engine idle speed, fuel pump operation, and the "Service Engine Soon" or "Check Engine" warning lamps. Some systems also have self-diagnostics built in and can either flash out trouble codes via the engine warning light or through a scan tool or code reader. An EFI system that controls more than just fuel delivery is often referred to as an engine-management system and is the most common type of design used today.

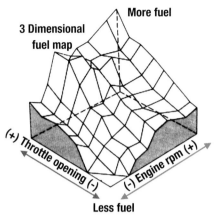

FIGURE 5 This three-dimensional fuel map illustrates how a typical EFI system controls fuel delivery. At the lower left is throttle opening and on the right is engine rpm. As both throttle opening and rpm increase, the amount of fuel delivered by the injectors is increased (top of fuel map) or decreased (bottom of fuel map). The reason the map looks to have mountains and valleys is due to camshaft design, cylinder head flow, piston stroke, and exhaust system design. All of these components factor into how much air flows into, and out of, the engine at any given rpm and throttle opening.

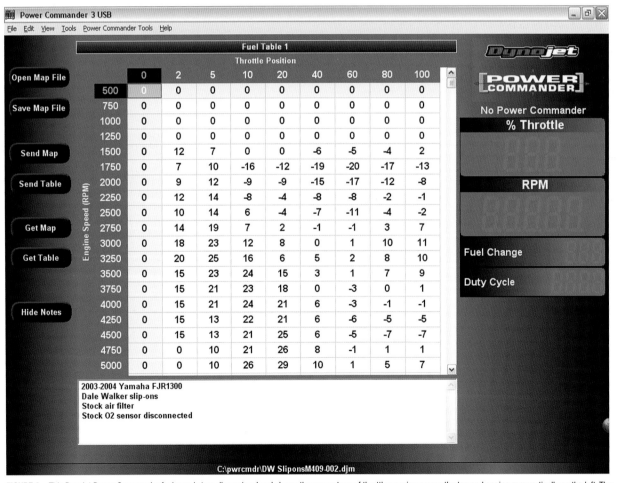

FIGURE 6 This Dynojet Power Commander fuel map is two-dimensional and shows the percentage of throttle opening across the top and engine rpm vertically on the left. The map is divided into cells where a "0" value represents no change from stock fueling. Positive numbers represent an increase and negative numbers are a decrease in fuel delivery at a given rpm and throttle opening. A base map is provided with each Power Commander application, and depending on the motorcycle application, maps are available for specific exhaust systems and other performance components. *Dynojet Research*

Whether an engine is carbureted or fuel-injected, it requires the same basic requirements: the correct amount of air and fuel at a given rpm and an ignition spark at the right time during the compression stroke. The operating concept of electronic fuel injection is simple. The ECU, or electronic control unit, is a small computer that performs two tasks: reading input signals from engine sensors and controlling fuel injector and ignition coil operation.

Typical EFI injectors are shown. They function like a variable main jet in a carburetor in that they have a range of fuel they can deliver based on how long they are turned on by the ECU. If engine size is increased substantially over the stock configuration, the fuel injectors may have to be sized up as well in order to keep up with fuel demand. This is similar to increasing main jet size in a carburetor or even changing the carburetor for units with larger bore sizes when cylinder displacement is increased.

Fuel delivery is controlled by how long the ECU turns on one or more electromechanical valves, commonly called fuel injectors. When the fuel injectors are turned on, they spray fuel into the engine. The amount of "On" time is called injector pulse width, and the longer this is, the greater the amount of fuel delivered to the engine. The ECU calculates the injector pulse width based on data received by the EFI system's sensors. In addition to injector on time, the ECU also calculates when to trigger the ignition coils that in turn produce a spark at the spark plugs.

Instead of going through a long list of sensor inputs and the resulting fuel delivery and ignition spark timing, we'll take a virtual test ride on an EFI-equipped motorcycle to illustrate how EFI systems operate.

TAKING EFI FOR A TEST RIDE

Our virtual EFI-equipped motorcycle uses all the latest digital fuel delivery technology. Not all EFI systems found on motorcycles use all of the sensors discussed in this example, and they differ in their fuel delivery strategies as well, but this hybrid system will illustrate how everything interrelates and operates as a complete engine-management system.

In order for the ECU to control the injectors and ignition timing, it must receive information about engine rpm, engine temperature, altitude, air temperature, and rider demands. This information is passed along to the ECU via the EFI system's sensors.

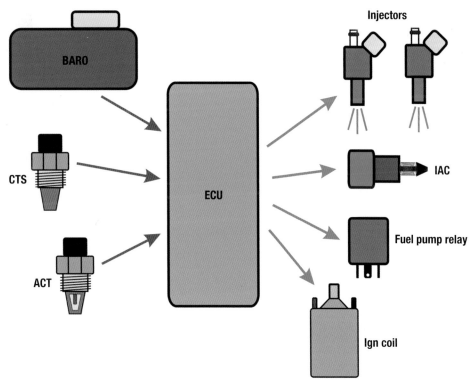

FIGURE 7 Just like a fast idle and choke circuits on a carburetor, coolant or air temperature sensors provide the ECU with input to control the injectors and deliver a rich fuel mixture (extra fuel) for cold starting. The idle air controller (IAC) adds extra air, increasing engine idle speed during cold start-up so the engine won't stall.

The ECU powers up the fuel pump (shown) via the fuel pump relay for about 2 seconds when the ignition is first turned on in order to prime the fuel system. As long as the ECU receives an engine rpm signal, it keeps the fuel pump relay energized. As a safety measure in case of a crash that could cause the engine to shut off, the fuel pump is turned off automatically by the ECU, preventing a possible fire. Fuel pumps on most EFI motorcycles are located in the gas tank. In a few applications, the pump is mounted somewhere on the frame under the tank.

STARTING

Imagine yourself on a fall day sitting on your new motorcycle, which is, naturally, equipped with the latest-greatest EFI system. When the ignition key is turned to the "on" position, the ECU turns on the fuel pump for 2 seconds to prime the fuel injectors. The fuel pump doesn't keep running at this point because the engine has not yet been started.

As soon as the ECU detects an rpm signal, it will keep the pump running. The ECU then checks in with the sensors for engine coolant temperature, oil temperature, air temperature, and barometric pressure. In our example, these sensors report the outside ambient temperature as cool (50 degrees F), and because the bike has been sitting overnight, the engine coolant and oil temperature are also 50 degrees F. Since your imaginary motorcycle was parked near the beach, the barometric pressure (BARO) sensor indicates to the ECU that barometric pressure is at sea level. When you push the start button, the ECU goes into "start" mode. Because the engine temperature is cold, and air pressure is at sea level, the ECU adjusts the injector's initial pulse width, or On time, in accordance with its internal software program to produce a rich fuel mixture for cold starting. The ECU also opens an idle air controller (IAC) that allows extra air to enter the engine, causing a fast idle. This keeps the engine from stalling, until it warms up. These functions take the place of the manual choke lever that your old carbureted bike had.

With the engine running, the ECU receives a signal from the crankshaft and camshaft position sensors. The crankshaft sensor sends an engine rpm signal and the camshaft sensor identifies which cylinder is next in the engine's firing order.

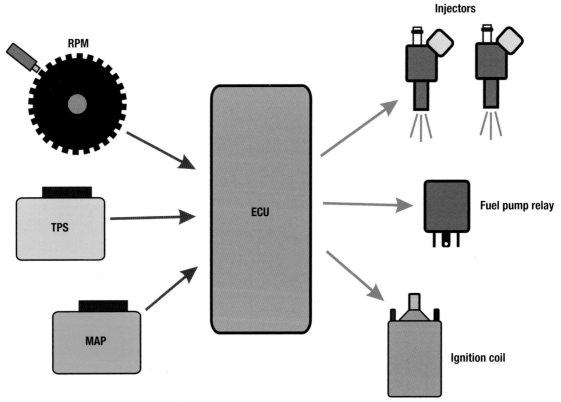

FIGURE 8 On the left are the three basic inputs—engine rpm, throttle position, and manifold pressure (engine load)—that determine both base injector pulse width (On time) and ignition timing. The manifold absolute pressure (MAP) sensor works like an electronic vacuum gauge, in effect telling the ECU how hard the engine is working or how much load is being placed on it. The TPS sensor sends the ECU rider demand information about how fast, and how far, the throttle is being twisted. The ECU's output signals control the fuel injectors, fuel pump relay, and ignition coil operation.

The ECU pulses the injectors (turning them on, then off) to keep the engine running. Fuel injectors atomize the high-pressure fuel stored in the fuel rail. Fuel is further atomized because it is spayed directly onto the back of the hot intake valve. During cold start-up, the ECU pulses all of the injectors every crankshaft revolution to help provide extra fuel for cold startup. Once the engine warms up, however, the injectors will be pulsed in the same sequence as the cylinder firing order—just like the spark plugs. Each injector is switched on just before the intake valve opens for that cylinder. This fuel-delivery strategy is called sequential port fuel injection. Sequential port injection decreases exhaust emissions while increasing horsepower and helps out in the fuel economy department as well.

WARMING UP AND RIDING

As the engine warms up, the fuel mixture must be leaned out, creating a mixture that has less fuel and more air. Based on the engine's coolant or oil temperature, the ECU turns on, or pulses, the injectors shorter amounts of time as the engine warms up. Also, the ECU lowers engine idle speed by signaling the idle air-control valve to close off an air passage in the throttle body.

When you're ready to head out, you pull in the clutch and put the transmission into first gear. As you release the clutch and start to twist the throttle, the ECU immediately changes ignition timing by advancing it. When the throttle is twisted more, the ECU checks several sensor inputs to determine injector pulse width and ignition timing. These include the throttle position sensor (TPS), manifold absolute pressure sensor (MAP), and crankshaft speed sensor.

This Harley-Davidson crank sensor (left) and camshaft sensor (right) provide the ECU with engine speed and cylinder identification information. The cam sensor is used for sequencing the firing or operation of the fuel injectors, as it identifies which cylinder is approaching top dead center on its compression stroke. This allows the ECU to pulse only that injector just before the intake valve opens for that cylinder. *Harley-Davidson of Frederick*

This throttle position sensor (TPS) monitors rider demand on a Honda 599. Notice that the sensor is adjustable, as illustrated by the slotted mounting holes. The mounting screws are a tamper-proof design and require a special tool to turn them. This is the factory's effort to keep owners from making unauthorized TPS adjustments. *Twigg Cycles*

The TPS senses how far and how fast the throttle is being opened by the rider. The MAP sensor measures engine vacuum, an indication of engine load or how hard the engine is working. The MAP sensor functions like an electronic vacuum gauge and measures intake manifold vacuum. The ECU uses TPS and MAP sensor inputs, as well as engine rpm, to determine base injector pulse width and ignition timing parameters.

The ECU does this by consulting its computerized internal dictionary, essentially looking up tables, to calculate all of its outputs. These tables contain information about how long to keep the injectors on for specific operating conditions. For example, if the throttle is opened at a moderate rate, causing engine rpm to increase slowly, the ECU increases the injector On time gradually. If the throttle is twisted rapidly, the ECU momentarily increases injector pulse width to provide an extra "shot" of fuel similar to the function of a CV carburetor's accelerator pump.

NORMAL OPERATING TEMPERATURE

Now you're riding down a country road, the engine is at normal operating temperature, and you're holding the throttle steady. The ECU goes into what is known as "closed-loop" operation. The interaction between ECU, fuel injectors, and oxygen (O_2) sensor is often called a "feedback loop" (it's also commonly referred to as "closed-loop control"). During closed-loop operation, the ECU pulses the injectors to inject specific amounts of fuel to maintain a specific air-fuel ratio. As the air-fuel mixture is burned in the engine's combustion chamber, the resulting exhaust gases travel through the exhaust system, where exhaust-gas oxygen levels are measured by an O_2 sensor. The O_2 sensor sends a signal voltage to the ECU, which then modifies the injector pulse width to maintain a 14.7:1 (14.7 parts of air to one part of fuel) air-fuel ratio. This air-fuel ratio is considered ideal for the catalytic converter to operate and

This OEM narrow-band oxygen sensor has a 12-volt internal heater, powered by the bike's electrical system. The heating element keeps the sensor at around 600 degrees so it operates accurately when the engine is at idle and not producing much exhaust heat.

reduce exhaust emissions. The sequence of "inject, combust, sense, and control" creates a feedback, or closed, loop of information.

You decide to take a side road that leads up into the mountains. In addition to basic fuel delivery, the ECU makes fine adjustments to injector pulse width based on outside air temperature and altitude. As you gain altitude, the barometric pressure sensor (BARO) changes the signal it sends to the ECU. As you ride higher, the surrounding air density decreases (less oxygen), and the ECU "leans out" the air-fuel mixture by decreasing the injectors' On time. This matches fuel delivery to the lower air density found at above sea-level altitudes.

At the same time the ambient outdoor air temperature drops due to the higher altitude. The air charge temperature (ACT) sensor signals the ECU to alter the fuel mixture to accommodate the colder air entering the engine. The fine adjustments caused by the BARO and ACT sensor's input allows the engine to run smoothly with optimum air-fuel ratios regardless of ambient temperature or altitude. Both BARO and ambient air temperature sensor inputs are used for "trim" adjustments by the ECU and have only a small effect on injector pulse width and overall fuel mixture.

In addition to regulating fuel control, the ECU is also continually adjusting ignition timing. Factors such as engine rpm, TPS, and MAP values all contribute to the ECU's decision-making processes regarding either advancing or retarding ignition timing.

For example, if partial throttle opening is used in conjunction with moderate engine rpm, ignition timing will be advanced to promote fuel economy. However, if the throttle is wide open but engine rpm is low, timing will be retarded to prevent engine ping or "knock." As engine speed increases, timing is advanced to its optimum setting for maximum power.

Speaking of knocking, our virtual system also uses a knock sensor that "listens" electronically to the engine to determine if the fuel mixture in any of the engine cylinders is detonating, which causes a pinging or knocking sound. The ECU is able to determine which cylinder is pre-igniting, or knocking, and then retards ignition timing for only that cylinder, thereby preventing damage to pistons during heavy engine loads at low rpm.

After your ride through the mountains, you return to sea level and travel along a country road approaching a quaint little town. A group of kids are crossing the street, so you slow your bike and come to a stop. As you roll off the throttle, the ECU recognizes the TPS signal for a closed throttle. The crank sensor indicates that the engine rpm is also decreasing. These operating conditions cause the ECU to shut off the fuel injectors. This is also known as fuel cut. Cutting off the fuel to the engine as it decelerates reduces exhaust emissions and keeps the exhaust from making a popping sound as many carbureted motorcycles do.

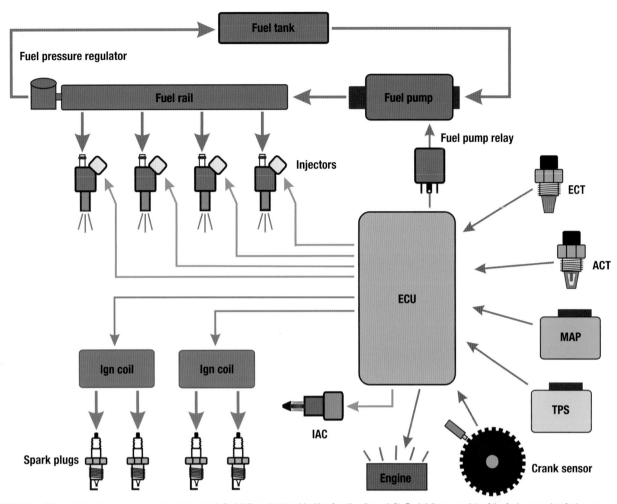

FIGURE 9 This typical engine-management system controls fuel delivery (top) and ignition function (lower left). Fuel delivery consists of the fuel pump relay, fuel pump, fuel rail, fuel pressure regulator and injectors, and the fuel tank. The input sensors are located on the right. The two additional ECU outputs are the idle air controller (IAC) for controlling engine idle speed and the check engine light. The check engine light can flash out trouble codes, warning the rider of a sensor or other system malfunction.

Heading out of town you pull alongside a shiny, new 600cc sportbike waiting at the stoplight. The road in front of you is straight and passes through open fields. As the rider glances over at you and revs his engine, the light turns green and you take off before he can react. You twist the throttle three-quarters open on your 1,300cc, sport-touring motorcycle and accelerate through first gear.

When the throttle is opened suddenly, the TPS signal voltage goes up instantly and the injectors are given a long On time, but only for an instant. This extra squirt of fuel is like that provided by a CV carburetor's accelerator pump. Unlike a carbureted engine, however, with EFI, just the right amount of atomized fuel is injected and is waiting at the intake valves just before they open. When the intake valves open, the cloud of fuel is pushed into the cylinder by the big blast of air coming from the wide-open throttle. This is one reason that EFI engines have better throttle response than carbureted bikes. You reach 60 miles per hour, shift into second gear and open the throttle all the way. The ECU looks at TPS, MAP, and rpm signals to determine the pulse width for its four injectors.

Meanwhile, onboard the sportbike, other technology is at work. Lighter motorcycles (especially 600cc race replicas) are prone to lifting the front wheel into the air when accelerating in lower gears if too much throttle is applied. To keep over-enthusiastic riders from flipping over backwards, the EFI system can limit power delivery to the rear wheel at low speeds in first, second, and even third gear.

As the clutch is let out in first gear, the ECU looks at a signal from the vehicle speed sensor (VSS) attached to the front sprocket cover. By comparing engine rpm to rear-wheel speed, via the rotation of the drive chain's counter sprocket, the ECU can determine if engine speed, throttle opening, and rear wheel speed are in line with what's needed to keep the bike from pulling a major wheelie.

Pictured is a vehicle speed sensor (VSS) on a Kawasaki ZZR 600. The sensor reads magnetic pulses from the countersprocket and sends a signal to the ECU. The ECU uses this input to operate the speedometer and control rear-wheel spin on hard acceleration. *Twigg Cycles*

To limit engine power, two throttle plates are used for each cylinder. Some manufacturers refer to their dual throttle designs as subthrottle valves. The rider operates the primary set of throttles, and a stepper motor, controlled by the ECU, actuates a secondary set of throttle plates. Instead of going round-and-round, a stepper motor rotates in precise steps and is controlled by pulses it receives from the ECU. Two TPS sensors are used to measure both the manually operated throttle and the computer-controlled throttle. The ECU delays the opening of the secondary throttle plates via the stepper motor to limit engine power output. As vehicle speed increases, the stepper motor opens the secondary throttles all the way. In this example, the secondary throttle plates are used to limit engine power output, but their main purpose is to provide the correct amount of air to the engine no matter what the rider does with the throttle opening. This type of system is also used for traction control on some sport motorcycles.

About a mile away, the road starts to climb a low hill, and when you hit 80 miles per hour you start to roll smoothly off the throttle. Still accelerating, the sport bike blasts past you doing more than 120 miles per hour. This is your neighborhood and you know that a state trooper sometimes waits just over the crest of the hill on the hunt for speeders. Sure enough, a few miles down the road you see flashing lights in the distance. You slow to the posted 45 miles per hour speed limit and head for home.

You've finally reached your destination—home. You pull into your driveway and turn off the ignition key. The ECU on your motorcycle goes to "sleep" and remains this way until you start the process over again by turning the key to the on

position. Any malfunctions in the system during your ride were stored in the ECU's memory as a trouble code. If the problem is serious enough, the ECU will turn on the Check Engine light the next time the bike is started.

During our virtual ride, the ECU, its various sensors, fuel injector, and ignition system operation was depicted in real time. In reality, all of this electronic "talking" and decision-making happens much faster than the description suggests.

Sensor inputs to the ECU can be processed at amazing rates of more than one million times per second. However, the rate at which ECU outputs change is much slower, only about 80 times per second. Because a rider can't open the throttle, accelerate, or change gears faster than the EFI system can process information, the operation of the engine-management system is seamless and invisible to the rider. Typically, EFI engines (1) start and run well whether cold or hot, (2) accelerate smoothly at any throttle opening, (3) get good fuel mileage, and (4) have reduced exhaust-gas pollutants when operating with a catalytic converter. As a result, electronically fuel-injected motorcycles offer better overall performance and exhaust gases that are often cleaner than the surrounding air, especially in large cities (can you say "smog"?) during summer months.

EFI VARIATIONS

There are several variations of EFI fuel-delivery strategies, injector locations, and throttle controls. While all these systems perform the basic functions covered earlier in this chapter, it's important to note some of the differences. Each motorcycle manufacturer designs EFI for its products differently, and a service manual is the best reference to discover the differences and details. Even if manufacturer X

One of four injectors on a Yamaha FJR1300. Each injector is sandwiched between the intake runner and a fuel rail. The fuel rail acts like a pressurized fuel storage tank for the injectors. Excess fuel is returned to the fuel tank via the fuel pressure regulator. *Twigg Cycles*

has essentially the same EFI system as manufacturer Y, the manufacturers usually name the components differently. The most effective way to sort out these differences is to take an elevated view of each system to find the similarities, then zero in on the specifics using a service manual.

SPEED DENSITY VS. ALPHA-N

Motorcycles use two types of EFI systems: speed-density and alpha-n. The difference between the two is how they determine the load being placed on the engine. The alpha-n system uses two basic inputs: engine speed and throttle position. The ECU for these systems monitors engine rpm and throttle movement to come up with a calculation that determines optimal injector pulse width, or On time. Rapid movement of the throttle along with increased rpm causes the ECU to lengthen injector pulse width. Alpha-n systems were used in early applications, since they only needed a moderate amount of computer processing power.

The speed-density system uses engine rpm (speed) and intake-manifold pressure (density) to sense engine load. Manifold absolute pressure, or MAP, sensors are connected to the intake manifold and operate like an electronic vacuum gauge. As the throttle opens, pressure in the intake manifold goes up, causing the ECU to add more fuel to the engine. Speed-density systems also use a TPS sensor but can deliver fuel more accurately than the older alpha-n systems because of the MAP sensor.

SEQUENTIAL EFI

While the injectors used in motorcycle EFI systems operate in the same manner, there are several computer strategies that control when fuel is injected. Early systems fired all the injectors once per crankshaft revolution, called batch injector firing. This design wastes fuel and doesn't provide an especially clean exhaust but does require less computing power and sensor input. An improvement over batch firing is bank firing, where injectors are triggered in pairs (on a four-cylinder engine) to fire in phase with the engine's firing order. These systems get better fuel mileage and run cleaner than batch firing systems, but they need a sensor to tell the ECU which cylinders are on their intake stroke and about to fire. Because of the need for lower emission engines, neither of these older systems has been used for several years.

All manufacturers today use sequential injection, where each injector is activated in accordance with the engine's sequential firing order—just like spark plugs. Unlike spark plugs, which are fired as the piston reaches the top of its stroke, sequential injection fires the fuel injectors just before the intake valve opens for each cylinder. These systems provide more accurate fuel delivery, and in turn helps reduce exhaust emissions, offers better idle quality, and gives increased fuel mileage.

PORT AND HIGH-MOUNT INJECTORS

Some sportbikes use two injectors per cylinder, with one injector taking care of fuel delivery for idle and mid-range engine operation, and another high-mount injector, or shower injector, for high-rpm operation. The reason for their use is the high velocity of airflow into the intake runner for each cylinder.

At high engine rpm (up to 14,000 rpm on some four-cylinder sportbikes), the air is moving so fast that fuel vapor may become stuck to the intake runner walls if injected between the throttle plate and intake valve, typically where port and lower-mount fuel injectors are located. The high-mount injector is placed above the throttle plates, slightly above the bell mouth of the velocity stack, where the airflow is moving slower. Adding fuel in this location gives the fuel more time to vaporize and remain in suspension with the airflow going into the intake tract.

Some two-cylinder sportbikes (like Ducati) may also use shower injectors for the same reason: high air velocity entering the intake tract. In fact, the volume per intake stroke on a two-cylinder engine when compared to a four-cylinder engine of the same displacement is twice as much, so the airflow velocity is even greater. The low-mounted injectors on both types of engines take care of fueling during low rpm and part throttle operation. These injectors have smaller openings for fuel delivery but can more precisely control the amount of fuel injected, especially for emission testing that manufacturers are required to perform for EPA certification. Having two sets of injectors offers better throttle response at low rpm, better fuel economy, cleaner exhaust emissions, and high rpm performance.

SINGLE AND DUAL THROTTLES

Some motorcycle manufacturers use dual throttles, or subthrottles (aka as "flies"), to control intake airflow at low engine rpm. These serve the same purpose as the secondary throttles on old four-barrel carburetors. Four-barrel carburetors used primary throttle plates to control low-speed air and fuel delivery. But when the driver mashed down the accelerator pedal, secondary plates would open, allowing more fuel to enter the engine. Without these secondary throttles, stomping on the accelerator could cause the engine to hesitate and possibly backfire through the carburetor if all four throttles were opened too quickly. The same is true with a motorcycle. If the rider twists the throttle too fast just off idle, the engine will end up with too much air and could backfire through the throttle bodies.

Subthrottles also play a part in emission control. Because of this, the ECU may overly control their use to precisely meter fuel at the expense of engine performance. This has caused many owners of sportbikes to modify, or remove, subthrottles for better engine performance. Traction control offered by some manufacturers also may use subthrottles to control engine power to the rear wheel.

DRIVE-BY-WIRE

Drive-by-wire, or as applied to a motorcycle, ride-by-wire, is a variation on the subthrottle. This system uses one or more throttle plates that are under direct control of the bike's ECU. More important, in ride-by-wire systems, there is no mechanical connection to the handlebar throttle grip used by the rider to control engine speed. The throttle grip sends a signal to the ECU, which in turn opens and closes the throttle plate(s) via a stepper motor. This keeps the rider from opening the throttle too fast for engine operating conditions, especially at low rpm. Just like dual-throttle designs, ride-by-wire systems are often too slow to open, and engine performance may suffer.

Pictured is a Harley-Davidson "Throttle-by-Wire" actuator. On motorcycles that use this type of system, there is no direct connection from the rider to the throttle plate. On 2008–09 H-D touring models, the throttle is operated by the ECU. There are no throttle cables used; a stepper motor opens the throttle. The throttle is operated based on what the rider is doing with the throttle—its position and how fast it's being twisted. A twist grip sensor (TGS) sends a digital signal to the bike's ECU which, in turn, controls the throttle via the stepper motor. *Dynojet Research*

This 2011 Yamaha YZF-R6 features some of the most current EFI technology. It was the first production motorcycle to use a fly-by-wire throttle system and has a Yamaha Chip Controlled Intake that automatically varies the length of the intake port runners based on inputs from the bike's ECU. The variable intake runners provide an extra boost in horsepower at high engine rpm. *Twigg Cycles*

Chapter 2
Aftermarket EFI Controllers

Dynojet's Power Commander III (right) and PC-V (left) offer owners the ability to take control of their motorcycle's fuel-injection system. These piggyback systems can add or subtract fuel based on engine rpm and throttle position, are easy to install, and come with a variety of fuel maps that accommodate aftermarket exhaust systems and other engine-performance modifications. *Dynojet Research*

In Chapter 1, we discussed motorcycle emissions and the need for manufacturers to adhere to federal standards regarding what comes out of motorcycle exhaust pipes. In the early 1980s, when emission regulations were first introduced, all motorcycles used carburetors, and, to meet the stricter emission rules, fuel settings were adjusted to minimize the amount of fuel used by engines at idle and part throttle. These lean air-fuel ratios caused engine-performance problems, and many motorcycles had poor idle quality, surged at part throttle, and often backfired through the exhaust when decelerating. Enthusiasts used jet kits to modify the carburetors on their bikes to solve these problems.

In the late 1990s, as original equipment manufacturers (OEMs) started to ramp up production of EFI systems to replace carburetors, the EFI systems still had to operate under the same constraints imposed by the EPA that carburetors did. Both EFI and carbureted bikes still ran too lean, and owners wanted a way to modify the new electronic fuel systems to address the issue. With a new demand in the marketplace for a way to fix factory EFI systems, the aftermarket started developing EFI controllers. As OEM fuel-injection systems became more sophisticated, so too did EFI modification products from the aftermarket. Today, riders can choose from a wide variety of products when they want to upgrade or modify their stock electronic fuel-injection systems.

ARE EFI CONTROLLERS LEGAL?

Companies that produce jet kits or EFI controllers have wrestled with the "legal-for-street-use" issue since they started producing these products more than 20 years ago. Because the federal government has never required motorcycles to be inspected regarding exhaust emissions and modifications to fuel delivery systems, jet kits and EFI controllers have been for the most part under the radar of the EPA and state emission-inspection agencies.

When purchasing jet kits, or EFI controllers, motorcycle owners receive warnings regarding their use including: "For Off-Road Use Only," "For Competition Use Only," or "Not Legal for Use on Public Highways." The reality was that owners simply wanted their motorcycles to run properly, and were not too interested in cleaning up exhaust emissions. People went ahead and installed these products despite the warnings. Because jet kits and EFI controllers filled a need, the sale of all types of fuel-delivery system modifiers skyrocketed.

As time went on, the disclaimers from the manufacturers of EFI controllers contained more "legalese," basically to cover their asses if a state or the EPA ever tried to hold them liable for selling products that violated federal or state emission laws. Here are a few examples from several companies whose names have been removed to protect the innocent:

- "Some _____ systems are intended for use only on competition vehicles not used on public highways. For systems legal for use on public highways, please refer to A.R.B. E.O. No. D-632-1 or click here."
- "Some vehicles modifications with _____ products must not be used on public roads and in some cases may be restricted to closed course competition. Those products not identified as U.S. EPA legal are intended for off-road or marine applications only. Not intended for use on emission-controlled vehicles."
- "The _____ EFI controller is not legal for use or installation on motor vehicles operated on public highways in the State of California or other states where similar emission control laws may apply. The user shall determine suitability of the product for his or her use. The user shall assume all risk and liability in violation of regulations and any incurred financial obligations due to vehicle inspections or emissions tests."

Still, many companies that produced EFI controllers tried to comply with emissions standards in California. As discussed earlier, California is the gold standard when it comes to setting the national agenda regarding emissions regulations. Using past history as a guide, aftermarket manufacturers calculated that if they could have their products approved for sale in the Golden State, the other 49 would not present a roadblock to sales. Unfortunately, the California Air Resources Board (CARB) was only used to dealing with automotive manufacturers, not smaller companies that produced products for a limited, small market, specifically, motorcycles. The amount of red tape, endless meetings (in Sacramento and Los Angeles), and unrealistic demands from CARB made it economically difficult, or impossible, to get

approval for EFI controllers or other products that modified anything involving ignition or fuel control on a motorcycle.

For example, if a manufacturer received approval of an EFI controller for a specific year, make, and model of motorcycle, and the next model-year of the same bike was identical (same engine, fuel system, and so on), CARB would require completely new testing for that model. Because CARB was not willing, or motivated, to learn how an industry other than the automakers operated, they were less than cooperative when dealing with the motorcycle aftermarket industry. One company was told that things would be much simpler if they sold their technology to Honda, Harley-Davidson, Yamaha, or Kawasaki, that CARB could then more readily approve these types of products.

Production and sales of EFI controllers and jet kits rolled along as they had for years until September 2007, when the California Air Resources Board decided that it was going to make an example of someone in order to halt the sale of illegal fuel-system modification components. That someone turned out to be Dynojet Research Inc. The CARB press release regarding their actions reads as follows:

DYNOJET RESEARCH INC. CASE SETTLES FOR $1,000,000

The Mobile Source Enforcement Section along with the Office of Legal Affairs has completed its investigation against Dynojet Research Inc., located in Las Vegas, Nevada. Dynojet was manufacturing an aftermarket part called the "Power Commander" that would alter the air-fuel mixture and the [ignition] timing on off- and on-road motor vehicles. By installing the Power Commander this would alter or modify the original design of the motor vehicle and would affect the emission control systems that were certified by the manufacturer through CARB. As part of the settlement it was agreed between both parties that Dynojet would not violate the Health and Safety Code with respect to the installation, sale, offer for sale or advertising of any device in California intended for use with, or as part of, any required motor vehicle pollution control device or system which alters or modifies the original design or performance of any such motor vehicle pollution control device or system. Dynojet has now certified a California version of the Power Commander that is legal for sale and use on California motor vehicles. Dynojet also paid penalties in the amount of $1,000,000 to the California Air Pollution Control Fund as part of the settlement.

To be fair, Dynojet was not doing anything above and beyond what other aftermarket companies were engaged in, but it was the biggest fish in the sea. The company had the

The Dynojet Power Commander (left) is a piggyback controller, in that it intercepts the injector signal from the motorcycle's ECU and modifies it. The ThunderMax takes a different approach and is a complete replacement for the stock ECU on many Harley-Davidsons. *Dynojet Research and Zipper's Performance*

most conspicuous magazine advertisements, and CARB used them to put other companies on notice that they were going to be paying attention to who sold what fuel-delivery system modification products in California.

As a result of this slap on the hand, Dynojet certified a version of its Power Commander EFI controller that was legal for sale in California. Today, other companies also offer two versions of their products: one legal for sale in California and another version for the rest of the 49 states. This is no different than the certifications for the motorcycles themselves, as OEMs have sold 49 state and California models since the 1980s.

TYPES OF EFI CONTROLLERS

There are two common types of aftermarket EFI controllers available today. The most common is the so-called "piggyback" design. These controllers operate as the name implies: They intercept the fuel injector signal from the stock ECU, modify the signal by adding or subtracting fuel values, then send the modified signal on to the fuel injector. It operates on top of

the stock EFI system, thus the name piggyback. Dynojet, Dobeck, FuelPak, Cobra, and others use this style of controller.

The other type of aftermarket EFI controller is a complete replacement of the stock ECU. ThunderMax, MoTeC, and other manufacturers offer ECUs that replace factory units.

PIGGYBACK CONTROLLERS

In Chapter 1, the general operation of EFI systems was discussed, along with the concept of how electronic fuel injectors are controlled. To review, injectors are either open (spraying fuel into the intake) or closed (no fuel delivery). All EFI systems power the injectors with battery voltage, and the ECU grounds the injector (completing the electrical circuit) to energize it. The length of time that the ECU grounds the injector is called injector pulse width, and it is measured in milliseconds, or one thousandths of a second.

Piggyback controllers receive power from the injector power wire, and they measure injector pulse rate to read engine rpm. They also measure injector pulse rate over time. The pulse rate vs. time ratio can be used by the controller to indirectly calculate several engine parameters, including acceleration, rider demand, and engine load. Using these two inputs (engine speed and pulse width), piggyback-style aftermarket controllers modify the injector pulse width, either causing it to be longer (adding more fuel) or shorter (taking away fuel).

Regardless of how they accomplish injector pulse-width modification, companies that manufacture and sell EFI controllers have several common goals: to make more power over stock EFI systems; to compensate for engine modifications like non-stock exhaust systems or other components; and to smooth out factory, EPA-mandated EFI fuel-delivery engine-performance issues.

The remainder of this chapter covers how several of these EFI controller manufacturers accomplish these goals. The examples of products outlined in this chapter represent only a few of the numerous companies that provide fuel controllers. We'll start with the originator of EFI controllers—Dynojet Research.

FIGURE 1 This is the sequence of events that take place when a piggyback controller is used with a stock ECU. Based on sensor input, the ECU calculates injector pulse width at 5 milliseconds for a given throttle position and engine rpm. The aftermarket controller intercepts the injector signal and modifies it by adding more injector On time. The controller's output to the fuel injector is 6 milliseconds—1 extra millisecond. This addition of fuel makes the difference between surging at part throttle or smoothing out the throttle transition between idle and part throttle.

Pictured are the male and female injector connectors used by Dynojet's Power Commander. The gray connector plugs into a stock fuel injector. The black connector plugs into the factory wiring harness, where it normally is connected to the fuel injector. The controller intercepts the stock ECU's signal to the fuel injector and modifies it based on the fuel map stored in its memory. *Dynojet Research*

FUEL INJECTOR PULSE

The following graphs illustrate what a typical fuel injector pulse, or signal, looks like on a digital lab scope. Each graph shows voltage over time, with time in milliseconds along the *x* (horizontal) axis and voltage on the *y* (vertical) axis. Charging-system voltage is at 14.0 volts. You can see the voltage drop to 0 when the injector is turned on, or is grounded, by the ECU. Notice that the duration of the voltage drop changes. The injector is grounded for about 2.5 milliseconds at idle, 5 milliseconds at steady part throttle, and 7 milliseconds under acceleration.

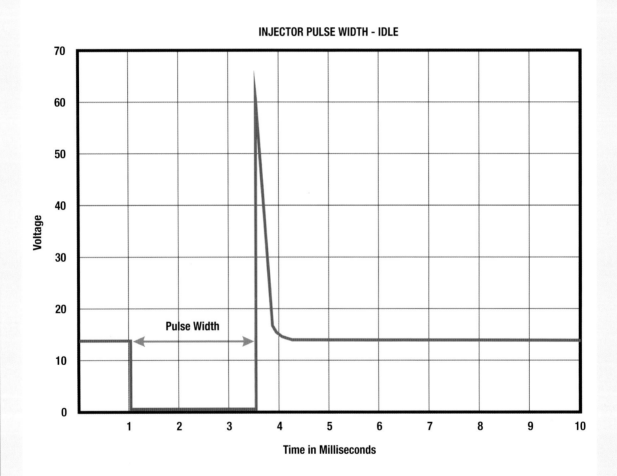

FIGURE 2 This graph of voltage vs. time shows what takes place on the fuel injector's ground wire when the ECU completes the circuit to ground, turning on the injector. Starting from the left, power to the injector is charging-system voltage (14.0 volts) when the injector is off. When the ECU grounds the injector, the voltage drops to 0. This energizes the injector's internal coil of wire, turning it into an electromagnet and opening the injector. When the ECU releases the ground, the magnetic field in the injector coil collapses and causes a voltage spike to more than 60 volts. The voltage returns to system voltage and the injector is ready for the next pulse from the ECU. The time between when the voltage drops to 0 and the start of the voltage spike is the pulse width, or injector on time. Thus, in this drawing, pulse width is 2.5 milliseconds (ms), or 2½ of 1,000ths of a second with the engine at idle.

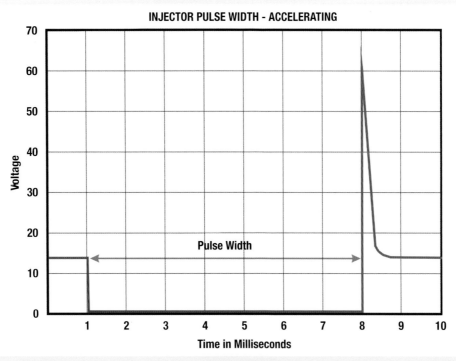

FIGURE 3 This graph illustrates how the pulse width is affected when the throttle is suddenly opened. The ECU reads inputs from its various sensors and grounds the injector for a longer period of time. This allows the injector to spray more fuel into the engine for a short time, making a smooth transition from idle to wide-open throttle. This pulse width for acceleration is 7 milliseconds and is similar to a carburetor's accelerator pump squirt of fuel into the intake manifold.

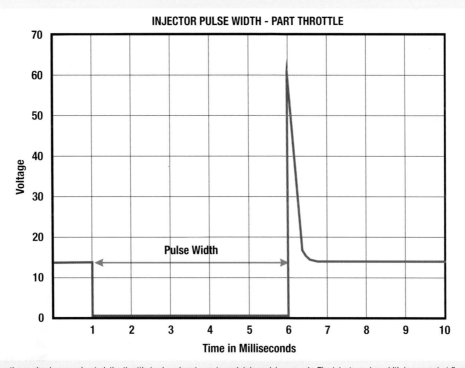

FIGURE 4 After the engine has accelerated, the throttle is closed part way to maintain cruising speeds. The injector pulse width is now set at 5 milliseconds for good fuel economy. These pulse width numbers are only used to illustrate basic operation of a typical EFI system. Actual pulse width numbers will vary from one motorcycle to the next.

Dynojet Research started its transition from producing jet kits for modifying carburetors to electronic modules that accomplish the same goals on electronically fuel-injected motorcycles. Today, Dynojet manufactures a host of products that modify EFI and ignition systems for all types of motorcycles. *Dynojet Research*

DYNOJET RESEARCH

In the early 1970s, Sun Electric, a manufacturer of automotive diagnostic-testing equipment, produced two-gas analyzers that could read hydrocarbon (HC) and carbon monoxide (CO) emissions, and many hot-rod tuners used these early units to fine-tune fuel mixtures produced by carburetors. As an auto-shop teacher many years ago, I had one of these analyzers and a Clayton chassis dynamometer as part of the school's equipment. These crude technologies got a workout tuning carburetors on hundreds of vehicles and were great teaching tools for my students. Sun eventually produced a portable, 12-volt unit that could be taken for a ride in the passenger seat. A 15-foot sniffer was shoved up the tailpipe, and HC and CO readings could be observed while on the road. Many enthusiasts used this early technology for tuning all manner of hot rods, and even the family station wagon.

One man who saw the value of using new technology and science for engine-performance tuning was Mark Dobeck, the founder of Dynojet. Dobeck had experience tuning English sports cars that used Skinners Union (SU) carburetors, which were similar to the CV carburetors motorcycles were using in the mid- to late 1970s. What they had in common with the CV carburetor was that both used a slide and jet needle to control fuel delivery. Dobeck used his knowledge of SU carburetors, with their oil-damped slide and applied it to CV carburetors on motorcycles.

Dobeck wanted to take advantage of the new portable two-gas analyzers for setting air-fuel ratios, but the portable analyzers were simply too large (about the size of a small TV) to carry on a motorcycle. Dobeck solved this problem by designing and constructing a "rolling road" that consisted of a heavy drum driven by a motorcycle's rear tire. Because the drum weighed several hundred pounds, a motorcycle engine's power output was tested every time the drum was accelerated. The history of dynamometers and how they operate will be covered in detail in Chapter 4, How to

The Dynojet Power Commander III USB can both add and subtract fuel from the base fuel map that comes pre-loaded into the controller. The unit can be connected to a laptop or be programmed via the three tuning buttons on the face plate. *Dynojet Research*

Measure Engine Performance. By using the rolling road and a two-gas analyzer, Dobeck was able to develop jet kits that fixed stock carburetion issues. In 1972, he founded Dynojet and started to mass produce CV carburetor jet kits for all types of motorcycles.

Early Japanese superbikes came equipped with CV carburetors that were, at the time, new to motorcycling. They were more difficult to tune than conventional carburetors, and replacing them was expensive. The Dynojet kits offered a cost-effective solution. Because Dobeck continued to develop his motorcycle chassis dynamometers, he could give his customers proof in the form of repeatable torque and horsepower numbers that his jet kits actually worked—something that was new to both the automotive and

motorcycle aftermarket industry. In fact, Dobeck is credited by many for making the hot-rodding aftermarket industry (both automotive and motorcycle) honest by making them back up their claims that using their products would increase engine power.

Dobeck sold Dynojet to a group of investors in 1997 and started a new company, Dobeck Performance, that currently manufactures fuel controllers. Today, Dynojet has 160 employees and a presence in 60 countries worldwide. They still make jet kits; however, these are being phased out as fewer carbureted motorcycles and all-terrain vehicles (ATVs) are produced that use this old technology. Just like the OEMs, Dynojet started making the transition from the production of jet kits that modify carburetors to electronic solutions that accomplish the same goals on electronically fuel-injected motorcycles. We'll take a closer look at Dynojet's electronic controllers starting with the Power Commander III USB.

Power Commander III USB

Dynojet's Power Commander has been around since 1998 and has applications for motorcycles from U.S., Japanese, and European manufacturers. Currently, Dynojet makes two Power Commanders, the Power Commander III USB for motorcycles manufactured in 2008 and earlier, and the Power Commander V for bikes made in 2009 and later.

The Power Commander III USB (PCIII USB) is a piggyback controller that plugs in line with a motorcycle's stock EFI fuel injectors. The factory EFI sensors and ECU base fuel map are used for basic fuel delivery. The PCIII USB modifies injector signals to change fuel mapping. Some applications also allow ignition-timing modifications as well. OEM-style connectors are used, and most applications do not require any cutting or splicing of wiring harnesses.

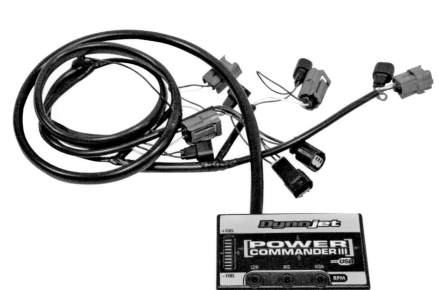

The PCIII USB shown is for a four-cylinder motorcycle. There are four pairs of injector connectors, one for each of the four stock injectors. Installation is simple: mount the controller under the seat, unplug all the injectors and plug in the PCIII's injector connectors, and plug the stock wiring harness connectors into the PCIII connector harness. While this application shows individual pairs of injector connections, some motorcycles may connect to the fuel injectors with a single plug. The PCIII comes with a base map installed for a specific motorcycle application. Other fuel maps are available on line. *Dynojet Research*

The PCIII USB allows a full range of fuel mapping modifications—as much as a 100 percent increase or decrease of fuel delivery over factory settings. Adjustments to the fuel map can be made in one of two ways: using a Microsoft Windows-based PC or laptop, or by using three pushbuttons and a series of LED lights mounted on the unit's faceplate. The PCIII USB does not make any permanent changes to the factory EFI system. When the Power Commander is removed, the motorcycle's stock settings take over and again control the EFI system.

The PCIII comes with Dynojet's Power Commander Control Center software on a CD. This software can also be downloaded from Dynojet's website. The software provides a platform for users to upload and download fuel maps from the PCIII and to modify them. A power-up adapter is included with each PCIII and uses a 9-volt battery to power the unit when it is not installed on a motorcycle. The ability to modify fuel maps without being inside a garage next to the motorcycle is a really nice feature, especially for users who don't own a laptop and instead interface with the PCIII using a desktop computer. The software allows users to compare two map files side-by-side in numerical form or a graphical display.

The "USB" in PCIII USB stands for universal serial bus and allows a quick, easy connection between the PCIII and a computer. The USB standard has been in existence since 1996 and is by far a vast improvement over older serial and parallel bus communications. Though none exists currently, it's conceivable that an iPhone or Android phone application could be developed for the Power Commander using its USB communication port.

When connected to a PC, the PCIII automatically establishes a communication link and the software displays the current map loaded into the PCIII. The software provides a place for the user to write notes regarding what the fuel map is for, changes made, tuning details, and other information. The PCIII USB stores the notes from the map in its onboard memory. When the PCIII is plugged into a computer, the map notes help identify which map is loaded. There are several features that the latest version of the PCIII USB has to offer including:

- Easier to use "Button Adjust" mode. Button adjustment has been improved over older Power Commanders, making it easier to use. It now features a startup delay that gives the user time to start the bike and then switch the PCIII USB into button adjust mode. When the high, mid or low rpm range buttons are pressed, the fuel cell ranges are displayed on the computer. Button adjustment allows the PCIII to be tuned without the use of a PC or laptop. A series of LEDs, next to the buttons, indicate how much fuel you are adding or subtracting from the base map for that rpm range.
- Individual cylinder adjustment. The PCIII USB has a "cylinder trim" adjustment feature that allows the user

to offset (add or subtract) fuel delivery to one or more cylinders. Additionally, for advanced users, the PCIII USB allows individual cylinder fuel mapping throughout the entire rpm/throttle position range. The ability to modify fuel maps for individual cylinders can help extract that last bit of power from the engine.

- Accelerator pump adjustment. The user can adjust accelerator pump attributes, such as the amount of fuel to add, the number of engine revolutions during which fuel is added, and the sensitivity of throttle movement under which the accelerator pump is activated. This feature can help eliminate hesitation when transitioning from idle to part throttle, or part throttle to full throttle. This feature is not necessary on all bikes, as some motorcycles are more prone to this problem than others.
- Harley-Davidson–only features. Rev X-tend provides the user with the ability to increase the engine's rpm limit over stock without having to modify the bike's ECU. Harley engines with aftermarket camshafts, cylinder heads, and other modifications can often take advantage of a higher rev limit. Another feature is Start Fuel, which allows the user to add additional fuel during startup. On heavily modified and large displacement (124 cubic inches or more) engines, extra fuel is sometimes required to ease starting. Start Fuel is a software-adjustable setting that makes it possible to increase or decrease the amount of fuel injected into the engine during cranking without making the idle overly rich once the engine starts.
- Accessories expansion port. A port that provides an easy way to connect accessories, including Dynojet ignition modules, Quick Shifter, Multifunction Hub, Pressure Sensor display, and LCD display screen. This feature allows the PCIII USB flexibility in use, and integrates it and other Dynojet products into a single, comprehensive system.

When a rider purchases a PCIII for a specific motorcycle, the PCIII comes loaded with a base map that has been developed to provide improvements for a stock engine with an OEM exhaust system and air filter. However, Dynojet supports the Power Commander with an extensive database of fuel maps for aftermarket components. Working with leading aftermarket intake and exhaust component manufacturers as they introduce new products, new maps are continually developed and tested at Dynojet's dynamometer facilities using its Tuning Link software.

Most stock motorcycles have factory maps that are not optimized for performance. Due to emission-related lean settings, they typically offer about 70 percent of the engine's performance potential. Adding an aftermarket exhaust and performance air filter without also changing the fuel map lowers the performance even further, to around 60 percent. With the installation of a PCIII and the supplied base map,

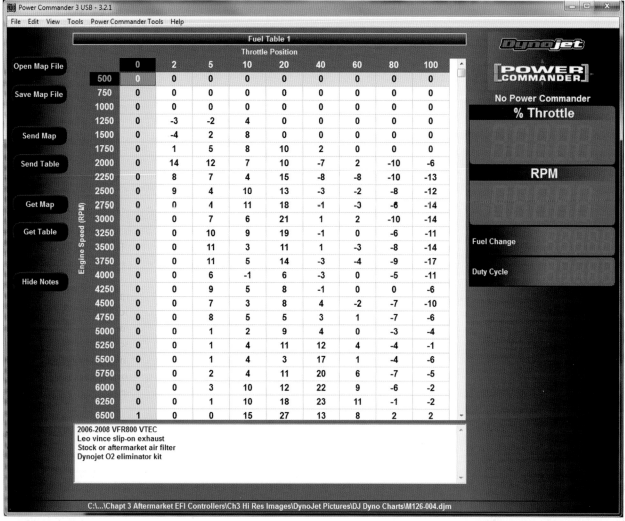

Fuel Table 1									
Throttle Position									
Engine Speed (RPM)	0	2	5	10	20	40	60	80	100
500	0	0	0	0	0	0	0	0	0
750	0	0	0	0	0	0	0	0	0
1000	0	0	0	0	0	0	0	0	0
1250	0	-3	-2	4	0	0	0	0	0
1500	0	-4	2	8	0	0	0	0	0
1750	0	1	5	8	10	2	0	0	0
2000	0	14	12	7	10	-7	2	-10	-6
2250	0	8	7	4	15	-8	-8	-10	-13
2500	0	9	4	10	13	-3	-2	-8	-12
2750	0	0	4	11	18	-1	-3	-6	-14
3000	0	0	7	6	21	1	2	-10	-14
3250	0	0	10	9	19	-1	0	-6	-11
3500	0	0	11	3	11	1	-3	-8	-14
3750	0	0	11	5	14	-3	-4	-9	-17
4000	0	0	6	-1	6	-3	0	-5	-11
4250	0	0	9	5	8	-1	0	0	-6
4500	0	0	7	3	8	4	-2	-7	-10
4750	0	0	8	5	5	3	1	-7	-6
5000	0	0	1	2	9	4	0	-3	-4
5250	0	0	1	4	11	12	4	-4	-1
5500	0	0	1	4	3	17	1	-4	-6
5750	0	0	2	4	11	20	6	-7	-5
6000	0	0	3	10	12	22	9	-6	-2
6250	0	0	1	10	18	23	11	-1	-2
6500	1	0	0	15	27	13	8	2	2

2006-2008 VFR800 VTEC
Leo vince slip-on exhaust
Stock or aftermarket air filter
Dynojet O2 eliminator kit

C:\...\Chapt 3 Aftermarket EFI Controllers\Ch3 Hi Res Images\DynoJet Pictures\DJ Dyno Charts\M126-004.djm

FIGURE 5 This PCIII fuel map is for 2006 to 2008 Honda VFR800 VETC motorcycles with Leo Vince slip-on exhaust and stock or aftermarket air filter. Engine pm is listed on the left and throttle position is across the top of the map. The numbers in each cell represent the percent change from the stock fuel map. Some cells have an increase in fuel (positive numbers) and others take fuel away (negative numbers) at that throttle position and rpm coordinates. *Dynojet Research*

engine performance typically increases to between 85 and 95 percent of the engine's full power-producing potential.

In addition to the base map, the Power Commander is supplied with a number of alternate maps on a CD-ROM (they can be downloaded from the company website). These maps cover specific combinations of exhaust systems and other modifications. The more popular the motorcycle is, the more maps are available for it. For example, a search on Dynojet's website for a 2000 Moto Guzzi V11 Sport produces four maps. A search for a 2006 Suzuki GSXR1000 delivers more than 50 maps. Another source for Power Commander maps are motorcycle forums on the Internet. No matter the make, model, or year of motorcycle, there is likely to be a forum for that specific bike. Many forum members dyno tune their bikes and have custom maps that they share via email with other members.

Dynojet's Power Commander V (PC-V) and PCIII USB side by side. The PC-V is smaller, making installation in tight spaces easier. The tuning buttons are gone from the PC-V as well. All adjustments are made via the Power Commander Control Center software. *Dynojet Research*

Power Commander V

The Power Commander V replaces the PCIII USB and is designed for 2009 and newer models. PC-V controllers are also available for a few popular motorcycles manufactured before 2009. Physically, the PC-V is smaller than the PCIII, and the fuel mapping buttons have been removed.

The PC-V functions much like the PCIII, but has enhanced features like off-the-bike-power supplied directly from a computer USB port instead of a 9-volt battery—a handy feature for desktop tuning. The PC-V also has an input for a map switch that allows the rider to switch between two internal fuel maps on the fly. A speed/gear input allows

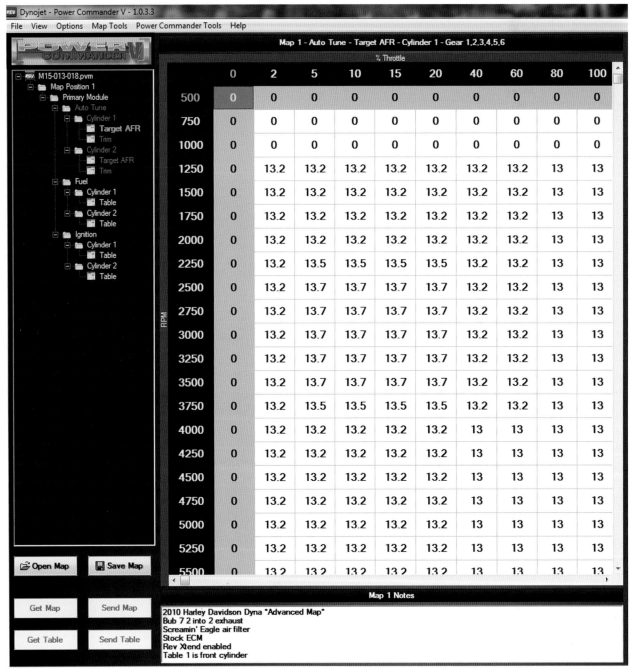

FIGURE 6 This Dynojet Auto Tune map displays the AFR targets for each rpm and percentage of throttle opening. As the motorcycle is ridden, the wideband O$_2$ sensor and PC-V compare the actual AFR with the target AFR and adjust the base map until they match. This operation is automatic and does not require the use of a dynamometer. If a dynamometer is used, the AFR base map will be filled in more quickly compared to simply riding the bike on the street. *Dynojet Research*

The Power Commander V has the ability to switch between two internal fuel maps. A switched input terminal can be connected to a switch on the handlebars, enabling the rider to select between maps. For example, you could have a map for power and another for fuel economy. *Dynojet Research*

The addition of Dynojet's Auto Tune Kit for the PC-V provides a wideband, closed-loop EFI tuning system. A target AFR map is loaded into the PC-V and the base map is modified as inputs are received from the Auto Tune module. Auto Tune is available with one wideband O_2 sensor, or for Big Twin engines, two wideband oxygen sensors in order to accommodate differences between cylinder fueling. *Dynojet Research*

for map adjustment based on gear position and speed, so the PC-V can have individual cylinder maps for each gear. For example, a four-cylinder engine with a six-speed gearbox could have 24 different fuel maps.

The PC-V can make fuel changes from -100 percent to +250 percent (the PCIII USB had a range of -100 to +100 percent) and uses 10 throttle position columns instead of the PCIII's 9. An analog input for a 0- to 5-volt signal (engine temperature, turbo boost, or other) can be used to alter fuel mapping based on the input of this signal, programming it into the Power Commander Control Center software. The accelerator-pump utility has increased adjustment and sensitivity ranges. Finally, the PC-V can interface with Dynojet's Auto Tune kit, providing wideband, closed-loop operation for the PC-V. This allows the PC-V to continually tune the fuel map based on a target air-fuel ratio (AFR) set in the unit's base map software.

Auto Tune Kit

The Auto Tune Kit interfaces with the PC-V and uses a wideband oxygen sensor for automatic fuel mapping as the motorcycle is ridden. The Auto Tune module plugs into the PC-V. If the motorcycle already has a factory oxygen sensor, it should be replaced with the Auto Tune's Bosch wideband sensor. If the bike has no OEM sensor, the Auto Tune kit comes with a bung that can be welded into the exhaust for installing the Bosch sensor.

The Auto Tune system uses the same technology that Dynojet's Tuning Link software uses for tuning air-fuel ratios on a dynamometer. A target AFR map is loaded into the PC-V. While the bike is ridden, the wideband sensor sends a signal to the PC-V that is interpreted as the AFR for specific throttle openings and rpm settings. The PC-V then alters the fuel map to match actual AFR to the target AFR.

Like the PCIII, the PC-V uses base maps, but with the Auto Tune module added, fine-tuning the fuel map is accomplished automatically. Large V-twin engines from many manufacturers often vary significantly in their fuel requirements between front and rear cylinders and therefore require individual cylinder maps. The Auto Tune kit for Harley-Davidson motorcycles has two wideband O_2 sensors, and the PC-V can map front and rear cylinders individually. The Auto Tune kit can be configured to run and correct AFR and fuel mapping at all times or, by using the map switch port on the PC-V, the rider can switch between tuning mode and base map settings.

The Power Commander LCD unit is a weather-resistant, active-matrix, color touch screen that connects to both the PCIII and PC-V. The unit can display all available data from the Power Commander via a quick-disconnect cable. Other features include switching between multiple maps, data logging (requires an optional SD memory card), and on-screen map adjustments. When other Dynojet controllers are added via the Multi-Function Hub, that data is available for display as well. The LCD can be removed from the motorcycle and programmed with a desktop computer or laptop. Maps can be downloaded and stored, and logged data can be viewed with the supplied software. The unit is upgradeable as new features become available. The LCD display can be mounted to any motorcycle using a Techmount Accessory Mounting system adapter available at www.techmount.com. *Dynojet Research*

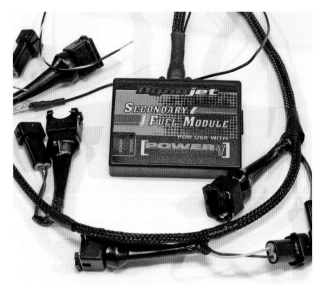

Dynojet's Ignition Module (lower left), PCIII USB (lower right), and Multi-Function Hub (top) are pictured. The Ignition Module is connected to the PCIII USB with a controlled area network (CAN) interface cable. The module uses OEM connectors to plug in-line of the stock ignition harness, so no cutting or splicing is required. Direct coil-driver technology is used, which allows a high degree of ignition timing adjustment via the Power Commander Control Center software. Ignition timing can be advanced or retarded up to 10 degrees based on throttle position and engine rpm. It's also possible to alter the timing for each cylinder individually. On some motorcycles, the module enables a feature called "Rev Xtend" that allows the user to increase the engine rpm limit from factory settings. The Multi-Function Hub provides users an interface through which one can add components to the PCIII or PC-V. In addition, it provides a means for both input and output signals to or from the PCIII. These could include map selection switch, gear position and speed input, boost input (turbocharged engines), and programmed outputs, including triggering of a solenoid (nitrous oxide system), relay, shift light, or air shifter. *Dynojet Research*

The Power Commander V Secondary Fuel Module lets owners take control of the high-mount injectors found on some race-replica sportbikes. The PC-V alone adjusts the lower injectors but cannot control the four upper injectors. The fuel module allows adjustment of the upper injectors by +250 to -100 percent fuel correction. In addition, using the gear position connection to the PC-V, the module and PC-V can adjust all eight injectors on a per-gear basis. There is also a "basic" mode that allows adjustment via a single fuel table that applies the requested fuel change to both upper and lower injectors at the same time. *Dynojet Research*

The Dynojet Quick Shifter allows full- or part-throttle clutchless upshifting. When road or drag racing, rolling off the throttle and pulling in the clutch lever to disconnect the engine from the rear wheel for a gear change takes time, slowing the motorcycle. The Quick Shifter allows the rider to keep the throttle fully on while shifting up in gears. For street riding, part-throttle clutchless shifting can be a benefit as well, especially in commuter traffic. The Quick Shifter works best for part-throttle shifting with the engine at or above 4,000 rpm. It operates by momentarily cutting off ignition signals from the ECU. This unloads the transmission, allowing an upshift without rolling off the throttle. The amount of "kill time" is adjustable in milliseconds via the Control Center software. There are three styles of Quick Shifter: shift rod pressure and tension sensor that mounts inline with the motorcycle's shift rod, linear travel sensor for motorcycles that don't use a shift rod, and a handlebar-mounted switch. *Dynojet Research*

Dobeck Performance

Mark Dobeck, founder of Dynojet, started Dobeck Performance in 1997 and began designing the Techlusion Fuel Injection (TFI) controller for on- and off-road motorcycles, ATVs, and other powersports machines. Introduced in 2002, the TFI is a piggyback-style EFI controller that can be adjusted without a laptop or PC.

Because many homegrown motorcycle technicians are familiar with how to tune carburetors when swapping aftermarket exhaust systems for stock ones, the TFI controller was designed to function much like a carburetor. For example, if a carburetor uses a 32.5-sized pilot jet to deliver fuel at part throttle and a 170 main jet for full throttle operation, a given AFR will result. An EFI system might use a 6-millisecond injector pulse width at part throttle and increase to 23 milliseconds at wide-open throttle to achieve the same AFR.

Remember, Dobeck was the inventor of the Dynojet jet kit when he owned Dynojet. By designing the TFI controller to mimic the fuel metering aspects of a carburetor, the TFI acts like an electronic jet kit. It uses injector pulse width, engine rpm, and rate of fuel required to determine how much

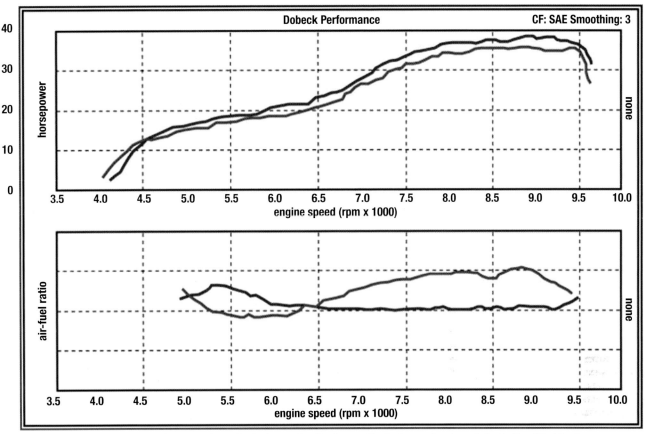

FIGURE 7 The upper graph represents horsepower for acceleration in second and fourth gears (blue line is second gear) on a Harley-Davidson V-Rod. Two horsepower curves are shown because of torque multiplication through the gearbox, causing the engine to work harder in fourth gear than in second. The lower graph indicates AFR in each gear. The AFR for fourth gear is lower (red line, more fuel) than for second gear. The Dobeck controller's load-based technology software calculates different AFRs for each gear based on the stock fuel map and the injector pulse width signal that it receives. *Dobeck Performance*

load is being placed on the engine during idle, part throttle, and wide-open throttle operation in all gears. In this way, the TFI uses the stock factory fuel map as a baseline and adds additional fuel to accommodate engine modifications.

The first TFI controllers used adjustable electronic pots (adjusted using a small screwdriver) to add fuel to the intake (you couldn't subtract fuel in early TFI models). Later Dobeck units (Generation 3 and up) use pushbuttons and a series of colored LED lights to indicate fuel adjustments. These more sophisticated GEN 3 and 3.5 controllers are also sold through private labelers including Battley Cycles in Maryland, Two Brothers Racing, Arlen Ness, FMF Racing, Jardine Products, and others. These controllers are programmed to adjust fueling by zones based on rpm and engine load as determined by fuel-injector pulse width.

There is an amazing amount of information to be gleaned from pulse width, or injector duty cycle, and the GEN3 and 3.5 controllers are sophisticated in their ability to correctly adjust AFR for engine modifications. Each zone for the GEN3 can be adjusted to determine how load sensitive

the zone is. Switch points that allow fuel mapping to change between zones can also be adjusted.

Initially, program baselines are developed at Dobeck through extensive dyno testing for each motorcycle application. Then, using the program baseline as a starting point, further development is performed by riding the motorcycle on the street and monitoring air-fuel ratios. This combination of dyno testing, street riding, and AFR measurements finalizes the program for each application. Once the unit is programmed, bike owners can make further adjustments using the pushbuttons and LED lights on the face of the controller.

ECU REPLACEMENT CONTROLLERS
Zipper's Performance Products—ThunderMax

Zipper's Performance Products has been manufacturing high-performance components for Harley-Davidson motorcycles since 1978. By educating its customers about how to achieve real performance gains, the company has positioned itself in the marketplace as an expert on engine modification and EFI

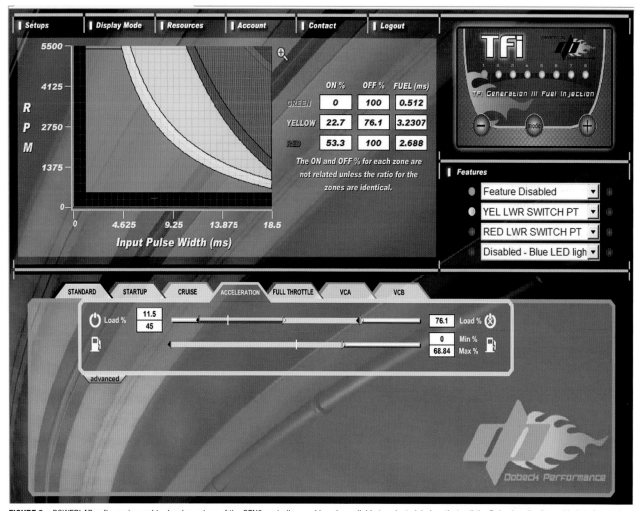

	ON %	OFF %	FUEL (ms)
GREEN	0	100	0.512
YELLOW	22.7	76.1	3.2307
RED	53.3	100	2.688

The ON and OFF % for each zone are not related unless the ratio for the zones are identical.

FIGURE 8 POWERLAB software is used to develop setups of the GEN3 controllers and is only available to private labelers that sell the Dobeck units. A graphic interface using combinations of sliders and check boxes customizes each controller for use on the rider's specific motorcycle. The colored graph shows the three zones as they relate to ECU input pulse width in milliseconds and engine rpm. The zones are cruise, acceleration, and full-throttle. Values are displayed to the right of the graph, and the controls for each zone are at the bottom, including startup, cruise, acceleration, and full throttle. *Dobeck Performance*

One sure way to know if your products perform as claimed is to go drag racing, and that's exactly what Zipper's did, starting in 1985. Using the weight of the motorcycle, quarter-mile elapsed time, and trap speed, engine power can be calculated—and the numbers don't lie. This 1996 Zipper's-sponsored, 114-cubic-inch V-Twin engine puts out around 180 horsepower—underpowered by today's standards but cutting-edge technology at the time. *Zipper's Performance Products*

systems. Zipper's has developed a complete line of engine and transmission assemblies that fit a variety of Harley-Davidson years and models.

Most powersports aftermarket companies develop their expertise through racing, and Zipper's is no exception. With more than 60 national and world records, plus five National Drag Racing Championships, Zipper's continues to be a major source of racing components, engines, and transmissions for many race teams. Its street engine kits offer different levels of performance to accommodate customer goals ranging from reliability and fuel economy to horsepower and acceleration.

When motorcycle manufacturers started transitioning from carburetor technology to electronic fuel injection, Zipper's knew it had to do the same to remain competitive Zipper's has many, long-standing alliances with other motorcycle aftermarket industry leaders, and the marriage of Zipper's technical advances with existing high-value products created new solutions to performance issues. For example, Zipper's teamed up with electrical engineering

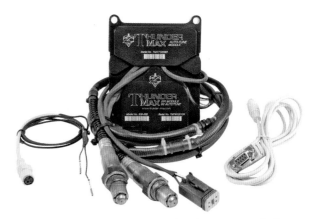

Pictured is the ThunderMax EFI Tuner with Auto Tune for a 2010 Harley-Davidson Sportster. The two oxygen sensors are Bosch wideband types and replace the stock narrow-band sensors. The cable to the right connects the ECU to a laptop or PC in order to allow base map loading and tuning. *Zipper's Performance Products*

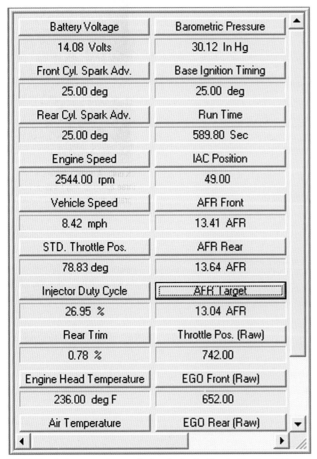

FIGURE 9 Engine parameters are displayed using the ThunderMax SmartLink software. Screens like this provide a wealth of information to the engine tuner, allowing fine adjustments for just about everything found in the engine-management system's ECU on late-model Harley-Davidson motorcycles. *Zipper's Performance Products*

experts at Thunder Heart Performance Corporation to develop EFI products that deliver performance, drivability, and efficiency. Not wanting to follow other aftermarket companies that produce piggyback EFI controllers, they spent more than three years developing and testing before releasing the ThunderMax EFI controller—a replacement for Harley-Davidson factory ECU or fuel-injection computer.

ThunderMax EFI Systems

ThunderMax EFI controllers are stand-alone replacements for Harley-Davidson stock ECUs. A complete ECU replacement overcomes the limitations of the stock system—and Harley's Race Tuner software—and allows complete flexibility in setting engine parameters and fuel map tuning. Unlike piggyback controllers that correct factory fuel maps, the ThunderMax allows changes to other engine functions, including startup fuel pulse, adjustable closed-loop air-fuel ratios and engine rpm targets, injector size compensation, automatic idle speed, acceleration pump simulation, ignition timing, rpm rev limits, throttle-by-wire control (2008 and newer Touring models only), speedometer calibration, adjustable warm-up settings, diagnostic code output (Digital Tech scan tool Compatible), deceleration pop control, engine temperature alarm, live monitoring and recording, running statistics and logs, fuel map analysis, and more.

The ThunderMax EFI controller is an Alpha-N based system and uses engine rpm and throttle position to calculate basic fuel delivery and ignition timing. Unlike the stock EFI system it does not use the factory MAP sensor. Harley's first EFI system (manufactured by Weber-Morelli) was an Alpha-N type system. In 2002, when the Motor Company introduced its replacement, the Delphi system, the new MAP sensor was quite an accomplishment, both from hardware and software engineering aspects.

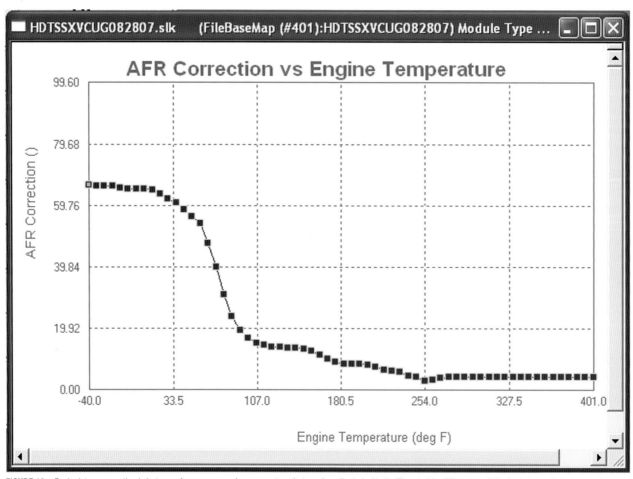

FIGURE 10 Fuel mixture correction is but one of numerous engine parameters that can be adjusted with the ThunderMax EFI system. This chart shows that at an engine temperature of 33 degrees F, the fuel system richens the air-fuel ratio 59 percent over the base fuel map. As the engine warms up, the mixture is leaned out until, at an engine temperature of around 220 degrees F, the fuel correction is only about 6 percent of the base map. These changes offer better cold running characteristics over the stock ECU. *Zipper's Performance Products*

All Harley engines have uneven cylinder firing intake pulses and use a common intake manifold, making the MAP sensor's job difficult. Smoothing out the intake pulse signals from the stock MAP sensor is a complex process, so the ThunderMax bypasses this input. Instead, the ThunderMax Alpha-N system uses far more rpm/throttle-position cells or blocks—close to 2,000—than the stock ECU uses in its look-up tables. Regardless of throttle position and engine rpm, there is a cell in the ThunderMax's look-up table to address rider demands for fuel in every condition. The abundance of rpm vs. throttle position information, plus a fast, on-board processor, makes fuel and ignition control seamless to the rider. This design also makes fuel map tuning more straightforward, and the system uses one less sensor input, which is one less thing to go wrong.

BASE MAPS

Because the stock ECU is replaced by the ThunderMax, there are no OEM base fuel or ignition maps for the ThunderMax

ECU to use for basic operation. Instead, the ThunderMax must have base maps uploaded into the controller before it can be used. This is easily accomplished with the Zipper's SmartLink Software that comes with each ThunderMax product, or base maps can be downloaded from the company website. Zipper's has an extensive library of base maps it has developed using thousands of combinations of aftermarket parts on motorcycles at their dynamometer facility. Their base maps take into account engine size, engine family (TwinCam or EVO), throttle bore and injector size, exhaust system installed, muffler type and model, air cleaner, camshaft profile and cylinder head modifications, piston type, and other engine modifications. Zipper's continues to develop new maps as soon as new aftermarket parts are available for Harley-Davidson models.

If there is no base map that exactly matches a combination of engine modifications, the SmartLink software allows the base map to be adjusted by (+/-) 20 percent for fuel mapping and 10 degrees of ignition timing adjustments.

Base Map Definitions

Ite...	Manufacturer	EngineType	Family	Throttle	Exhaust	Muffle
382	HarleyDavidson	96ci	TwinCam A&B	Stock HD TC 06-07 all, 08 FX (25° Inj)	2:1 D+D Fat Cat	Model = FL
383	HarleyDavidson	96ci	TwinCam A&B	Stock HD TC 06-07 all, 08 FX (25° Inj)	Stock HD FL Head Pipe	KW HP+ Mu
384	HarleyDavidson	96ci	TwinCam A&B	Stock HD TC 06-07 all, 08 FX (25° Inj)	True Dual Rinehart Full System	N/A
385	HarleyDavidson	96ci	TwinCam A&B	Stock HD TC 06-07 all, 08 FX (25° Inj)	Stock HD FL Head Pipe	Stock HD Mu
391	HarleyDavidson	96ci	TwinCam A&B	Stock HD TC 06-07 all, 08 FX (25° Inj)	2:1 D+D Fat Cat	Model = FL
392	HarleyDavidson	96ci	TwinCam A&B	Stock HD TC 06-07 all, 08 FX (25° Inj)	Stock HD FL Head Pipe	KW HP+ Mu
393	HarleyDavidson	96ci	TwinCam A&B	Stock HD TC 06-07 all, 08 FX (25° Inj)	True Dual Rinehart Full System	N/A
394	HarleyDavidson	96ci	TwinCam A&B	Stock HD TC 06-07 all, 08 FX (25° Inj)	Stock HD FL Head Pipe	Stock HD Mu
396	HarleyDavidson	96ci	TwinCam A&B	Stock HD TC 06-07 all, 08 FX (25° Inj)	True Dual Rinehart Full System	N/A
397	HarleyDavidson	96ci	TwinCam A&B	Stock HD TC 06-07 all, 08 FX (25° Inj)	2:1 D+D Fat Cat	Model = FL
401	HarleyDavidson	96ci	TwinCam A&B	Stock HD TC 06-07 all, 08 FX (25° Inj)	Stock HD FXST Head Pipe	KW HP+ Mu
402	HarleyDavidson	96ci	TwinCam A&B	Stock HD TC 06-07 all, 08 FX (25° Inj)	Stock HD FXST Head Pipe	Stock HD Mu
403	HarleyDavidson	96ci	TwinCam A&B	Stock HD TC 06-07 all, 08 FX (25° Inj)	Stock HD FXD Head Pipe	KW HP+ Mu
404	HarleyDavidson	96ci	TwinCam A&B	Stock HD TC 06-07 all, 08 FX (25° Inj)	Stock HD FXD Head Pipe	Stock HD Mu
411	HarleyDavidson	96ci	TwinCam A&B	Stock HD TC 06-07 all, 08 FX (25° Inj)	Stock HD FXD Head Pipe	KW HP+ Mu
412	HarleyDavidson	96ci	TwinCam A&B	Stock HD TC 06-07 all, 08 FX (25° Inj)	Stock HD FL Head Pipe	D+D FL Slip
522	HarleyDavidson	96ci	TwinCam A&B	Stock HD TC 06-07 all, 08 FX (25° Inj)	Stock HD FL Head Pipe	Stock HD Mu
523	HarleyDavidson	96ci	TwinCam A&B	Stock HD TC 06-07 all, 08 FX (25° Inj)	True Dual Rinehart Full System	N/A
524	HarleyDavidson	96ci	TwinCam A&B	Stock HD TC 06-07 all, 08 FX (25° Inj)	Stock HD FL Head Pipe	KW HP+ Mu
525	HarleyDavidson	96ci	TwinCam A&B	Stock HD TC 06-07 all, 08 FX (25° Inj)	2:1 D+D Fat Cat	Model = FL
544	HarleyDavidson	96ci	TwinCam A&B	Stock HD TC 06-07 all, 08 FX (25° Inj)	Stock HD FL Head Pipe	KW HP+ Mu
546	HarleyDavidson	96ci	TwinCam A&B	Stock HD TC 06-07 all, 08 FX (25° Inj)	Stag Duals V&H Big Shot w/PC	N/A
554	HarleyDavidson	96ci	TwinCam A&B	Stock HD TC 06-07 all, 08 FX (25° Inj)	True Dual FL Headpipe	D+D FL Slip

Clear Filters   Close   Excel Export

FIGURE 11 The SmartLink Base Map Definitions screen shown is a partial list of possible combinations of engine families, throttle body and injector sizes, and exhaust systems for a particular motorcycle. Any of these base maps can be further modified to suit specific engine-tuning requirements. Fuel maps can be uploaded into the ThunderMax controller via a laptop of desktop computer. *Zipper's Performance Products*

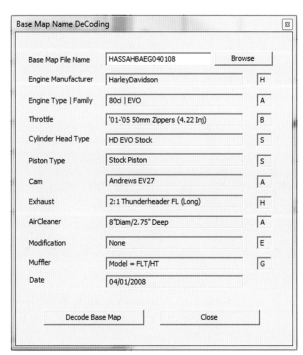

FIGURE 12 A tuner can download Zipper's base maps. This screen decodes the map file and displays the parameters. This Harley-Davidson FLT fuel map is for a bike using an Andrews EV27 cam, aftermarket air filter, Thunderheader exhaust system, and a stock 80-cubic-inch EVO engine. *Zipper's Performance Products*

Other engine parameters, including idle adjustment, rpm limit, speedometer calibration, accelerator fuel enrichment, crank fuel, decel fuel cut (to prevent exhaust popping on deceleration), and engine temperature alarm (turns on check engine light if engine overheats) are also easily adjustable with the click of a mouse.

THUNDERMAX AUTO TUNE FEATURE

All ThunderMax Auto Tune EFI systems incorporate a wideband, closed-loop system that continually tunes the ECU's fuel map. If the user adds an exhaust system, changes camshafts or makes other engine modifications, the Auto Tune system adjusts the actual AFR produced by the ECU to match the target AFR in the base map. Two Bosch wideband, five-wire oxygen sensors (one for each cylinder) constantly provide AFR feedback to the ECU, which then updates the base map to optimize performance. In effect, the Auto Tune feature produces a custom fuel map every time the motorcycle is ridden.

As an engine runs mile after mile, it ages—piston rings, valves, and other parts experience normal wear. The Auto Tune compensates for normal wear by adjusting actual AFR readings to match target settings. With the ThunderMax EFI system constantly learning and adjusting

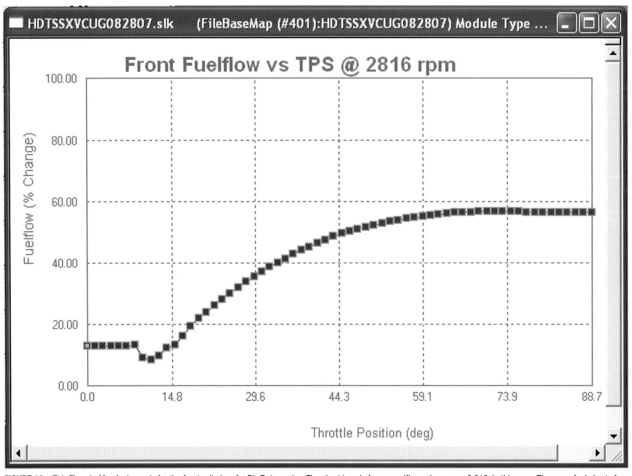

FIGURE 13 This ThunderMax fuel map is for the front cylinder of a Big Twin engine. The chart is only for a specific engine rpm—2,816, in this case. There are fuel charts for engine rpm at 256 intervals all the way from idle to redline. This amount of granular detail produces fuel maps that offer superior performance over stock ECUs and factory fuel maps. The horizontal axis of the chart is the throttle position in degrees of opening. The vertical axis is the percent of change for fuel flow. As illustrated, the percent change in fuel flow increases as the throttle is opened. *Zipper's Performance Products*

for changes from its sensors, performance tuning is always kept at optimum levels. The Auto Tune O$_2$ sensors can be installed on model years that already have O$_2$ sensor bungs (threaded holes in the exhaust pipes for the sensors) in the exhaust system. Some aftermarket exhaust manufacturers supply their pipes with the bungs installed. Bungs can also be welded onto any exhaust system that doesn't have them.

The software inside the ECU has user-selectable AFR targets for 32 rpm pages, or in intervals of 256 rpm. Each rpm page has 64 target points. Combined, more than 2,000 points, or targets, are matched by the Auto Tune system. The default AFR for all points is 13:1, which provides a balance between power and fuel economy. Users who want to optimize fuel economy can adjust the target AFR for a leaner mixture (13.8) for part throttle and low- to mid-rpm ranges. If power output needs to be optimized, the target AFR can be set for full throttle and high rpm. Auto Tune can adjust AFR up to 50 percent from the installed base map.

The ThunderMax Auto Tune module uses two wideband oxygen sensors and plugs into the ThunderMax controller. These sensors can be installed in place of the stock O$_2$ sensors. On bikes that do not come equipped with oxygen sensors, bungs can be welded into the exhaust system to accommodate the ThunderMax wideband sensors. *Zipper's Performance Products*

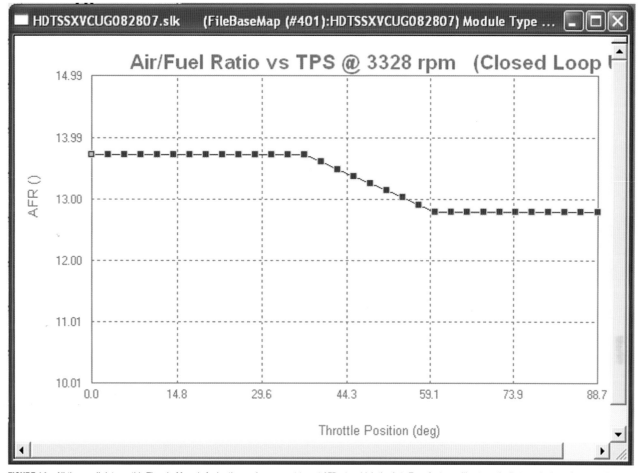

FIGURE 14 All the small dots on this ThunderMax air-fuel ratio graph represent target AFRs, to which the Auto Tune feature will automatically tune the base fuel map. This chart shows the TPS range values for 3,328 rpm. AFR targets start at 13.8:1 and start to richen up the AFR at around 35 percent of throttle position. At 59 percent of throttle position opening, the AFR is at 12.8:1 for maximum engine power. *Zipper's Performance Products*

The ThunderMax EFI module (with blue connector) has an Auto Tune module attached to it to provide a wideband closed-loop feedback system. Later versions of the ThunderMax have the Auto Tune function built into the EFI controller. *Zipper's Performance Products*

Users should initially use the base map that is the closest match to the engine modifications used, in order to minimize the time Auto Tune takes to match the AFR targets. Auto Tune "learning" controls can be set regarding how much learning, or feedback modification, can be made per riding session. This range is 0 to 50 percent and the default setting is 5 percent. If a faster learning curve is desired, the learning number can be set higher. Another parameter is the total amount of learning regardless of the number of riding secessions. This range is 0 to 50 percent, with 20 percent as the default. In addition to fuel adjustments, idle air-control settings can be adjusted during initial setups and are automatically adjusted thereafter.

THUNDERMAX APPLICATIONS

Zipper's ThunderMax EFI has applications for many late-model Harley-Davidson motorcycles. The ThunderMax system has four variations:

This is the complete ThunderMax EFI system for a Harley-Davidson VRod. The CD-rom has the SmartLink software used to upload fuel maps to the controller. The Auto Tune module plugs into the controller and the two wideband O_2 sensors take the place of the stock sensors. *Zipper's Performance Products*

- **ThunderMax EFI with Auto Tune.** The motorcycle must be equipped with exhaust bungs for installation of the wideband oxygen sensors. Stock wiring harness is retained, and there are no wires to cut or splice, as the installation of the ThunderMax ECU is plug-and-play.
- **ThunderMax 50 with Auto Tune.** Similar to the ThunderMax EFI except the unit has been certified by the California Air Resources Board and is legal for sale in California. Specific fuel and ignition timing targets are locked for certification. Even with these constraints, the Auto Tune feature can still compensate for changes in overall engine airflow increases and still meet emissions requirements. For example, if an aftermarket exhaust system has been installed, the fuel system would normally be too lean for good performance. The Auto Tune function increases the amount of fuel added to match the higher airflow gained by the exhaust but remains within the emission AFR targets.
- **ThunderMax TBW with Auto Tune.** This unit is specifically designed for 2008 to 2010 FL Touring models that use Harley's Throttle-by-Wire (TBW) system. On these motorcycles, there is no throttle cable used to operate the throttle-body butterflies. The ECU controls a stepper motor that opens and closes the butterflies. The factory TBW EFI systems have slow or poor throttle response. The ThunderMax TBW system addresses this issue, giving crisper throttle operation and making the motorcycle easier to ride.

- **ThunderMax VRod.** The unit is installed using the VRod's factory wiring harness. The system has the same features as the ThunderMax EFI system.

The following Harley-Davidson models will work ThunderMax EFI systems:

- 2008 and newer FL Touring models (Throttle By Wire)
- 2001 and newer Softail®, 2004-up Dyna®, 2002 to 2007 FL Touring
- 2007 to 2011 Sportster
- 2008 and newer XR1200
- 2002 and newer V-Rod

THUNDERMAX MAGNETI MARELLI CONVERSIONS

The ThunderMax Marelli Conversion Kit is a complete replacement for Harley-Davidson's first EFI system, developed jointly by the Motor Company and Magneti Marelli. These early systems did not perform well, and even the motorcycle press blasted them for not being ready for public consumption. The Marelli system suffered from hard starting, rough idle, overheating, and hesitation when accelerating. In fact, several aftermarket carburetor kits were available to replace the poorly running EFI system—a backward step for technology.

The ThunderMax conversion kit includes all the components required to replace the stock system. It allows

The ThunderMax Magneti Marelli Conversion Kit is a complete replacement for the Motor Company's EFI system on 1995 to 1998 EV and 1999–2001 Touring models. The gains in performance and rideability between the stock EFI system and the conversion kit make it like owning a different motorcycle. The stock fuel tank and wiring harness are retained for the conversion, making installation simple. *Zipper's Performance Products*

The ThunderMax Auto Tune module is bolted directly to the ThunderMax controller. This allows the system to operate in a closed-loop mode as the system modifies the base map AFR. Two wideband oxygen sensors are also included in the kit. *Zipper's Performance Products*

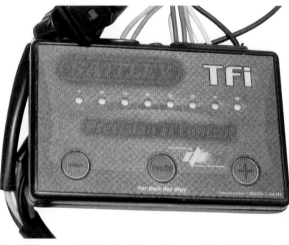

Dobeck Performance sells its fuel controllers under several private labels. Pictured is a GEN3 unit from Battley Cycles, located in Maryland. Battley develops fuel-mapping programs for their GEN3 controllers that are specific to year, make, model, and engine modifications. The controller is also adjustable by the end user if, for example, they were to change exhaust systems after the initial installation. *Battley Cycles and Dobeck Performance*

the retention of the factory wiring harness and fuel tank, making installation straightforward. The kit covers 1995 to 1998 Evolution engines and Twin Cam 88 engines from 1999 to 2001. The ThunderMax Auto Tune module can be added to the conversion kit, bringing to the conversion kit all the adjustability and advantages found on the other ThunderMax applications.

THUNDERMAX AUTO TUNE MODULE

The ThunderMax Auto Tune Module allows earlier versions of the ThunderMax EFI to be upgraded to include the automatic tuning capabilities. The module can also be added to the Marelli Conversion Kit. The Auto Tune Module kit comes with the module and two wideband, five-wire oxygen sensors. Some applications will require that bungs be welded to the exhaust in order to mount the O_2 sensors.

Chapter 3
Catalytic Converters, Air-fuel Ratios, and Oxygen Sensors

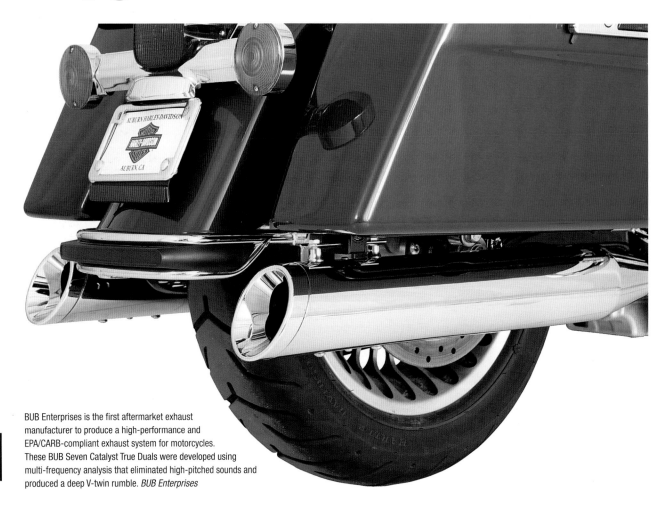

BUB Enterprises is the first aftermarket exhaust manufacturer to produce a high-performance and EPA/CARB-compliant exhaust system for motorcycles. These BUB Seven Catalyst True Duals were developed using multi-frequency analysis that eliminated high-pitched sounds and produced a deep V-twin rumble. *BUB Enterprises*

This chapter will focus on how catalytic converters (CATs), oxygen sensors, and air-fuel ratios (AFRs) interrelate in modern motorcycle engine-management systems. By taking a detailed look at the chemistry of what goes on in an internal combustion engine and what comes out as byproducts of the combustion process, we will explain how a catalytic converter operates. We'll also explore how the engine control unit (ECU), oxygen sensor, and the fuel-injection system use exhaust gas oxygen content to control the AFR and its subsequent effect on the catalytic converter's ability to reduce emissions. In addition, air-fuel ratios for performance and wideband O_2 sensors for fuel mixture tuning will be discussed.

CATALYTIC CONVERTERS

The catalytic converter is a major player in the effort to reduce the bad stuff emanating from a motorcycle's exhaust. We'll start by exploring what chemical elements are used by an internal combustion engine to make power, how they are processed, what comes out of the engine's exhaust, and, finally, what happens inside a catalytic converter.

An internal combustion engine breathes air that contains 78 percent nitrogen and 21 percent oxygen. Nitrogen molecules (N_2) are inert, which means they simply take up space and do not burn in the combustion process. All internal combustion engines create power from their ability to extract oxygen molecules (O_2) from the air-fuel mixture. The oxygen molecules combine with hydrocarbons from gasoline and then burn during combustion. The combustion process creates heat, which causes the nitrogen gas in the combustion chamber to rapidly expand and push the piston down the cylinder, which then rotates the engine's crankshaft. Engines with high compression ratios, long-duration camshafts, superchargers, turbochargers, and large displacements create more power because they convert greater amounts of fuel and oxygen into heat.

No matter how cleanly an engine burns, only the addition of a catalytic converter (CAT) can actually eliminate the unwanted byproducts of combustion. To understand why the CAT is a necessary component for engines to meet emission regulations, we need to understand how the combustion process works.

Gasoline is made mostly from hydrocarbons, which, when combined with oxygen and burned, produces heat. If piston engines were 100 percent efficient, all of the HC and O_2 molecules would be burned in the combustion process,

and only water (hydrogen bonded with oxygen—or H_2O), nitrogen, and carbon dioxide would be left. Unfortunately, even the most state-of-the-art combustion chamber designs are not 100 percent efficient in burning all the air and fuel completely, and harmful unwanted gases always remain in the exhaust. These chemical leftovers are emitted from the exhaust system in the form of three hazards: carbon monoxide (CO), hydrocarbons (HC), and nitrogen oxides or NO_x.

The first of these is the harmful gas carbon monoxide, which is colorless, odorless, and poisonous. Carbon monoxide is what kills people when they leave a car running inside a closed garage. The next unwanted byproduct of combustion is unburned fuel, or hydrocarbons, also called volatile organic compounds (VOC). The last unwanted hazards are nitrogen oxides, or NO_x, as they are commonly called. NO_x is a generic term for the reactive gases that contain nitrogen and oxygen atoms, nitric oxide (NO) and nitrous dioxide (NO_2). The x at the end of NO_x is a variable encompassing these two possible combinations. NO_x is produced when fuel is burned at the high temperatures that take place at part throttle operation, when mixtures have less fuel and more oxygen. When combined with HC, NO_x produces smog, and on a hot summer day it makes people's eyes sting and makes breathing difficult.

Catalytic converters have been equipped on all cars and light trucks since the early 1980s. Automotive CATs used before 1981 were the oxidizing type and were called two-way

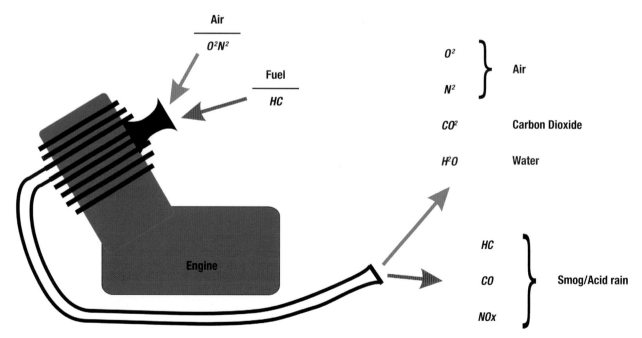

FIGURE 1 This illustration shows what goes into an engine (nitrogen and oxygen) and what comes out. Ideally, if all the air and fuel were burned completely, the resulting gases would be oxygen, nitrogen, carbon dioxide, and water (in blue and green). Unfortunately, even after more than 100 years of perfecting combustion-chamber design, this process is still not as efficient as it could be. Consequently, unburned fuel, or hydrocarbons, carbon monoxide (CO), and nitrogen oxides (NO_x) are still emitted as exhaust gases, as shown in red. A catalytic converter's job is to convert these unwanted gases into less harmful substances.

converters. Since 1981, all CATs used on automobiles are three-way designs. Unlike cars, current motorcycle emissions systems can use either a two-way or three-way catalytic converter design.

The difference between the two types comes down to which harmful gases they remove from the exhaust. Two-way converters remove only hydrocarbons, or HC and CO. Three-way catalytic converters remove HC and CO, plus NO_x. Both types are constructed using an extruded honeycomb core. The core, or substrate, is sprayed or dipped and then subsequently coated with precious metals, including platinum, palladium, and rhodium. Platinum and palladium accelerate the oxidation of HC and CO so they won't exit the tailpipe and pollute the atmosphere. The use of rhodium in a three-way CAT helps reduce NO_x emissions.

In order for a CAT to start converting harmful exhaust emissions into more desirable compounds, it must be hot, around 500 degrees F, which is known as the "light-off" temperature. Normal operating temperatures for catalytic converters range between 750 to 1,500 degrees F or higher. A CAT should normally last the lifespan of an engine. However, if the fuel system consistently runs an AFR that is too rich, or the ignition system continually misfires, the temperatures within the CAT can increase to more than

2,500 degrees F, which will shorten its lifespan or destroy it. Other factors affecting converter longevity are the use of leaded fuel, excessive engine oil burning, or the presence of antifreeze in the exhaust from a blown head gasket or cracked cylinder head.

CONVERTING BAD INTO GOOD

A three-way catalytic converter removes or eliminates all three harmful gases from exhaust emissions using two separate catalyst stages—reduction and oxidization. This two-stage design is also known as a dual-bed converter.

The reduction catalyst processing stage is the first stage that all exhaust gases must pass through, and its function is to ideally eliminate, or at least reduce, NO_x emissions. A NO_x molecule is composed of one atom of nitrogen and one or two oxygen atoms. By using the elements platinum and rhodium, the reduction catalysts rip the nitrogen atom out of the NO_x molecule, thus freeing the oxygen. The free nitrogen atoms bond with each other to create N_2 (nitrogen gas).

The free oxygen molecules are then passed into the second stage, or oxidization stage, of the catalytic converter where they will be put to good use. This second process reduces HC and CO from exhaust emissions by converting the oxygen freed from the NO_x molecule in the first stage.

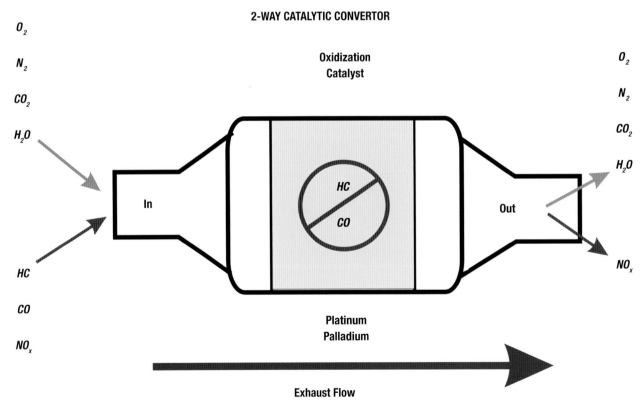

2-WAY CATALYTIC CONVERTOR

O_2

N_2

CO_2

H_2O

Oxidization Catalyst

In

HC
CO

Out

Platinum
Palladium

O_2

N_2

CO_2

H_2O

NO_x

HC

CO

NO_x

Exhaust Flow

FIGURE 2 This drawing illustrates how a two-way CAT operates. The chemicals on the left are what is coming from the engine into the CAT, and those on the right are the end result of the convertor's chemical conversion. The platinum and palladium contained in the honeycomb section of the CAT oxidize the incoming gases of HC and CO, converting them into oxygen, nitrogen, carbon dioxide, and water. Two-way CATs are sometimes called a single-bed converter, because they only have one catalyst element.

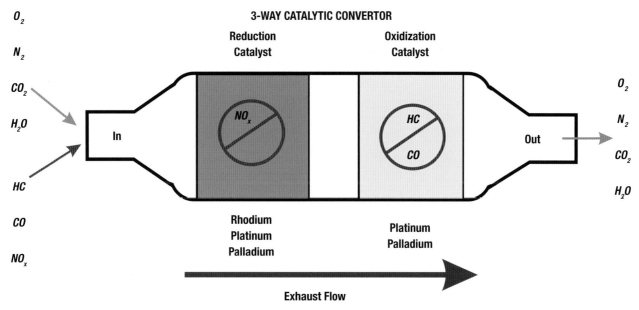

3-WAY CATALYTIC CONVERTOR

Reduction Catalyst

Oxidization Catalyst

O_2
N_2
CO_2
H_2O
HC
CO
NO_x

In

NO_x

HC

CO

Out

O_2
N_2
CO_2
H_2O

Rhodium
Platinum
Palladium

Platinum
Palladium

Exhaust Flow

FIGURE 3 This three-way CAT has two separate elements. The first is the reduction catalyst (left) that breaks up the nitrogen from the NO_x molecule and creates oxygen. The oxygen is sent on to the oxidization catalyst, where it is used to reduce HC and CO through an oxidizing process. Because a three-way CAT has two catalysts, it's often called a dual-bed converter.

Pictured is the catalyst honeycomb substrate inside a BUB Seven muffler. These catalytic converters use more precious metals than stock mufflers, ensuring they meet CARB and EPA specifications, while at the same time providing high-flow exhaust capacity. The BUB CATs flow 30 percent more exhaust gases than the stock CATs from Harley-Davidson and provide an 11 percent increase in engine horsepower with the proper EFI fuel modifications. *BUB Enterprises*

Catalytic converters used on motorcycles only reduce harmful emissions during two operating conditions: idle and part throttle. During these operating modes, the AFR has to average 14.7 to 1, or 14.7 parts air to 1 part fuel by weight. AFRs are commonly expressed as X:Y; in this case, the desired ratio is 14.7:1. This air-fuel ratio is called stoichiometric, because it is the mixture of fuel and air that has the potential to burn completely. AFRs for outright performance will be covered in more depth later in this chapter.

Based on input from an oxygen sensor, ECUs attempt to maintain the ideal average AFR of 14.7:1 during idle and part throttle. Fuel injection systems constantly vary the air-fuel mixture between slightly rich and slightly lean, however. This variation in air-fuel mixture allows enough oxygen to exist in exhaust gases for the oxidization catalyst stage of the catalytic converter to convert HC and CO into harmless water and carbon dioxide.

Automotive CATs are highly efficient, and the exhaust gases coming out of them are so clean that, when sniffed by a five-gas analyzer, typical readings register 0 detected presence of HC, CO, and NO_x. When teaching auto shop classes in the mid-1980s on hot, smoggy days in southern California, I could hold the five-gas analyzer's exhaust probe up in the air and read 1 or 2 percent HC in the atmosphere. When the probe was inserted into the exhaust of a running car equipped with a CAT, the analyzer would read 0 percent HC coming out of the tailpipe. (In fact, cars are now so effective in cleaning exhaust gases that the rate of suicide from breathing engine exhaust has dropped significantly.) This efficiency comes at a price, in that converters used on cars are rather large and heavy—two design attributes that don't work especially well on a motorcycle. Conversely, because catalytic converters that fit into the exhaust system on a motorcycle are small, they don't work as well in reducing emissions as those used on automobiles.

FIGURE 4 This drawing shows the logic for closed-loop control. The O_2 sensor senses exhaust-gas oxygen content; the ECU compares this information to an internal reference table, then corrects the fuel injector On time. The injectors deliver fuel to the engine, and the process starts all over again—a closed loop of information.

Figure 4 depicts what is known as a feedback loop, or closed loop, that takes place during part throttle or at idle. In a feedback loop, fuel is injected into the engine, where it is then burned. An oxygen sensor then *senses* the oxygen content in the exhaust gas and passes this information on to the ECU, which then references its internal data tables regarding ideal air-fuel ratios. The ECU *compares* the existing fuel conditions against the ideal, and finally adjusts or *corrects* the fuel mixture by varying injector pulse width. Thus, this informational loop consists of **sense** (oxygen sensor measures oxygen content in the exhaust), **compare** (ECU consults internal data tables regarding actual oxygen and fuel content needed to average the ideal ratio under the current operating conditions), and **correct** (ECU varies the amount of fuel the injectors deliver to the engine). This continuous feedback loop is necessary to maintain the precise AFRs required by catalytic converters.

Since this continuous information gathering and operation adjusting process is endless, it's often referred to as a "closed-loop" mode of operation. Open-loop is any engine-operating mode when the ECU is not in closed-loop. Starting, accelerating, decelerating, and wide-open throttle are all open-loop modes of engine operation.

It is interesting to note that all through the 1980s, and midway through the 1990s, automotive textbooks and service manuals claimed that the catalytic converter's ability to eliminate HC, CO, and NO_x was sufficient to completely rid the earth of pollutants from automobiles. During this time, CO_2 was not considered harmful, because it occurs naturally in the atmosphere. It wasn't until the late 1990s that governments realized that simply removing harmful chemicals from automobile and motorcycle emissions is not sufficient to solve the problem of global warming. Today, most scientists worldwide agree that manmade CO_2 emissions are the primary cause of rising temperatures on earth. Ironically, the more efficient an internal combustion engine is at burning fuel, the higher the CO_2 levels it produces.

Added to the irony is the fact that the larger the engine, the greater amount of CO_2 it produces. One of the emission-related benefits of choosing a motorcycle over a car for transportation is that it produces less CO_2 due to smaller engine sizes. The use of smaller, more fuel-efficient engines on motorcycles and small cars, as well as hybrid engines that use a combination of battery power and a gasoline- or diesel-powered engine looks to be promising for effective pollution control and reduction of greenhouse gases, at least for the immediate future.

Parts is parts, and these are the ones that make up the closed-loop feedback system. From left are pictured an ECU, fuel injector, and oxygen sensor (with the wire). Early automotive applications that featured closed-loop control used an electro-mechanical carburetor instead of a fuel injector to vary fuel mixture to the engine.

Not to be outdone by the auto industry with their hybrid automobiles, there are several zero-emission (electric) motorcycles on the market today. KTM's Freeride zero-emission off-road and supermoto motorcycles are both powered by electric motors that offer performance comparable to a 125-cc two-stroke engine. The motor is a permanent magnet synchronous design and is powered by a lithium-ion plug-in battery. The motor puts out about 30 horsepower and will propel the Freeride to a top speed of 43 miles per hour. The battery can be charged in 1.5 hours. *KTM North America*

Zero Motorcycles offers the Zero S on-road all-electric motorcycle. Using an advanced monitoring system, each cell in the lithium-ion power pack (battery) is individually controlled during discharging and charging. An onboard charger is used that can bring the batteries back to life in just under four hours. The motorcycle has a 50-mile range. Because of the high torque available from the electric motor, the transmission has only one gear and no clutch. *Zero Motorcycles*

AIR-FUEL RATIOS FOR EMISSIONS

Exhaust gas analyzers (EGA) have been around for years. These diagnostic tools can measure two, three, four, or five exhaust gases, depending on the sophistication level of the model used. While the cost of these tools (typically upward of $3,000) is customarily beyond the budgets of most shade-tree mechanics, knowing how they are used by professional technicians at a dyno-tuning facility is helpful in understanding and interpreting exhaust gas readings cited in engine-performance dyno runs.

The five-gas AFR graph shown in Figure 5 provides the easiest explanation and illustration of the relationships between exhaust gases and how air-fuel mixtures affect them. As discussed earlier, an average AFR of 14.7:1 produces the most efficient and complete burning of the air-fuel mixture during combustion. This is the target for an EFI system to average at idle or cruise in closed-loop operational mode. The graph illustrates why the air-fuel ratio of 14.7:1 produces the lowest level of HC, CO, and NO_x emissions. As the AFR gravitates toward the rich side of the ideal 14.7:1 ratio, both hydrocarbons (HC) and carbon monoxide (CO)

emissions start to rise. Since CO is a byproduct of incomplete combustion, it is only produced when insufficient oxygen is present in the combustion chamber. Therefore, the presence of CO always indicates a rich air-fuel mixture. Insufficient oxygen in a rich mixture will also cause HC to rise, since not all of the fuel can be burned. Exhaust gas NO_x levels are low in a rich mixture, because combustion chamber temperatures aren't high enough to produce NO_x.

In lean AFR mixtures, or those that tend to the lean side of the ideal 14.7:1 ratio, CO is close to, or at, 0 percent, because sufficient oxygen is present to support complete combustion. Therefore a CO reading of close to 0 and an O_2 reading of more than 0 indicates an AFR on the lean side of ideal. False lean air-fuel mixture readings can be caused by a malfunctioning air injection system or leaks in the exhaust system.

As the air-fuel mixture becomes more lean (less fuel, more air), the molecules of hydrocarbons become spaced farther apart, rendering combustion via ignition from the spark plug more difficult. As hydrocarbon molecules become even more widely spaced, because even less fuel is present,

EXHAUST GAS READINGS

The graph in Figure 5 provides a quick reference for interpreting exhaust gas readings produced by a five-gas analyzer. At 14.7:1, the air-fuel ratio is ideal for combustion, since harmful, unwanted HC (in the form of raw, unburned fuel), CO, and NO_x are at their lowest levels.

As the AFR moves toward the rich side of ideal, HC and CO start to rise, and O_2 drops to 0. This is because there is too much fuel for the amount of oxygen present during combustion. All the oxygen is consumed, but there's a lot of fuel left over. CO rises because it is the unwanted result of incomplete combustion—caused by too much fuel and not enough air. When the AFR indicates a rich fuel mixture, combustion temperatures are relatively low, and NO_x production will be 0.

When the fuel mixture tends toward the lean side of ideal, CO is 0 because enough oxygen is present for complete combustion. However, if the AFR moves further to the lean side of 14.7:1, too much oxygen will be present and not enough fuel to support combustion. This can cause what is known as a "lean misfire," a condition that occurs when there is not enough fuel in the air for the spark plug to ignite the mixture. Lean misfires cause extremely high levels of HC from unburned fuel to exit the cylinder. When the engine misfires due to lack of fuel, unburned oxygen levels will increase. In addition, lean AFRs cause combustion temperatures to rise, creating NO_x.

The only gas that is at its highest level at 14.7:1 is CO_2. Therefore, CO_2 can be used as a combustion efficiency indicator. Too rich or too lean causes CO_2 levels to decrease, as the combustion process becomes less efficient.

Many motorcycle performance tuners make extensive use of exhaust gas readings when adjusting air-fuel ratios in fuel maps. Most motorcycle-related exhaust gas samplers don't display NO_x, but many will, at a minimum, take readings of HC and CO.

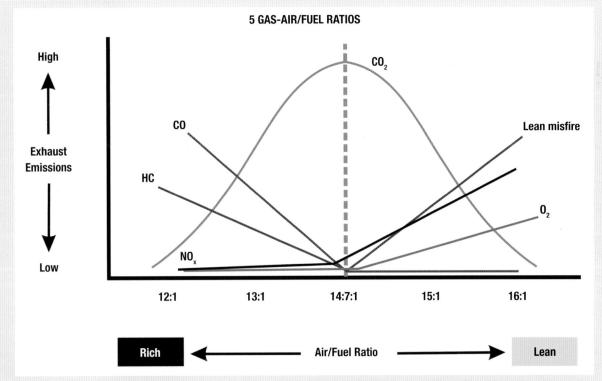

FIGURE 5   This graph shows the five exhaust gases as they relate to emissions. The dashed line above the 14.7:1 AFR identifies stoichiometric air-fuel ratio, the point at which all the air and fuel are consumed in the combustion process. This is where harmful gas emissions are at their lowest and CO_2 emission is at its highest, indicating efficient combustion.

a lean misfire will occur if the spark plug fails to ignite the air-fuel mixture. When this occurs, raw, unburned fuel passes directly into the exhaust gases, causing HC readings to skyrocket. O_2 readings will also continue to rise as the AFR becomes leaner. In addition, NO_x emissions also increase whenever air-fuel mixtures are on the lean side of ideal because there is excess oxygen present during combustion. A lean mixture burns hotter than a rich air-fuel mixture, and these high temperatures will produce NO_x as a byproduct of the combustion process.

So far we've only looked at the three bad gases: HC, CO, and NO_x. Now let's take a look at carbon dioxide (CO_2). CO_2 is often overlooked as an exhaust gas, but it does have value for air-fuel mixture fine-tuning. CO_2 readings peak in output at the average ideal 14.7:1 air-fuel ratio. The higher the CO_2 percentage present, the more efficiently the engine is combusting air and fuel. Since CO_2 readings flatten out at their peak, it can often be difficult to tell on which side of the ideal 14.7:1 air-fuel ratio (either rich or lean) the air-fuel mixture falls. Levels of carbon monoxide are required to determine when CO_2 is at its highest point—exactly the same point at which the engine is most efficient. CO_2 is at its maximum when CO readings first drop to 0 percent. By looking at CO percentages in conjunction with CO_2 percentages, peak CO_2 can be determined. CO_2 levels can tell you how efficient an engine is and how close to ideal its fuel mixture is.

The five-gas AFR graph shows readings obtained from exhaust gases coming directly from the engine. Exhaust gas readings sampled at locations after a catalytic converter, or at the tailpipe itself, will be "masked" by the operation of the catalytic converter. This is because the converter's job is to eliminate HC, CO, and NO_x gases from exhaust emissions, leaving only small amounts of O_2 and CO_2 present instead. In addition, air injection systems should be disabled when taking exhaust gas readings for tuning purposes. Air injection normally operates only during cold engine operation, but a leak in the system could cause a false oxygen reading.

Besides using a five-gas analyzer's exhaust reading to tune EFI systems, it can also uncover other engine problems. By holding an analyzer's sampling probe just above the level of coolant present in a radiator (naturally, with the radiator cap removed), any reading that detects the presence of hydrocarbons could indicate a possible blown head gasket or cracked cylinder head. Technicians must be careful performing this test, since sucking coolant up into the probe will ruin the five-gas analyzer test machine. Another mechanical-condition test can be performed by inserting a five-gas analyzer's sampling probe into a crankcase breather hose, oil dipstick hole, or oil filler hole; high HC readings from this test can indicate worn piston rings or other cylinder sealing problems that cause excessive crankcase blowby.

AIR-FUEL RATIOS FOR PERFORMANCE

Figure 6 shows air-fuel ratios that produce maximum engine power are different than those used to produce the cleanest exhaust. For maximum power, the goal inside the combustion chamber is to extract or consume all of the oxygen present. This chemical process is more of a sure thing when a slight

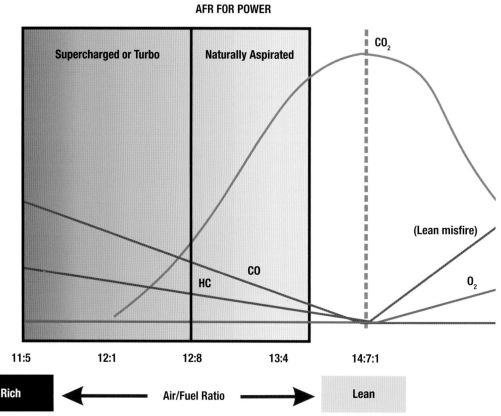

FIGURE 6 When tuning for performance, air-fuel ratios are on the rich side of 14.7:1. The Rich/ Lean scale at the bottom has been shifted toward the rich side of 14.7:1 and is relative to the target AFRs typically used to modify motorcycle EFI systems for maximum engine power. Some tuners may use CO percentage instead of AFR to adjust EFI systems. In general, CO readings should be around 3 percent for idle and cruise and 4 to 6 percent CO represents maximum power.

amount of excess fuel is added. In other words, a slightly rich mixture uses all the O_2 and produces the most power. Adding fuel beyond this point will not make more power, because all the oxygen is already being used. In fact, adding more fuel at this point will reduce power output, because it produces progressively lower combustion temperatures and thus lower cylinder pressures. Excessive fuel will also foul spark plugs, causing a rich misfire condition.

An additional benefit of a slightly rich mixture for power is that combustion temperatures will be somewhat lower. This will lessen the possibility of engine detonation, or knock, which if left unchecked and allowed to continue can over time damage piston ring lands or burn a hole in the piston itself. Twenty years ago, engine combustion chamber technology was not as refined or sophisticated as today's designs. Before modern cylinder head designs, an AFR of 12.5:1 was considered to produce the most power. Modern motorcycle engine design has come a long way since the 1990s, and many factors make engines able to combust air and fuel more rapidly and efficiently. These improvements include high-atomizing EFI injectors, high-energy ignition systems, advanced combustion and piston crown design, and other factors. Because of technological advances, the AFRs for best power are now in the range of 12.8:1 to 13.4:1 for normally aspirated engines. Turbocharged or supercharged engines require an even richer mixture of 11.5:1 to 12.1:1 for the most power.

AIR-FUEL RATIOS AND LAMBDA

So far, air-fuel ratios have been discussed in terms of "parts" of air related to "parts" of fuel. For example a mixture with an AFR of 13.4 parts of air and 1 part fuel would be expressed as 13.4:1 (13.4 to 1). There is another method used to define AFRs that some tuning software and wideband oxygen sensor tuning kits use—Lambda. Wideband O_2 sensors are discussed in detail later in this chapter, but for reference, a wideband O_2 sensor and accompanying software can detect air-fuel ratios over a range of 10:1 to over 20:1. The factory O_2 sensors found on motorcycles are called narrow-band sensors and are only able to deal with AFRs slightly on either side of 14.7:1, the mixture used for cleaning up emissions.

The reason that it's important to have an understanding of what lambda is has to do with how wideband oxygen sensors operate. Neither wide nor narrow-band oxygen sensors actually measure the air-fuel ratio of combustion. Instead, they measure lambda values. The 11th letter in the Greek alphabet, the lambda letter looks like this "λ". Lambda is the ratio of oxygen vs. fuel left over in the exhaust after combustion. Lambda values are often converted and displayed on a gauge or in software as an air-fuel ratio. Lambda values are specific to the fuel being burned, and values will be different for gasoline, E10 (gasoline with 10 percent ethanol), propane, methanol, and others. This is why O_2 sensors are sometimes referred to as lambda sensors, because that is what they do—measure λ values. Lambda sensors "sense" the oxygen content in exhaust gases and report this condition in units, or values of lambda.

The λ measurements indicate if there was more fuel than oxygen or more oxygen than fuel in the exhaust after the mixture was burned. When exactly enough fuel is combined with the available free oxygen, the mixture is chemically balanced and is called stoichiometric. A gasoline AFR of 14.64:1 (rounded off to 14.7:1) burned during combustion would generate a lambda reading that indicates a complete burn of all the fuel and air, or stoichiometrically (stoic) perfect combustion. The lambda value for a gasoline AFR of 14.7: is λ 1.00. If a slightly different fuel was used, like E10, the stoic AFR is 14.08:1, which would generate a different λ value of .957. Another automotive example is E85, used on flex-fuel

AIR/FUEL RATIOS

11.5	12.0	12.5	13.0	13.4	13.6	13.8	14.0	14.5	14.7	15.2	15.7
.782	.816	11.5	.884	.911	.925	.938	.972	.986	1.0	1.03	1.06

Lambda values λ

FIGURE 7 This chart shows relative air-fuel ratios vs. lambda values for gasoline. A lambda value of 1.0 equals a stoichiometric mixture (numbers in green). A lambda less than 1.0 is a rich mixture and lambda of greater than 1.0 is a lean air-fuel ratio. Lambda is indicated by the Greek letter λ. Other types of fuel will have different values. A λ 1.0 value always represents when the correct amount of fuel is combined with available free oxygen and both are completely burned in the combustion process.

vehicles. Gasoline that is mixed with 85 percent ethanol has a stoichiometric number of 9.76:1, and the resulting λ value would be .663.

As discussed, the λ value changes for different types of fuel. So how does the lambda sensor know what type of fuel is being used? The answer is it doesn't. For the lambda sensor to report the correct λ value, the wideband gauge, controller, or software on a laptop needs to be programmed according to the type of fuel to be measured. The default for most of these components is to use the value of gasoline. The controller multiplies the measured lambda by 14.7 to come up with a gauge reading. Most wideband gauge kits and some software use AFR numbers to indicate rich vs. lean intake mixtures. This can become confusing if a fuel other than gasoline is used.

For most street-tuning situations on motorcycles, the only fuel used is gasoline. Having some E10 in the fuel tank is a possibility, however. Instead of trying to convert gasoline AFR values to E10 AFR values for the purposes of fuel mapping, using lambda values is easier to interpret. Some software programs even have a drop-down menu list where the user can select the type of fuel.

Whenever possible many experienced tuners use lambda values to view exhaust burn conditions and thus fuel mixture. Using lambda instead of AFR numbers lets the tuner monitor the mixture purely in terms of what is actually being measured by the wideband oxygen sensor. Using lambda, the tuner doesn't have to remember what AFRs are correct for max engine power or fuel economy. When tuning for fuel economy the lambda will be around 1.00, while tuning for wide open throttle the lambda value should be around .850. Turbocharged or supercharged engines would require a lambda value in the .780 to .810 range. Unfortunately, there are not many wideband gauges that can display lambda. Software programs for a PC or laptop are somewhat more flexible, and many can display either AFR or lambda.

There are some factors that can affect AFR or lambda readings that have nothing to do with the air-fuel mixture entering the engine. Many motorcycles have an air injection system (AIS) that, if not working correctly, could affect AFR when tuning. The AIS is only supposed to operate when the engine is cold, adding fresh, filtered air to the exhaust. The extra oxygen helps get the CAT up to operating temperature quickly. If the system has a leak, or is always on because it's broken, the extra oxygen will result in a different AFR or lambda number when tuning. Even if the bike is not being tuned, the ECU and narrow-band O_2 sensor will see this extra air or oxygen and try to compensate for it by adding fuel to the engine. This will cause an overly rich mixture, possibly fouling the spark plugs or, if the condition exists long enough, ruining the catalytic converter.

Another potential problem is an exhaust leak. Neither narrow nor wideband O_2 sensors take into account exhaust leaks. They just read excessive oxygen in the exhaust, causing incorrect tuning AFR numbers or a too-rich mixture caused by the ECU reacting to the false sensor readings.

THE "BEST" AFR?

So what is the correct AFR number to make maximum horsepower? That depends on whom you ask, the day of the week, and phase the moon is in. In other words, there are too many factors to provide a pat answer to fit all applications. Is the engine being tuned for maximum power, safe operation, or fuel economy? Fuel economy is easy to get one's head around, in that the less fuel added to the mixture, the better the miles per gallon will be. AFRs in the range of 14.4:1 to 15.2:1 (λ .979 to λ 1.03) are in the ballpark for maximum miles per gallon. Because max fuel economy is only achieved at part throttle (around 10 to 30 percent of throttle opening depending on the motorcycle), AFRs can be lean without causing engine damage in the form of ping or knock. On the other hand, AFR for best power is a constant, ongoing debate. Just type "Best air-fuel ratio for my _____" (fill in year, make, and model of a car or motorcycle) into an Internet search engine to see how many opinions are out there.

Concerning AFRs for full power and engine safety, tuning on the side of a little too rich keeps the combustion process from going into melt-down. An AFR of 13:1 (λ .884) is widely accepted to be a good place to start for normally aspirated engines, and 12:1 (λ .816) is good for motorcycles equipped with turbochargers or mechanically driven superchargers. Add more fuel than this, and the engine may suffer another problem. Excessively rich mixtures can wash the oil film off the cylinder walls, causing accelerated piston ring ware. In addition, the extra fuel will eventually fuel-foul the spark plugs.

Selecting AFRs for full power will be different for each motorcycle. In fact, there will be differences between the same year, make, and model because of manufacturing tolerances within the engine. Because of these variables, if one wants to achieve maximum power through experimenting with AFRs, the only sure method is to put the motorcycle on a chassis dyno and measure power output.

Keep air-fuel ratios in perspective when trying to make the most power possible. If an engine's AFR is set only by looking at the highest torque produced, the resulting AFR may be in the 14.1 to 15.1 range. It is a fact that these lean settings will make the max power for most engines, but there's a price to pay—literally. While these settings may make the most power on a naturally aspirated engine, they are not considered "safe" by most tuners. If the bike is going to be used for competitive drag or road racing, the owner probably expects to rebuild the engine at least once per racing season

While these oxygen sensors look similar, their function and operation are quite different. The narrow-band sensor (left) can only react to AFRs between 14.4:1 to 14.9:1 and is typical of stock O_2 sensors. The wideband O_2 sensor (right) can change its output over a wide range of air fuel ratios from 10:1 to over 20:1, making it an excellent fuel-mapping tuning tool. *Zipper's Performance*

and the cost of engine parts and labor is figured into their racing budget. If, however, the motorcycle is for street use, with an occasional track day, most owners are willing to sacrifice the few horsepower that they might get by running lean and instead opt for an air-fuel ratio that will help their engine last and run safely for many years.

Another factor to take into account when measuring AFRs, especially those that are on the edge of causing engine meltdown, is the accuracy of the measuring equipment. Wideband oxygen sensors don't last forever, and tend to lose accuracy over time. Some designs need to be calibrated periodically as well. Also, where the exhaust sample is obtained can make a difference in precise readings. Gas velocities in the exhaust stream may vary, and the location of the wideband O_2 sensor may result in different readings at various engine rpm. At some dyno-tuning facilities, an exhaust sniffer is inserted into the muffler to obtain AFR readings. At low rpm the engine may not produce enough exhaust gas to displace all of the residual air in the muffler and a false lean exhaust reading may be a possibility.

FACTORY NARROW-BAND OXYGEN SENSORS

So far, we have explored the chemistry of air and fuel as they are consumed by the engine and how a catalytic converter operates. It's important to keep in mind that the reason we

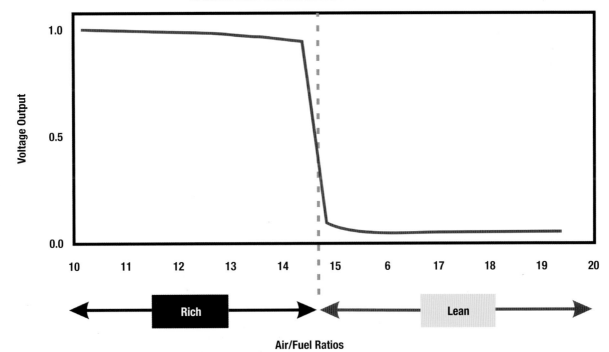

NARROW BAND OXYGEN SENSOR VOLTAGE OUTPUT

FIGURE 8 As shown by the drawing, the voltage output (vertical axis at left) on this narrow-band oxygen sensor switches from rich (0.9 volts) to lean (0.2 volts) only at AFRs that are close to 14.7 to 1. While this design performs well for keeping fuel mixtures within the operating capabilities of the catalytic converter, it won't work at all for measuring AFRs for performance tuning.

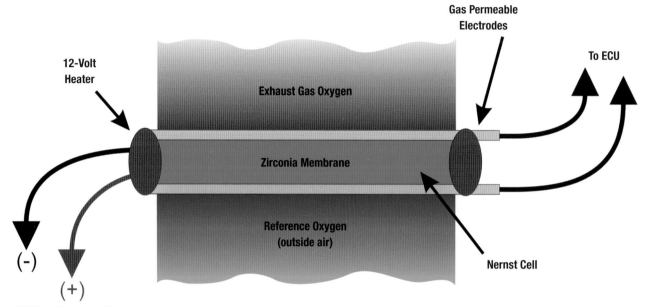

NARROW BAND O$_2$ SENSOR

FIGURE 9 This drawing illustrates how a typical four-wire narrow-band O$_2$ sensor operates. The two wires going to the ECU are the ground and signal wires that indicate oxygen content in the exhaust gas. A voltage output of 0.9 volts means the mixture is slightly on the rich side of ideal, and a voltage reading of 0.1 volts indicates an AFR just to the lean side of 14.7:1. Oxygen sensors must be hot in order to operate, and under certain operating conditions, exhaust gases alone do not produce enough heat to accomplish this. Therefore, some oxygen sensors use an internal heating element. The other two wires (left) are power and ground for the sensor's 12-volt heater.

have EFI engine-management systems at all is to provide proper air-fuel ratios to keep catalytic converters operating at peak efficiency. The key to having precisely the correct amount of air and fuel burning inside a combustion chamber and then exiting the engine as exhaust gas, and eventually passing through a catalytic converter, is the oxygen sensor. We'll start with a discussion of the two types of commonly used factory O$_2$ sensors equipped on motorcycles today—zirconia and titania sensors.

The most common type of oxygen sensor is manufactured using zirconium dioxide. The zirconia O$_2$ sensor is based on a solid-state electrochemical fuel cell, called a Nernst cell. This cell has two gas-permeable electrodes that provide an output voltage corresponding to the quantity of oxygen in the exhaust relative to that in the atmosphere. Here's how it works: When oxygen content in the exhaust gas is low (a rich air-fuel mixture), the difference between the level of exhaust gas oxygen and the level of oxygen in the atmosphere is high, causing the sensor to produce a relatively high voltage—between 0.45 volts to 0.9 volts. Conversely, when the O$_2$ sensor detects a high exhaust gas-oxygen content (a lean air-fuel mixture) and compares it with the oxygen in the outside atmosphere, the difference is smaller, so consequently, lower voltages are generated—between 0.1 to 0.45 volt. The output voltage is then interpreted by the ECU as too much fuel (rich) or too little fuel (lean). The ideal reading that the

ECU is trying to obtain is an average of 14.7:1, and it does this by varying the AFR slightly on either side of 14.7:1.

The other type of oxygen sensor is a titania O$_2$ sensor. It operates somewhat differently from a zirconia-type sensor, but the end results are the same. Instead of producing a small voltage, a titania O$_2$ sensor uses a reference voltage from the ECU and then adjusts its internal resistance based on the oxygen content found in the exhaust gas. A titania sensor's resulting voltages are similar to those of a zirconia sensor. A rich fuel mixture produces higher voltages (above 0.45 volts), while a lean fuel mixture with a little less fuel produces lower voltages of less than 0.45. Titania sensors are less common than zirconia sensors.

Both oxygen sensor types must be hot (600 degrees F) before they can function. Oxygen sensors have to rely on hot exhaust gases to maintain optimal operating temperature levels. Exhaust heat required to operate O$_2$ sensors is dependent to how close they are placed to the engine's cylinder head exhaust port. If the sensor is located too far downstream of the exhaust port, it may cool off and not provide accurate readings. This is especially true when the engine is at idle. To solve this problem, manufacturers use an O$_2$ sensor with an internal 12-volt heater. Heated O$_2$ sensors can also warm up faster from a cold start condition and start feedback-loop control sooner. Both the heated and nonheated types can be found on motorcycles.

CATALYTIC CONVERTERS, AIR-FUEL RATIOS, AND OXYGEN SENSORS

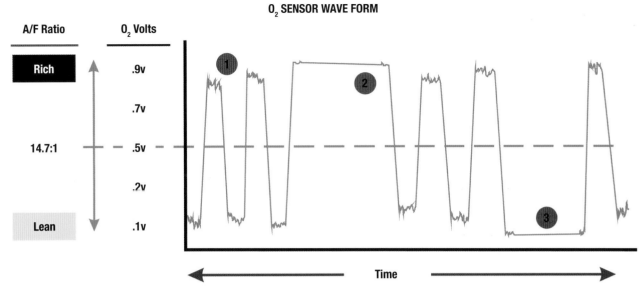

O₂ SENSOR WAVE FORM

A/F Ratio	O₂ Volts
Rich	.9v
	.7v
14.7:1	.5v
	.2v
Lean	.1v

Time

FIGURE 10 This graph shows an oxygen sensor's waveform as displayed on a lab oscilloscope. In this example, the engine is at 3,000 rpm with a steady throttle. Position number 1 indicates the O_2 sensor is operating in closed-loop mode because voltage keeps fluctuating up and down, reflecting continuous fuel correction adjustments made by the ECU. The average of this voltage output is around .45 volts. When the throttle is snapped open (position number 2 on the graph), O_2 sensor voltage rises to 0.9 volts, indicating a rich fuel mixture. Between position numbers 2 and 3 on the graph, the fuel system returns to closed-loop operational mode with the engine at idle. Position 3 on the graph indicates a lean air-fuel mixture when the throttle is suddenly closed.

This narrow-band O_2 sensor is one of two on this BMW 1200 boxer engine. Using two sensors provides the ECU with more accurate exhaust gas oxygen samples and thus a more precise fuel control for lower emissions. *Bob's BMW*

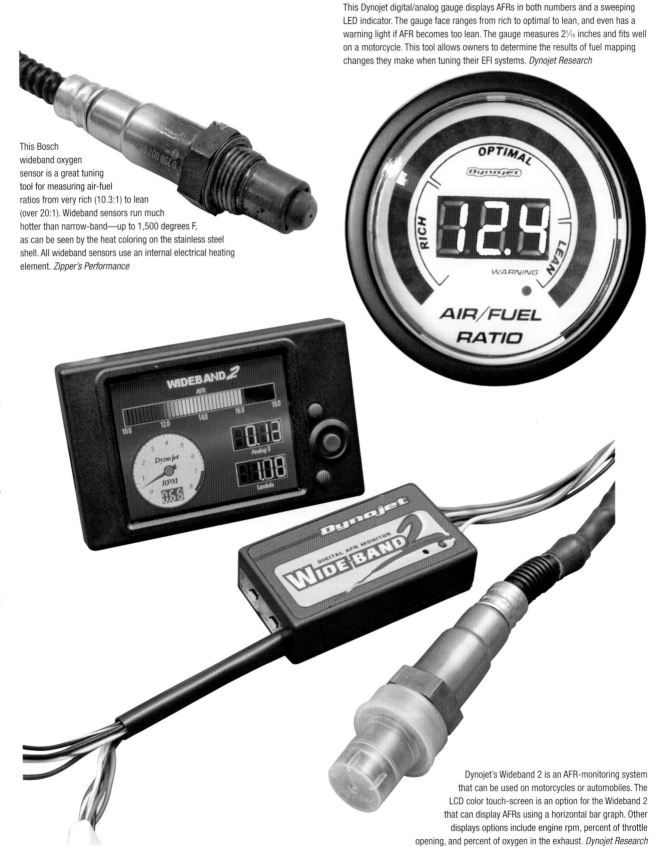

This Dynojet digital/analog gauge displays AFRs in both numbers and a sweeping LED indicator. The gauge face ranges from rich to optimal to lean, and even has a warning light if AFR becomes too lean. The gauge measures 2¹⁄₁₆ inches and fits well on a motorcycle. This tool allows owners to determine the results of fuel mapping changes they make when tuning their EFI systems. *Dynojet Research*

This Bosch wideband oxygen sensor is a great tuning tool for measuring air-fuel ratios from very rich (10.3:1) to lean (over 20:1). Wideband sensors run much hotter than narrow-band—up to 1,500 degrees F, as can be seen by the heat coloring on the stainless steel shell. All wideband sensors use an internal electrical heating element. *Zipper's Performance*

Dynojet's Wideband 2 is an AFR-monitoring system that can be used on motorcycles or automobiles. The LCD color touch-screen is an option for the Wideband 2 that can display AFRs using a horizontal bar graph. Other displays options include engine rpm, percent of throttle opening, and percent of oxygen in the exhaust. *Dynojet Research*

WIDEBAND OXYGEN SENSORS

While stock oxygen sensors perform well in providing information to the ECU for processing fuel correction, they won't work at all for motorcycle fuel mapping. Because of their limitation to only operate right at the stoichiometric AFR range, they are incapable of indicating richer mixtures—the specific ones required for EFI modifications. A variation on the zirconia O_2 sensor, called the wideband sensor, was introduced by Robert Bosch in 1994 for use on automobiles.

Based on the zirconia sensor, the wideband design uses additional circuits to indicate oxygen content in the exhaust. Within the wideband sensor is an electronic circuit that has a feedback loop control in the form of a gas pump that produces an electrical current used to keep the electrochemical zirconia cell voltage output constant. In this way, the gas pump current level directly indicates the oxygen content of the exhaust gas. This output eliminates the rapid rich/lean cycling output of narrow-band sensors. The latest wideband sensor is the five-wire Bosch LSU 4.2 that operates over an AFR range of 10.3 to more than 20 to 1. These sensors also react much quicker to changes in the exhaust gases than older wideband sensors, making them ideal for use in fuel map tuning.

The wideband oxygen sensor is a combination of the zirconia narrow-band sensor plus some additional components (see Figure 11). The Bosch LSU 4 wideband sensor's elements consist of a heater cell, conventional narrow-band sensing Nerst cell, and an oxygen pump cell. Except for the oxygen pump cell, the sensor's other components (heater, reference, and Nerst) are similar to the narrow-band O_2 sensor. The voltage output of the Nerst cell switches at 0.45 volts (stoichiometric 14.7:1) to either rich (1.0 volts) or lean (0.2 volts). Unlike a stock sensor that generates its own voltage, the Nerst cell relies on a reference voltage from the wideband controller. Within the wideband sensor, the Nerst cell compares the partial pressure of oxygen within the pump cell cavity to that of ambient air. The sensing range of the Nerst cell is relatively narrow (14.5 to 14.9 AFR).

The engine's exhaust gas is continually diffused into the pump cell cavity through a small hole, called a diffusion gap. The pump cell pumps oxygen into or out of the cavity, depending on the direction of current (either negative or positive) from the pump cell. As shown in Figure 12, the pump current changes as AFR changes. For rich conditions below 14.7:1, the current is negative; for AFRs above 14.7:1, the current is positive. When the AFR is at stoic (14.7:1) the current output is at 0, neither negative nor positive. The pump cell cavity is maintained at stoichiometric conditions by the Nerst cell. A digital signal processor changes the nonlinear relationship between oxygen pump current and AFR into a linear 0- to 5-volt output, as shown in Figure 13.

WIDEBAND O_2 SENSOR

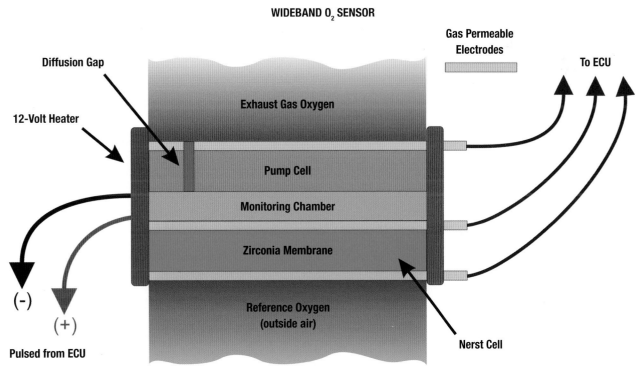

FIGURE 11   This schematic of a wideband O_2 sensor uses a varying voltage signal of 0 to 5 volts input to the controller, indicating oxygen content in the exhaust gas. Wideband sensors use heating elements to keep the sensor's temperature around 1,500 degrees F (twice the operating temperature of a narrow-band sensor). On some sensors, power to the heater is pulsed by the ECU to control the heating element's temperature.

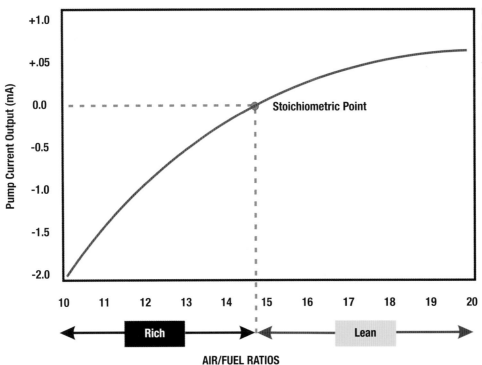

FIGURE 12 A wideband O_2 sensor's pump cell current changes with air-fuel ratio. At AFRs below stoich, the current is negative, and at AFRs above stoich the current is positive. The wideband controller converts this milliamp current into a varying voltage output signal of 0 to 5 volts, with less than 0 indicating rich mixtures and above 0 indicating lean mixtures in relationship to the ideal stoic mixture.

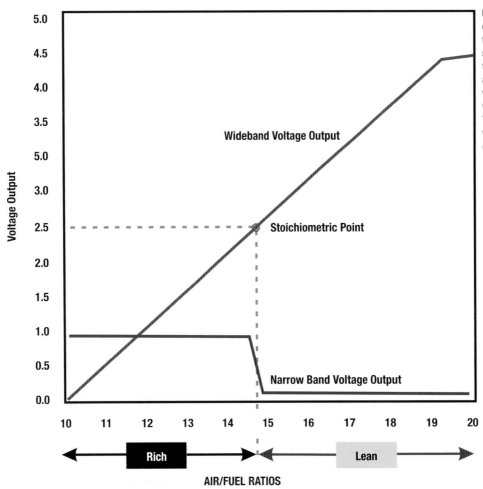

FIGURE 13 This chart shows the differences in voltage outputs between the wideband and narrow-band O_2 sensors. Voltage outputs are vertically on the left of the graph, and air-fuel ratios are horizontally along the bottom. The wideband measures AFR directly over a wide range of air-fuel ratios (pink line). The narrow-band sensor only switches voltages at the stoichiometric point (purple line).

Another difference between narrow- and wideband sensors is the heating element. The narrow-band sensor's heater maintains operating temperature at around 600 degrees F, and it takes up to 10 minutes to reach this temperature. The wideband heating element operates around 1,200 to 1,500 degrees F and heats more rapidly, around 1 minute or less. Power for the heater on the wideband sensors is not a constant 12 volts like the narrow-band sensor's heater. Wideband heaters use a pulse-width modulation that turns the heater current on and off at a 30-hertz rate (30 times per second). Identifying the heater wires is problematic in that some wideband sensors use a constant 12 volts to the heater with the ECU pulsing the ground side of the circuit, and others have a constant ground and pulse the power side of the circuit. When 12 volts are being pulsed to the heater, a voltage meter reading on the power wire will not display 12 volts but a lower reading, 6 to 8 volts. The voltmeter reading is the average of the pulsing 12-volt input. If the meter used has a frequency function it will show the pulses, verifying the presences of the ECU heater control and, thus, the heater-control wire.

There are some things to be careful of when using a wideband O_2 sensor on a motorcycle. Racing gasoline will severely limit the sensor's life, and you'll be purchasing another in short order. Engines that burn oil or have an overly rich mixture (exhaust blowing black smoke) will limit the sensor's ability to accurately read AFR. While usually not a problem, excessive exhaust backpressure will affect sensor readings. And, finally, always make sure the wideband sensor's heater circuit is working whenever the engine is running. Without power to the internal heating element, hydrocarbon residues from the exhaust may clog the sensor and it will have to be replaced.

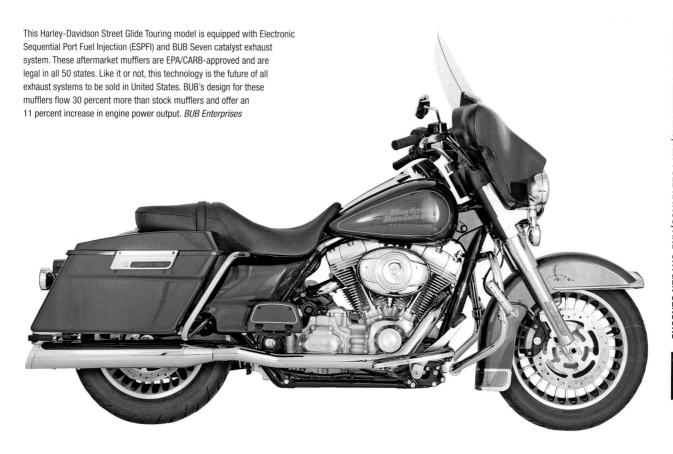

This Harley-Davidson Street Glide Touring model is equipped with Electronic Sequential Port Fuel Injection (ESPFI) and BUB Seven catalyst exhaust system. These aftermarket mufflers are EPA/CARB-approved and are legal in all 50 states. Like it or not, this technology is the future of all exhaust systems to be sold in United States. BUB's design for these mufflers flow 30 percent more than stock mufflers and offer an 11 percent increase in engine power output. *BUB Enterprises*

Chapter 4
How to Measure Engine Performance

Before the late 1700s, horses were the primary means of power for agriculture and transportation needs. With the advent of the steam engine, the use of horses started a long decline, and, by 1920, they were not used in significant numbers to perform work in the United States. Pictured is Becky VanGorder, a member of the Endless Mountains Draft Horse Club, plowing with her two Percheron draft horses. DJ, the white horse, and Donnie provide 2 horsepower, just enough power to pull the plow through the field. *Photo courtesy of Bob Gusciora*

HORSEPOWER

This chapter will explore the science, and art, of measuring an engine's power output, commonly called horsepower. How much power an engine produces has been a subject surrounded by controversy since the advent of the steam engine in the late 18th century. Defining the elusive horsepower number has always come down to whom you ask and what machine (dynamometer) was used to measure it. To complicate things even more, there are more than a few definitions of horsepower. Gross, brake, shaft, effective, indicated, relative, SAE Gross, DIN, JIS, ECE, ISO, advertised, rear wheel, and others are all terms used to define horsepower. To understand and get practical use from engine power measurements, horsepower needs to be put into historical perspective.

"Show me the money!" Horsepower measurement from its inception has been a somewhat questionable proposition. The dollars and cents of measuring an engine's power is easy to understand. For example, if an engine made by company A makes 100 horsepower and company B makes an engine that produces 108 horsepower, and both engines sell for the same price, which is more desirable? This question applies not only to engines themselves but anything that can be bolted onto an engine, like motorcycle exhaust systems. Many aftermarket exhaust manufacturers advertise that their systems will increase the power output of an engine by some amount. If two similar systems claim different power increases, one will have an advantage in the marketplace.

Honda, Harley-Davidson, Suzuki, Kawasaki, Yamaha, Ducati, Triumph, KTM, and other motorcycle manufacturers are all trying to sell products, and, if horsepower is a factor in the sales equation, more can only be better, right? Read the latest review of any motorcycle in an enthusiast magazine, and either rear-wheel or crankshaft horsepower will more than likely be listed. We use it to compare similar bikes in a particular class; we use it to determine which class we're interested in to begin with. It's only logical that the higher the horsepower number your product registers, the more it will sell.

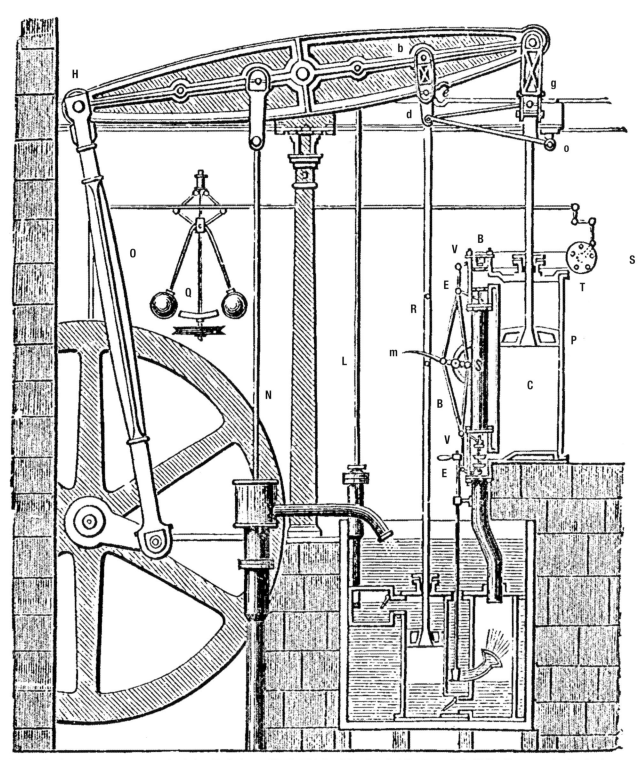

This drawing shows a beam-type steam engine designed by Boulton and Watt in 1784. Here is how it worked: The steam cylinder (C) fills with steam and pushes the piston (P) up, moving the balance beam. The connecting rod (O) then rotates a wheel that transmits power to perform work. From *A History of the Growth of the Steam Engine* by *Robert Thurston, 1878*

(ft-lbs)

Horsepower is measured using a device called a dynamometer, or dyno for short. Every company that manufactures dynamometers has a practical reason to steer potential customers away from their competition by pointing out why the other guy's dyno produces inflated horsepower numbers. Higher horsepower measurements are more desirable, but only if they're real. No motorcycle manufacturer, or aftermarket parts manufacturer, wants to be caught lying to us. Just the same, businessmen have been screwing around with horsepower calculations since the early 1800s.

In 1712, Thomas Newcomen designed the first commercially successful steam engine. It was not very efficient and had limited uses, mostly pumping water out of deep mines. In 1764, Scottish inventor and mechanical engineer James Watt came up with a vastly improved steam engine that used 75 percent less coal than the Newcomen engines. Watt's business plan was to collect royalties from his customers based on one-third of the savings in coal that an older steam engine of similar size consumed. This worked for customers who had existing steam engines and could track their use of coal, but mine operators who still used horses to get their work done needed a different way to calculate what they would pay for upgrading to the cutting-edge technology of Watt's steam engine.

Watt's plan to entice these mine owners to purchase one of his steam engines depended on how many horses the owners could replace, and that depended on how much work a single horse could perform over a period of time. If a horse could hoist a bucket of coal weighing 366 pounds up a mineshaft at the rate of 1 foot per second, in one minute the horse could raise the bucket 60 feet. With this information, Watt calculated that the horse could raise 21,960 pounds one foot in one minute, or 366 × 60 = 21,960 pounds per foot per minute (lb/ft/min). Other engineers at the time placed the number as high as 27,500 lb/ft/min.

Watt experimented further and, in 1782, found that a brewery horse (a large breed) was able to produce 32,400 pounds-feet of work per minute. Watt rounded that number up to 33,000 pounds-feet per minute and that became the standard, which is still used today. In addition to the 33,000 lb-ft per minute number, 550 lb-ft per second is also used (33,000/60 = 550).

Few horses of even the largest breeds can pull that much weight for any length of time, and speculation started that Watt had exaggerated the number to his advantage for the purpose of overvaluing his steam engine's capabilities. Another view is that Watt was just applying good marketing techniques by comparing horses, a familiar form of power and effort at the time, to new technology: the steam engine.

HORSEPOWER DEFINITIONS

We know that, from its earliest use, horsepower numbers have been prone to exaggeration by manufacturers of engines. To further complicate the issue, there are numerous definitions of the term *horsepower* that have been used in the past and currently. Here are some of the ways horsepower is defined.

Indicated horsepower is the theoretical power that a piston engine can produce, with the assumption that it is 100 percent efficient in the conversion of expanding gases in its cylinders into mechanical power. In the 1800s, this measurement was accomplished by calculating the pressure developed in steam engine cylinders. A device called an engine indicator was used, thus the name "indicated" horsepower. This figure doesn't account for any mechanical losses, and actual power output is generally 70 to 90 percent less than the indicated number.

SAE gross horsepower is defined by the Society of Automotive Engineers and is the standard that American auto manufacturers used to rate their engines prior to 1971. Power was measured from an engine running on a dyno that had been carefully prepared specifically for testing. The engine used for testing is configured differently than if it were installed in a car, in that it has no alternator, fuel pump, or mufflers. In addition, the engine is not connected to a

$$\text{Power} = \frac{\text{work}}{\text{time}} = \frac{\text{force} \times \text{distance}}{\text{time}} = \frac{(180\ \text{lbf})(2.4 \times 2\pi \times 12\ \text{ft.})}{1\ \text{minute}} = 32{,}572\ \frac{\text{ft. Lbf}}{\text{minute}}$$

FIGURE 1 This is Watt's formula for calculating how much work a horse could perform. He calculated that a single horse could turn a mill wheel 144 revolutions in an hour, or 2.4 times each minute. If the mill wheel was 24 feet in diameter (12-foot radius), the horse would have to travel about 180 feet to turn the wheel. If the average horse could pull with a force of 180 pounds, the total work the horse could accomplish is equal to 32,572 foot-pounds in one minute.

$$\text{Horsepower} = \frac{\text{Ft. / lb. Per min}}{33{,}000} = \frac{DW}{33{,}000\ t}$$

$$HP = \frac{DW}{33{,}000\ t} = \frac{60 \times 5000}{33{,}000 \times 3} = 3.03\ hp$$

FIGURE 2 The upper equation is the basic formula for finding horsepower. D = the distance the weight is moved; W = the force in pounds required to move the weight through the distance; and t = the time in minutes required to move the weight through the distance. The lower equation shows the amount of horsepower required to raise a weight of 5,000 pounds a distance of 60 feet in three minutes—3.03 horsepower.

HOW TO MEASURE ENGINE PERFORMANCE

transmission but is directly connected to the dynamometer, so there is no power lost from turning all the gears inside a transmission. The horsepower measured was not reflective of what the same engine installed in a car could produce.

SAE gross horsepower numbers could be exaggerated up or down, depending on what marketing goal a manufacturer was trying to achieve. For mass-produced engines, the number was adjusted upwards. For some high-performance muscle cars, the number was decreased, due to problems with the insurance industry and the premiums they might charge customers for higher horsepower numbers.

Brake horsepower, or bhp, is similar to SAE gross horsepower in that it measures engine power at the flywheel and doesn't count accessory or drivetrain (transmission, driveshaft, rear end differential) losses. Actual horsepower at the drive wheels is always less than brake horsepower. The term *brake horsepower* is derived from the water-brake type of dynamometer (discussed later in this chapter) used to measure engine power. The term is still commonly used in the United Kingdom.

SAE net horsepower (Hp) replaced gross horsepower in 1972, and is the current standard for rating power of engines sold in the United States. Horsepower is measured at the flywheel, but the engine is equipped with a full exhaust system, charging system, and emission controls. This caused many manufacturers to publish vastly different horsepower numbers for engines built a few years apart, even though they were the same in every other aspect, giving the appearance that manufacturers had de-tuned the engines when in fact they were just using a different measurement standard.

To muddy the waters further, some loss of published power could actually be attributed to emission-control equipment and lower-compression engines that used regular unleaded fuel instead of high-octane leaded gasoline. But the change from SAE gross to SAE net horsepower kept the auto insurance, environmental, and safety groups happy, because it lowered overall horsepower numbers and gave the perception that auto manufacturers were being more responsible corporate citizens.

SAE net may also be referred to as factory horsepower. Because the SAE net measurement is commonly used to rate motorcycle engines, it is the standard we use in this book.

SAE-certified horsepower was introduced in 2005, and its goal was to reduce the fudge factor that SAE net horsepower numbers from the manufacturers often produced. The basic difference between the two is that an independent observer must be present when an engine is measured on a dyno. Engine power numbers that use this standard can be advertised as SAE-certified.

PS, or *Pferdestärke* (translated as "horse strength" from German), is commonly used in Europe and Japan in both the automotive and powersports industries. PS is always measured at the drive wheels (rear wheel on a motorcycle), so it will always be less than SAE Net.

DIN horsepower is a German standard and is measured at the flywheel instead of at the rear wheels. It is similar to the SAE net standard in that the engine is equipped with all the accessories it would have when installed in a car or truck.

Watts are sometimes used by European and Japanese motorcycle manufacturers to designate the power output of their engines. One horsepower is equal to 745.7 watts. Sometimes electrical horsepower is designated as hp(E) on electric motors; however, most electric motors are rated in watts instead of horsepower.

ENGINE TORQUE

Torque is the "twisting" energy that an engine produces. In addition, torque as a force can also be used to describe a pushing or pulling motion. In pure engineering terms torque is also called moment or moment of force and is defined as energy required to rotate an object (an engine's flywheel for example) about its axis. We'll keep the definition of torque simple in this book and define it as the twisting force at an engine's crankshaft or flywheel. Torque is measured in "foot-pounds" (ft-lbs), which is the common terminology in the United States and used to specify the tightness of a bolt or rotational output of an engine. Torque is also referred to as "pounds-feet" and the difference, or confusion, created by the two terms is in what they technically define. The foot-pound is often used to describe the muzzle energy of a bullet in the study of ballistics in the United States as well as the twisting force created by an engine or electric motor. In 1892, an English physicist coined the term pounds-foot to minimize the confusion with foot-pounds as a unit of work. The two terms are still confusing and either is often used when describing torque. Foot-pounds will be used in this book to refer to torque as it is the common American terminology. Some motorcycle manufacturers will list engine torque in Newton meters (N, or N-m), which is equal to .737 of a foot-pound. For example, a BMW S 1000 RR engine produces 112 N-m of torque and when multiplied by the conversion factor of .737 produces 83 ft-lbs of torque (112 × .737 = 82.5).

MEASURING TORQUE

Home technicians who work on their motorcycles or automobiles are familiar with measuring torque as it pertains to tightening a nut or bolt. A torque wrench measures how much twisting force is applied to a fastener. The torque wrench indicates torque in foot-pounds or inches-pounds. When tightening a bolt, a torque wrench doesn't read the final torque value until the bolt stops turning. This type of torque is called static torque, because there is no acceleration involved when tightening a bolt. Dynamic torque is different than static torque in that it involves acceleration.

Actually, when a bolt is tightened, both dynamic and static torque are present, but not at the same time. As long as a bolt is turning, or rotating, dynamic torque is present. Once

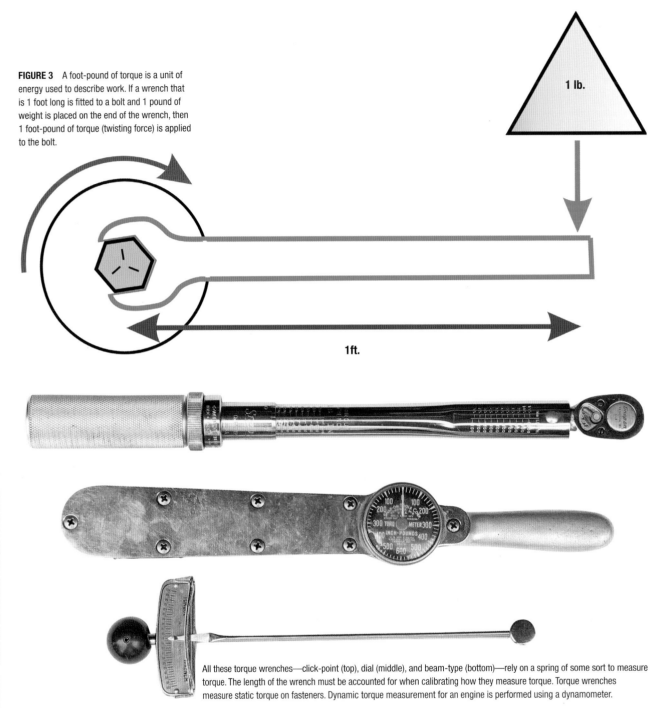

FIGURE 3 A foot-pound of torque is a unit of energy used to describe work. If a wrench that is 1 foot long is fitted to a bolt and 1 pound of weight is placed on the end of the wrench, then 1 foot-pound of torque (twisting force) is applied to the bolt.

1 lb.

1ft.

All these torque wrenches—click-point (top), dial (middle), and beam-type (bottom)—rely on a spring of some sort to measure torque. The length of the wrench must be accounted for when calibrating how they measure torque. Torque wrenches measure static torque on fasteners. Dynamic torque measurement for an engine is performed using a dynamometer.

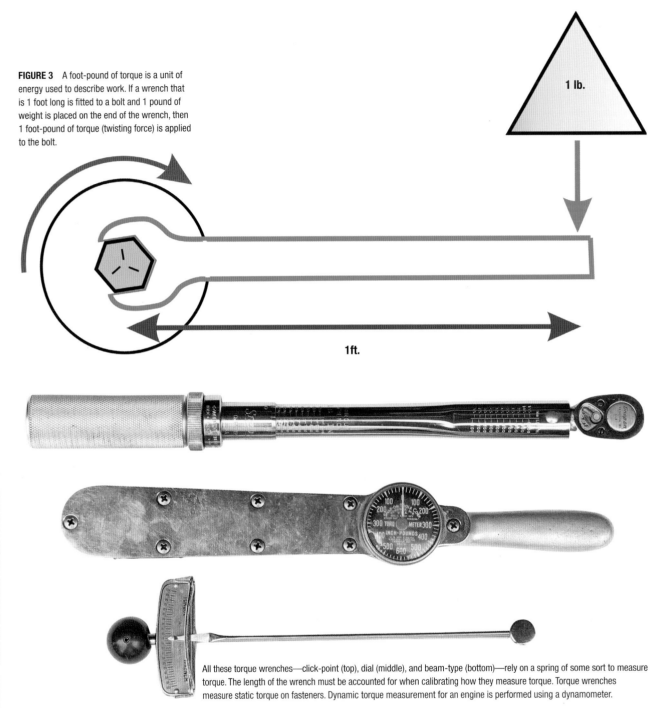

the bolt stops turning, static torque is now being applied. If you use a beam-type torque wrench (pointer or dial), dynamic torque can be observed, as the needle maintains some degree of torque reading while the bolt is rotated. As soon as the bolt stops turning, static torque is read on the torque wrench. Static torque is also applied to a fastener when loosening it.

An engine can produce both static and dynamic torque. For example, if a motorcycle is being ridden using a steady throttle opening on a flat surface, the type of torque produced by the engine is static, because there is no acceleration of the engine. When the throttle is opened and the bike accelerates, the torque produced is dynamic. In this book, torque, whether static or dynamic, is defined as the twisting force created from a running engine. Torque can be measured from the engine's crankshaft, transmission output shaft, or, most commonly, at the rear wheel of a motorcycle.

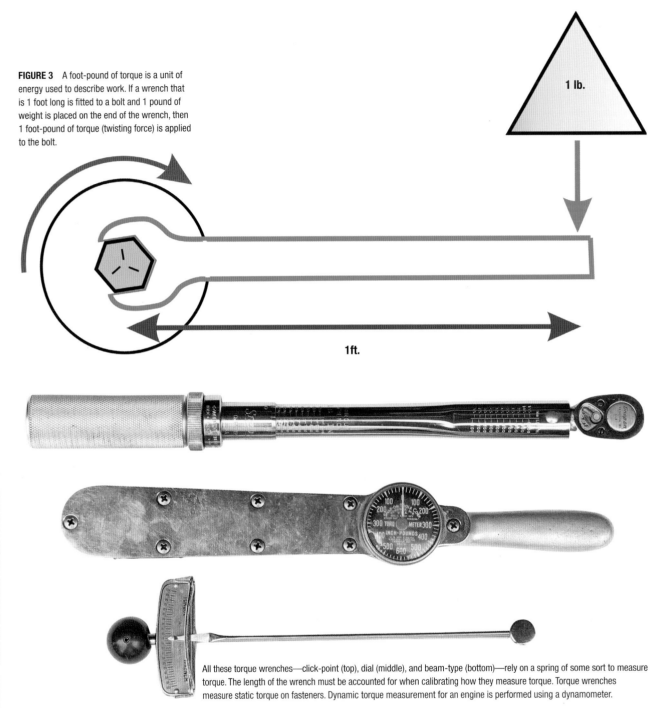

HOW TO MEASURE ENGINE PERFORMANCE

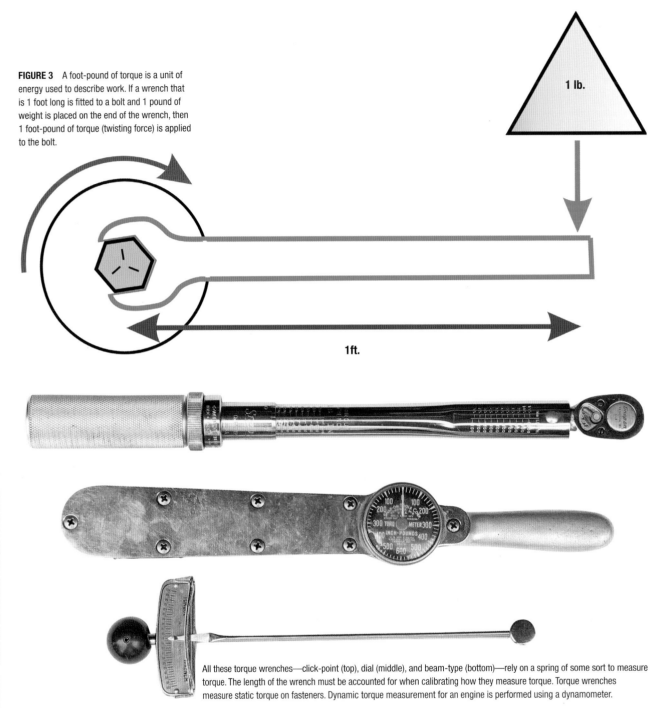

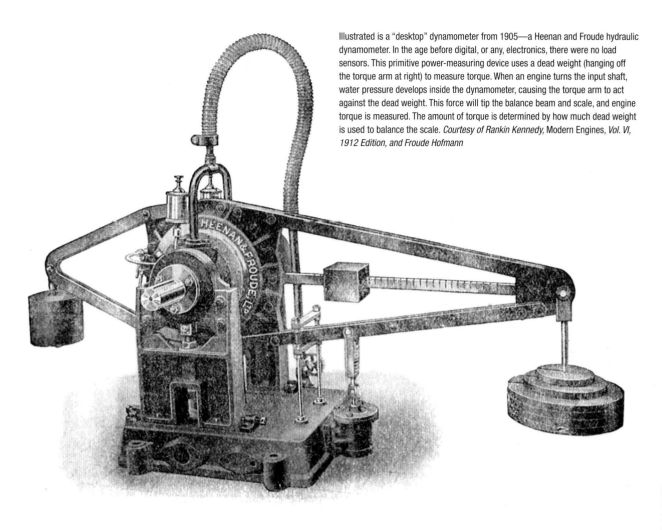

Illustrated is a "desktop" dynamometer from 1905—a Heenan and Froude hydraulic dynamometer. In the age before digital, or any, electronics, there were no load sensors. This primitive power-measuring device uses a dead weight (hanging off the torque arm at right) to measure torque. When an engine turns the input shaft, water pressure develops inside the dynamometer, causing the torque arm to act against the dead weight. This force will tip the balance beam and scale, and engine torque is measured. The amount of torque is determined by how much dead weight is used to balance the scale. *Courtesy of Rankin Kennedy, Modern Engines, Vol. VI, 1912 Edition, and Froude Hofmann*

WATER BRAKE DYNAMOMETER

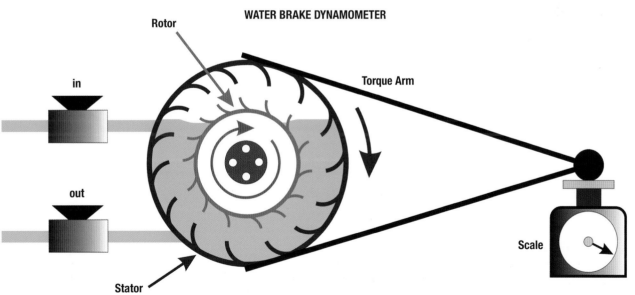

FIGURE 4 This drawing shows how a water brake dynamometer operates. The engine's crankshaft is coupled to the hub (located in center, with four holes), which is connected to the rotor. When the rotor turns (red arrow), its vanes throw water out against the vanes in the stator, creating resistance against the turning rotor. The stator can't turn but does move enough to cause the torque arm to press on the scale. The more twisting force the engine applies to the rotor, the more weight is placed on the scale, indicating a higher torque reading. Inlet and outlet valves (left) control the amount of water inside the water brake, and add or subtract to the load placed on the engine. A modern water brake dyno uses an electrical or digital load cell instead of a mechanical scale.

DYNAMOMETERS FOR MOTORCYCLES

There are two basic configurations for dynamometers that measure the power of motorcycle engines, engine and chassis. Engine dynamometers are used to measure power directly at the engine's crankshaft or flywheel. The engine is tested without its transmission or drivetrain connected. In other words, the engine is not installed in a motorcycle but on a test stand. For the majority of riders, removing the engine for this type of testing is too costly and impractical. The chassis dynamometer measures power at the motorcycle's rear wheel, and the bike is simply ridden onto the chassis dyno test stand and strapped down.

Of the four types of dynamometers discussed below, the water brake and eddy current types can be configured as either chassis or engine dynamometers. The electric motor designs (AC or DC) are used as engine dynos only. The last type, the inertia dynamometer is only used in the chassis configuration.

Water Brake and Hydraulic Brake Dynamometers

The first dynamometer was invented in 1821 by Gaspard de Prony. The de Prony brake, as it was called, was used to measure the performance of engines and other types of machines. Dynamometers have been widely used since the late 1800s to measure the torque of steam engines. The water brake dynamometer, sometimes mistakenly called a hydraulic dynamometer (hydraulic dynamo-meters work on the same principle as water brake dynamometers but use hydraulic fluid instead of water), is the oldest type of design and is still used today. Water and hydraulic brake-power absorption units can accommodate anything from a Briggs and Stratton lawnmower engine that makes 2 horsepower to marine diesel engines that make considerably more. The Froude Hofmann model RLS295 hydraulic dynamometer can absorb 39,440,000 foot-pounds of torque and 650,000 horsepower. Since most motorcyclists will never see a hydraulic dyno, we will concentrate on the

This Froude Hofmann hydraulic dynamometer measures power for marine engines. It can absorb 39,440,000 foot-pounds of torque and 650,000 horsepower. It is more than 9 feet in diameter (see worker on scaffold for scale). If you think this is big, you should see the engine that it connects to. This dynamometer's cost? A mere $4 million. Despite its size, it operates in the same general way that all water brake dynamometers do. *Froude Hofmann*

William Froude was born in England in 1810, and in 1877 he invented the hydraulic dynamometer, or water brake. Pictured is a large version of a water brake circa 1900, a model FA7 Froude Hofmann. The torque arm is easily visible to the right and looks to be almost 15 feet long. The company was established in 1881 and is still in business designing and manufacturing high-technology specialized test equipment. It produces power-measurement products for engines used on ships, automobiles, aircraft, even motorcycles. *Froude Hofmann*

water brake dynamometer as it functions in essentially the same manner.

A water brake dynamometer basically consists of two half couplings, a rotor and a stator (see Figure 4). The stator is stationary and the rotor is connected to the engine's flywheel on an engine dyno or on a roller on a chassis dyno. The rotor and stator have semicircular-shaped vanes that direct the flow of fluid as the engine turns the stator. Water flowing around the vanes creates a torque reaction through the dynamometer casing, or stator, which is free floating so that a slight rotational movement takes place when under load. The outer housing doesn't rotate because a torque arm holds it in place. The arm is called a torque arm because it "feels" 100 percent of the engine's torque trying to rotate the outer housing as the engine tries to twist or load it.

Before electronics, a scale was used to measure the load from the torque arm. Today, a load cell transducer or strain gauge converts the force applied to the arm into a digital signal that is sent to data-acquisition software on a laptop or PC. Engine loading, or how much the stator is resisting the engine's torque, is controlled by varying the level of water in the rotor housing using adjustable inlet or outlet valves. Raising the water level increases the rotational drag of the water brake's rotor, applying more resistance or load to the engine.

By design, the water brake is an inefficient pump and uses the engine's power to make hot water. Large water brake dynos can require a cooling tower the size of a building to dissipate the heat from the water, while smaller versions can use a garden hose. The Froude Hofmann RLS295 can't use either of these cooling methods—it needs a large lake or ocean to dissipate the heat it creates when under load.

Electric Motor Dynamometers

An electric DC or AC motor can both provide power absorption and drive an engine in order to measure frictional

(ft-lbs)

Dynamometers were developed for the automobile industry as a tool for engine development. In general, they function as power-absorption units, and the best of them can simulate real road conditions. Thanks to modern software, a good dynamometer can put an engine through its paces as if it were out in the real world driving on a highway. *Froude Hofmann*

torque or produce real-world road conditions. An engine can be coupled to an electric motor to drive it, essentially turning the assembly into a DC generator. The electrical output of this DC generator can then be calculated and converted into torque measurements. The electric motor dynamometer can also work in reverse in that it can drive an engine to determine its frictional horsepower losses. Large AC electric motors are also used to provide load absorption.

Electric motor dynamometers are very accurate and can regulate engine speed within a couple of rpm and have the ability to adjust engine loading from 0 to 100 percent in microseconds. They also have several disadvantages and are only used for serious, laboratory-grade engine development, generally by motorcycle or auto manufacturers. First, they are expensive. Another disadvantage is the weight of the

dynamometer's armature, which acts like a giant flywheel connected to the engine. This rotating mass makes anything other than steady-state load testing problematic since it takes considerable power from the engine being tested to accelerate the heavy rotor.

Eddy Current Dynamometer

Similar to a DC generator power-absorption unit, the eddy current, or electromagnetic brake, dynamometer also uses electricity to place a load on an engine. The difference between the eddy current and the DC generator is that the eddy current unit does not generate electrical current. The engine under test is connected to the dyno's input shaft, spinning a metallic rotor that creates a magnetic field. When current is increased to the dyno's internal electromagnetic coils,

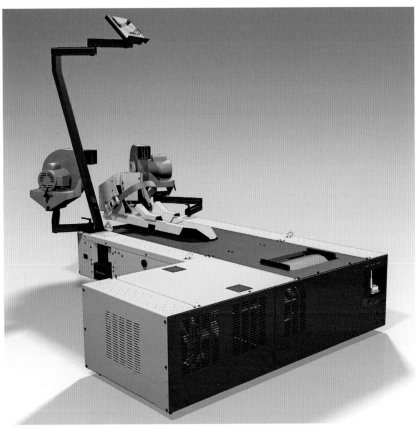

This Dynojet 250i load-control dynamometer can hold engine speed steady at any throttle opening while testing a motorcycle engine. The dyno can measure up to 750 horsepower at speeds of 200 miles per hour. It can also be configured to run sweep tests, like an inertia dynamometer. This type of dynamometer is available in portable designs (pictured) and in-ground installations. *Dynojet Research*

Pictured is a Dynojet Control panel for their WINPEP 7 software. This software allows the user to create custom gauges that have both analogue and digital displays. *Dynojet Research*

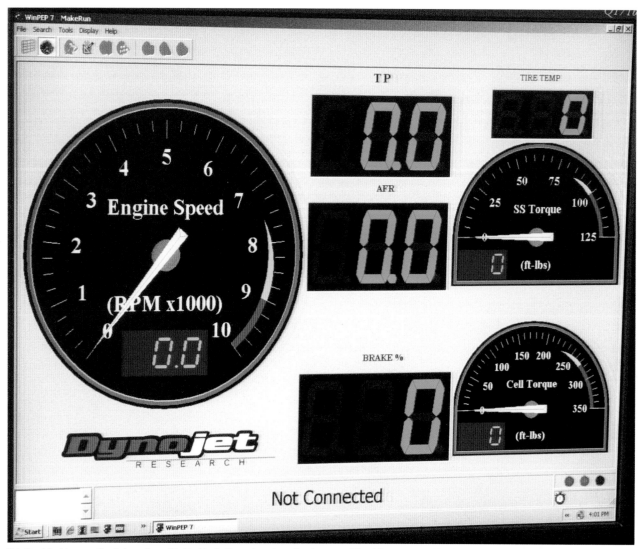

This Dynojet eddy-current load-absorption unit is ideal for testing motorcycle engines because of its quick response and loading capabilities. The electromagnetic coils can be seen next to the heat-absorption rotor. The rotor looks like a car's disk brake and has large cooling fins and passages to dissipate the heat created by a loaded engine. *Dynojet Research*

the rotor shaft becomes harder to rotate and thus loads the engine. Torque load is measured using a strain gauge similar to those used on water brake dynamometers.

Since the rotor gets hot as the dyno resists the engine's power, it must be cooled. Eddy current dynamometers used for testing motorcycle engines are usually air-cooled by a contraption that looks like an oversized automotive brake rotor with large cooling fins.

Eddy current dynos are accurate and offer the flexibility to perform both steady-state load testing and acceleration sweep testing.

Inertia Dynamometer

There are basically two kinds of dynamometers in use for testing motorcycle engines today, load and inertia. Load dynos

(eddy current and water brake) measure torque and have been discussed. The most common design of dynamometer is the inertia type, which doesn't actually measure torque but instead calculates it by measuring acceleration.

An inertia dyno calculates an engine's power output by measuring the time it takes for the motorcycle's rear tire to accelerate a heavy steel drum. Force at the surface of the drum is measured indirectly by measuring its acceleration from one revolution to the next. Force is calculated using Newton's second law: Force = Mass × Acceleration. Because the mass, or weight, of the drum is known, force (horsepower) can be calculated. A typical dyno run begins with the engine running just over idle, in fourth or fifth gear with the rear tire turning drum. When the throttle is opened, the engine accelerates the dynamometer's drum as engine speed increases to redline.

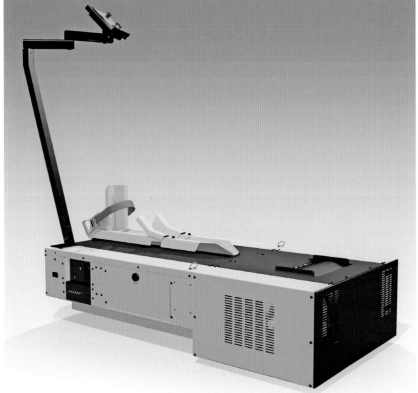

ABOVE Pictured is a torque cell that connects the stationary and movable components of a Dynojet eddy-current load unit. As the engine is loaded, the rotor, coupled to the engine (or roller on a chassis dyno), pushes against the housing that holds the electrical coils passing through the torque cell. The cable connected to the torque cell goes to the data-acquisition system, where the dyno operator can view torque in real time, an advantage when performing fuel map tuning. *Dynojet Research*

LEFT The Dynojet 200i is a chassis dynamometer that provides a quick way for motorcycle dealers and independent repair shops to diagnose a variety of performance problems and verify repairs. It comes with an atmospheric-pressure module that provides a correction factor to ensure consistency between dyno runs made at different times and under varying conditions. *Dynojet Performance*

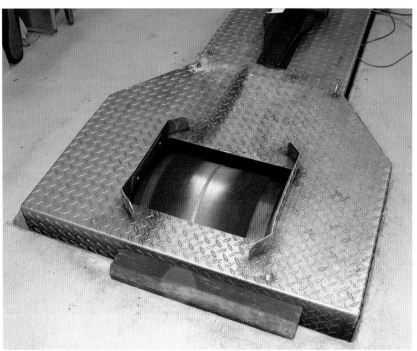

LEFT   This in-ground inertia dynamometer's roller weighs several hundred pounds and has an abrasive surface to keep a motorcycle's rear tire from slipping during a dyno run. The rate of acceleration of the roller is measured and that data is used to calculate horsepower. *Battley Cycles*

BELOW   This is the operator's panel that controls basic dyno functions of a Dynojet dynamometer. The two white buttons move the roller up and back in order to accommodate motorcycles with different wheelbases. Blue buttons are for the right and left engine-cooling blowers. The red and green buttons on the right are for dynamometer load control, and the big red button is in case something bad happens and the dyno run has to be stopped quickly. *Dynojet Research*

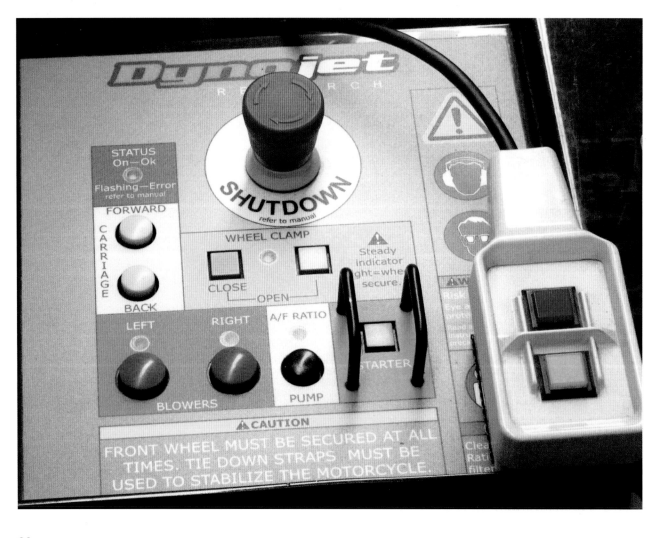

This Harley-Davidson Sportster is having an aftermarket exhaust system installed. A wideband oxygen sensor will be used to adjust the AFR to match the increase in airflow created by the less restrictive exhaust system. *Zipper's Performance*

Computer software used with inertia dynos can accurately measure acceleration of the drum over small increments of time and calculate a value for torque. Using torque and engine rpm rear wheel horsepower can be calculated.

THE VEYPOR—DO-IT-YOURSELF DYNAMOMETER

Don't have $40,000 for a dynamometer to see if all those engine upgrades on your motorcycle really did anything? Don't want to spend $250 or more to have your bike's power measured at the local dyno-equipped shop every time you change something? The Veypor and the VR2, from Nonlinear Engineering, are cost-effective alternatives to dynamometer testing. They are motorcycle data acquisition tools that offer riders a wealth of information. They can measure and plot horsepower and torque curves between two rpm levels in any gear. They also time quarter-mile runs and provide trap speeds. You can measure 0 to 60-mile-per-hour times, ⅛-mile times, top speed, and peak horsepower and torque.

The tool uses internal accelerometers that start timing for these features automatically. After performance runs are completed, data can be plotted on a graph. The VR2 can even upload data to PC software for more detailed analysis. Other features include a fuel toolbox with a simulated gas gauge, lap timer, programmable shift light, G acceleration meter, gear indicator, and others. Both the Veypor and VR2 will work on any motorcycle (or car for that matter). The VR2 offers additional features like lap delta time display, drag coefficient, and extended data logging. Both units are offered with an optional aluminum case that looks good on cruisers. Each unit comes with a Ram Ball universal mounting system that makes installation easy. A 9-volt AC power supply is also included, so the Veypor can be programmed using a PC or laptop computer.

Every time engine upgrades like an exhaust system, high-performance air filter assembly, or Dynojet Power Commander and fuel map are added to a motorcycle, there is always the question as to how effective the modifications are. These types of mods typically offer incremental increases in horsepower and torque, and judging if they work or not by the seat of your pants during a ride is somewhat subjective. An ideal measurement tool for the do-it-yourselfer, is the Veypor and VR2, good alternatives to traditional dynamometer testing. These units can provide a wide variety of power-related numbers and graphs, including horsepower and torque. *Nonlinear Engineering*

In the dynamometer mode, performance is measured between a start and stop rpm in third or fourth gear. To take this measurement, the rider opens the throttle below the start rpm and closes it after passing the stop rpm. The Veypor logs the data automatically. After the run, the unit enters the graphing mode, in which the screen displays horsepower, torque, and rpm, plus measurements over time including rpm, horsepower, velocity, and G-force. *Nonlinear Engineering*

CALCULATING HORSEPOWER

Horsepower and torque have already been discussed separately, and in this section they will be looked at together. In engineering terms, power output is expressed as torque multiplied by its rotational speed around an axis. An engine's horsepower output is in reality a calculation where engine torque produced is multiplied by the engine's speed. In order to use foot-pounds of torque and engine rpm to calculate horsepower, several numerical conversions need to take place. The formula for horsepower is Torque × Engine Speed, divided by 5,252, equals horsepower.

$$Horsepower = \frac{Torque \times rpm}{5252}$$

The number 5,252 is the result of lumping several conversion factors together into one number. One horsepower is defined as 550 foot-pounds of work per second, or 33,000 ft-lbs per minute. Engine power is equal to its torque times its angular velocity, and to convert angular velocity to engine rpm it needs to be multiplied by 2 pi (3.14159 × 2). So now we have Hp = 550 ft-lbs/ seconds × 2 pi. If this equation is rearranged it looks like this: Hp = (Torque × rpm × 2 pi) / 33,000/minute. This can be simplified further as 33,000 / (2 × 3.14159) = 5,252—the constant in the horsepower formula. On all graphs that show horsepower and torque curves, the two curves always intersect at 5,252 rpm because at that rpm the two will always be equal.

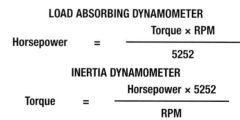

LOAD ABSORBING DYNAMOMETER

$$Horsepower = \frac{Torque \times RPM}{5252}$$

INERTIA DYNAMOMETER

$$Torque = \frac{Horsepower \times 5252}{RPM}$$

FIGURE 5 Load-absorbing dynamometers, like the eddy current design, measure torque and calculate horsepower. Inertia dynos measure horsepower and calculate torque. Watt's formula for power works either way—if torque and rpm are known, horsepower can be calculated. If horsepower and rpm are known, torque can be calculated.

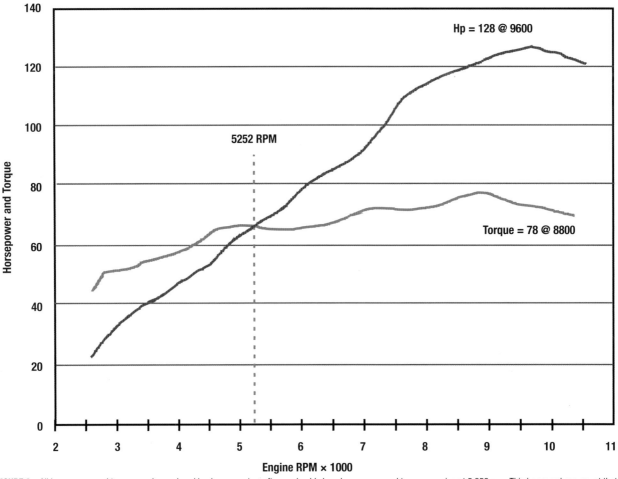

FIGURE 6   All horsepower and torque graphs produced by dynamometer software should show horsepower and torque crossing at 5,252 rpm. This happens because, at that rpm, torque and horsepower are always equal to each other. In addition, below 5,252 rpm torque will always be higher than horsepower, and above 5,252 rpm horsepower will always be higher than torque. A chart that doesn't show these characteristics has a "math" problem and is highly questionable.

HOW TO MEASURE ENGINE PERFORMANCE

HORSEPOWER VS. TORQUE

One activity that many motorcyclists participate in is benching racing, using horsepower and torque numbers to compete verbally with one another. Many times the statement "Torque creates acceleration, not horsepower" is made, often by cruiser owners whose motorcycles are low in the horsepower department, when compared to sportbikes, but generally they have higher torque numbers. This thinking, while it may make some kind of intuitive sense, is incorrect. Horsepower and torque are linked by the fact that horsepower is calculated from torque in foot-pounds and engine rpm (Hp = T × rpm / 5,252). Because of this formula, horsepower and torque are dependent on one another in relation to engine power.

Before we discuss how torque and horsepower are related, let's have a quick review of work, power, and torque. Work is the application of force over a distance. If a 10-pound weight is lifted 20 feet, 200 foot-pounds of work has been accomplished (10 × 20 = 200). Power is the application of

work within a finite time. So 550 ft-lbs of work in 1 second equals 1 horsepower. Torque is a twisting force applied to a bolt or an engine's crankshaft. A wrench fitted to a rusted bolt that is 1 foot long with a weight of 92 pounds tied to the end would exert 92 foot-pounds of torque on the bolt. Because the bolt is not moving, no work or power is present. Hypothetically, when the bolt breaks free it still requires 92 foot-pounds of force (torque) to keep it turning, so, for every revolution of the wrench, 92 pounds of force is applied over a distance or rotation. That distance is two times pi, or 2 × 3.14 = 6.28 feet—the circumference of the circle that the end of the wench makes as it turns the bolt. It's only when the bolt is moving that work is being performed. If the wench is turned fast enough to rotate once per second, then 550 foot-pounds of work-per-second is being accomplished, which is equal to 1 horsepower.

For an engine, torque is always listed at specific rpm because, like the rusted bolt, no work or power is produced unless the engine is turning. Once an engine is turning fast

HARLEY VS. DUCATI

The horsepower and torque graph in Figure 7 compares horsepower and torque for two very different motorcycles: a Harley-Davidson Road King and a Ducati 1098. Both engines have a V-twin design, but the similarity ends there. Since this is a fantasy horsepower and torque graph, let's assume for the moment that these two engines are installed in identical bikes and ridden by riders who weigh the same. The Harley engine makes 78 ft-lbs of torque at 4,200 rpm and the Ducati engine makes 62 ft-lbs at 10,400 rpm. If you were to bet on a drag race between the two bikes, and you think more torque will win the race, you'd lose. Here's why.

Both motorcycles will leave the starting line and run neck-and-neck for a short distance. When the Harley engine reaches its rpm redline (around 6,000 rpm), the rider will have to shift into second gear to continue the race. At that shift point, the motorcycle with the Harley engine is traveling around 40 miles per hour. At the same point in the race, the motorcycle with the Ducati engine is still accelerating in first gear and won't have to shift into second until over 12,000 rpm. When the 1098 engine makes the first-to-second-gear shift, his speed will be around 74 miles per hour—almost twice the speed of the motorcycle with the Harley engine. Even though the Harley engine can deliver 40 more foot-pounds of torque and has more initial "push" to get the motorcycle launched, the bike with the Ducati engine can go twice as fast in each gear. Every time the respective riders shift into a higher gear, torque and horsepower are reduced due to the gear ratio becoming higher. To win an all-out drag race, the engine that doesn't have to be shifted as often will win. The Ducati engine that makes more horsepower at a higher rpm wins the race.

Back to reality. Each of these V-twin engines and their respective motorcycles are designed for different purposes. The Ducati is a road-race replica, weighs around 370 pounds, and is intended for track use and occasional street riding. The Harley-Davidson is only for street riding, and as a cruiser weighing in at 850 pounds, doesn't need to be ridden fast to be enjoyed. Although both of these motorcycles feature a V-twin engine, that's where the similarities end. The Harley engine has a longer stroke, smaller valves and intake tract, and a heavier flywheel. This engine design fills its cylinders (volumetric efficiency) at close to 100 percent at low rpm, providing lots of low-end torque—ideal for the type of motorcycle it powers, especially getting all that weight moving from a stop. The trade-off is that it runs out of breath at higher rpm. This is due to both the use of smaller valves and the camshaft design. Cylinder filling becomes less and less efficient as engine speed increases, causing torque to drop. The upside is that the Harley is easy to ride on the street, because the large, flat torque curve between 2,000 and 5,500 rpm means the bike doesn't require much shifting.

The Ducati has a short stroke that allows the engine to rev much higher, and the large intake tracts and valves promote cylinder filling at high rpm. The camshaft design's duration and valve overlap does not fill the 1098's cylinders with air and fuel below 6,000 rpm, but starting at around 9,000 rpm, cylinder filling is at 100 percent and probably over 100 percent at 12,000 rpm. For the Ducati to use its 149 horsepower, the gearbox has to be shifted constantly in order to keep the engine in this 9,000- to 12,000-rpm range—not an easy ride on the street.

The total weight of a motorcycle dictates engine design to some extent. The Ducati weighs around 370 pounds without the rider. It doesn't take as much low-end torque to get the lightweight sportbike going when compared to the Harley-Davidson that weighs in at 850 pounds.

For both bikes, the chart shows that each engine's torque drops after a certain rpm. This is due to the fact that, as rpm increases, the cylinders don't fill with air as well as they do at lower engine rpm. Cylinder filling is directly proportional to torque production. Horsepower continues to increase even after torque begins to decrease because horsepower is a product of rpm and torque. After torque reaches its peak, the amount by which it decreases is initially small enough not to offset the still increasing rpm. Therefore, overall horsepower will continue to increase until the drop in torque becomes large enough that it outweighs the increase in rpm. This can be seen in both engines' graphs, but it takes place at different places along the rpm scale—higher for the Ducati and lower for the Harley-Davidson.

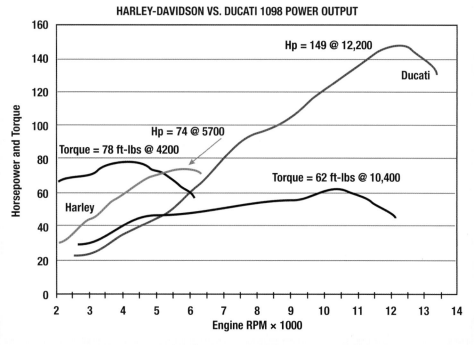

FIGURE 7   This chart is unique in that it compares a Harley-Davidson V-twin engine's horsepower and torque to a Ducati 1,098 V-twin sport bike engine—something that will never be seen in any motorcycle magazine.

enough, the force exerted against a load (like accelerating the drum on an inertia dynamometer) and the speed at which its work is being accomplished can be measured. Even with this fixed relationship between horsepower and torque, some riders state that a certain engine has a lot of power but is low on torque. Keeping in mind that the connection between torque and horsepower is the rotational speed of the engine, a four-cylinder sportbike engine might generate 149 Hp at 12,200 rpm with torque peaking at 62 foot-pounds at 10,400 rpm (see Figure 7). By comparison, a V-twin engine might make 74 Hp at 5,700 rpm and make 78 foot-pounds of torque at 4,200 rpm. The V-twin's torque at 4,200 rpm is greater than the sportbike's torque at 10,400 rpm, but the sportbike engine makes up for this difference with more engine speed (6,000 rpm more) that translates into higher horsepower.

Figure 7 shows how each engine's horsepower and torque characteristics are designed for a specific use. The V-twin cruiser makes 45 more foot-pounds of torque right off idle. Both torque and Hp are higher on the cruiser up to its redline of 6,500 rpm, and only at 7,000 rpm does the sport bike make more horsepower. The sport bike never reaches the V-twin's torque at any point in the chart. It is common sense that a 150-horsepower sportbike will be faster than a 74- Hp cruiser. But the cruiser makes way more torque, so why is the sportbike faster?

Before that question is answered, let's look at another example of how torque and horsepower relate. Two identical V-twin cruisers trying to pass a truck on the interstate. Both motorcycles are ridden by riders who weigh the same, and their engines are identical. At 60 miles per hour, both riders pull out into the left lane to pass an 18-wheeler. Rider A believes that acceleration is caused by torque and he knows from reviewing a dyno chart for his bike that at 2,500 rpm the engine will continue to produce torque until 4,200 rpm (see Figure 7). He leaves his motorcycle in fifth gear and starts to pass the truck. Rider B believes that horsepower, not torque, causes acceleration and he downshifts his motorcycle into third gear to make his pass. When he downshifts, the engine is now turning at 3,500 rpm. He, too, has looked at the same chart as Rider A and knows that torque from his engine will decrease at that engine speed, but his horsepower will increase. When passing the truck, Rider A accelerates at a constant rate as his engine torque increases. Rider B accelerates at a faster rate than rider A, but his torque is decreasing while his horsepower is increasing. Which rider passes the truck first? Even if you don't ride a V-twin cruiser you probably know the answer: Rider A, who downshifted into third gear.

Rider A is taking advantage of gearing to make more rear wheel torque than Rider B. His engine's torque is the same as the other bike's but because he is in third gear his rear tire is applying more torque to push his motorcycle forward. This is because engine torque is multiplied (increased) by the gear ratio of the selected gear. On any motorcycle, acceleration is always fastest in the lowest gear. As the rider shifts into successively higher gears, acceleration—or G force—starts to drop off.

For example, if a rider is in second gear and whacks the throttle open, how hard does he have to hold onto the handlebar grips in order to keep from falling off the back of his motorcycle? When in fifth or sixth gears, how hard does he have to hold on? Not as much, because there is less G force or pulling power from the rear wheel in the higher gear. Engine torque provides the pushing force to accelerate a motorcycle, but that force is transmitted through a gearbox and drivetrain. The gear ratios in the transmission divide the engine rpm and the torque, with higher gears producing less rpm and less rear-wheel torque at a given speed.

Torque produced by the engine always happens at some given speed, and the combination of torque and rpm (speed) are really what define power. To make more power, the engine has to turn faster (Rider A passes the truck with his engine spinning at 3,500 rpm vs. Rider B, whose engine is turning at 2,500 rpm). Horsepower is the rate at which work is performed, and torque is the amount of work or force an engine can produce. For making power, it is always better to make torque at a higher rpm than a lower rpm.

HORSEPOWER VS. TORQUE, AN EXTREME EXAMPLE

At the start of the industrial revolution, before the advent of steam power, water wheels were used to power everything from grain and sawmills to factories. A water wheel is similar to an internal-combustion engine in that it rotates and produces torque. A water wheel is a good example of lots of torque but very little horsepower. If a particular water wheel produces 2,500 foot-pounds of torque and turns 10 rpm (remember these wheels are big—30 feet in diameter and larger) and we apply the formula for horsepower, the result looks like this: 2,500 × 12 / 5,252 = 4.7 horsepower. Even though the massive waterwheel looks like it should produce a lot of horsepower, in fact it does not due to its slow speed. A motorcycle with only 4.7 Hp would not go very fast, even with 2,500 foot-pounds of torque. Performance would be limited by how fast the engine could perform work—in this case not fast at all. This example proves once again that horsepower is a function of time and the faster (rpm) an engine (or water wheel) can perform work, the more horsepower it makes.

This illustration from the book *De Re Metallica* (nothing to do with the rock group), written by Georgius Aricola in 1550, shows a water wheel being used to lift ore out of a mineshaft. Water wheels were used in mining not only for hoisting but also to crush ore in the process of refining gold and other metals. *From* De Re Metallica *by Georgius Agricola*

GEAR RATIOS

The examples used in this sidebar on gear ratios relate to Harley-Davidson motorcycles, but the theory and formulas used will apply to any brand of bike. Many owners of older Harley-Davidson motorcycles will often have their high-mileage engines rebuilt when they reach a point where performance starts to go downhill. When faced with having to buy new parts or machine original ones, it's often the practice to upgrade and modify stock components so that the end result produces more horsepower and torque. Just as many engines that are not worn out are rebuilt with the same idea in mind—more power. Whatever the reason for increasing the power output of an engine, changing the overall gearing may enhance an engine rebuild/upgrade project even further. If your goal is for an all-out, stoplight-to-stoplight racer, then lowering overall gearing with your newly "built" motor will turn your ride into a full-on street racer.

However, most riders want more than just a stump puller for transportation. While lowering overall gear ratios (more on this later) will increase acceleration, it also increases engine rpm when cruising the interstate at 75 miles per hour. Faster spinning engines vibrate more, get poor fuel economy, and wear out faster than an engine that drops rpm in high gear to a more relaxed pace.

With an engine that makes more power than stock, acceleration will not be affected much by changing the final gear ratio to lower the engine rpm for cruising. One obvious way to accomplish this is to add another gear to the transmission—turn a four-speed into a five, or a five-speed into a six. Transmission kits are available to replace the stock gear clusters to obtain the extra gear, or a complete replacement of the entire transmission with a five- or six-speed unit will do the same thing. The downside is cost, as these types of kits range from $1,700 to $2,500 and complete transmissions cost between $2,100 and $5,100. Six-speed versions of both kits and complete units are the more expensive. The bottom line is that adding an extra gear to an existing transmission can cost as much or more as rebuilding or upgrading an engine. In this section, we're going to take a more low-buck approach to lowering engine rpm for relaxed interstate travel by changing the primary or secondary gearing.

When one of your riding buddies tells you that he's lowered his motorcycle's gearing, and you ask him exactly what that means, he'll typically just say that it feels faster from a stop. Many riders can easily relate to making more engine power. It makes us accelerate faster, but when it comes to making gearing changes that affect how power is transmitted from the engine to the rear tire, and thus changing wheel torque and engine rpm, things become more complex. Terms like *gear ratios*, *primary gearing*, *final drive gearing*, and *overall gear ratios* are not self-explanatory.

GEARING

To understand the basics of how gearing in a motorcycle works, simply picture a lever that could be used to lift an object. An example is an 8-foot-long 2 × 4 used to lift a large rock. When the 2 × 4 is placed under a 100-pound rock, and another piece of wood is used as a fulcrum, it takes less than 100 pounds of force to lift the rock because that force is multiplied along the length of the 2 × 4. The old adage that you don't get something for nothing holds true with our rock-lifting example. The end of the lever under the rock will only lift it up a few inches, while the end with the force applied must move several feet—basically a trade off of distance for force. When a couple of toothed gears take the place of the rock and lever, the same thing happens. Torque from the drive gear is multiplied in the output of the driven gear, but the trade off is the driven gear will turn less distance than the drive gear—just like the 2 × 4 lever and rock. The difference between how much each gear turns relative to the other is called a gear ratio.

A gear ratio is simply a way to show the relationship between two sets of gears, pulleys, or sprockets. If the small gear in a gear set has 24 teeth and the larger gear has 32 teeth, the gear ratio can be calculated by dividing the number of teeth on the smaller gear into the number of teeth on the larger gear or 32 divided by 24 equals 1.33. This means that the larger gear will turn 1.33 times slower than the smaller gear, using a gear ratio of 1.33 to 1. This is written as 1.33:1. Another example is the rear sprocket and counter sprocket on the secondary drive on a Harley. If the counter sprocket has 36 teeth and the rear sprocket has 70 teeth, the ratio between the two sprockets is 1.94:1. Using this knowledge, we will figure out the overall gear ratio to determine engine speed vs. rear-wheel speed.

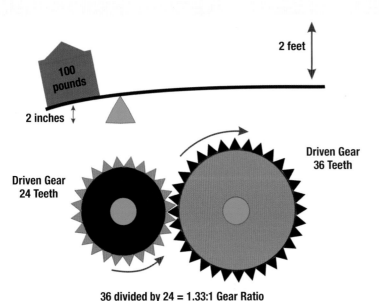

2 feet

100 pounds

2 inches

Driven Gear 36 Teeth

Driven Gear 24 Teeth

36 divided by 24 = 1.33:1 Gear Ratio

FIGURE 8 Two meshing gears work just like a lever for lifting a heavy weight. The difference between lever movements is called lever ratio and the difference between gear rotations is called a gear ratio.

Before we discuss overall gear ratios, we'll take a quick look at transmissions and how they match engine rpm and power output to road speed. Gears inside a motorcycle transmission or gearbox transmit power from the input shaft that is connected to the engine via the clutch to the output shaft where a counter sprocket (chain drive) or counter pulley (belt drive) is located. Each gear within the transmission is achieved using a pair of gears that are meshed with each other. Because the gears are always in contact with each other, the transmission is called a "constant mesh" transmission. Each gear set inside the transmission is in reality a different length of lever arm that transmits power between the engine and rear wheel.

Instead of lifting rocks, each pair of gears multiplies the engine's torque as it applies it to the rear wheel and lowers engine rpm. A typical Harley-Davidson can weigh in at more than 850 pounds. Add a couple of riders and the engine's torque has to get 1,200 pounds of man and machine moving from 0 miles per hour to road speeds. As you can see in the drawing, the lever ratio for first gear is longer because the engine's torque, or twisting force, needs to be multiplied many times to get things moving. Once the motorcycle and rider are in motion, say 15 miles per

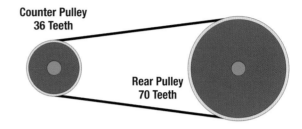

70 divided by 36 = 1.94:1 Pulley Ratio

FIGURE 9 Two gears that mesh together or two pulleys connected via a toothed belt are the same in that they both have a ratio to one another. The belt (or chain) allows the pulleys to turn in the same direction, and they can be located farther apart than gears.

hour, the transmission can shift into second gear where the lever ratio is a bit shorter. This is because it takes less power from the engine to accelerate the weight of the bike from 15 to 30 miles per hour than it did from 0 to 15 miles per hour. When the second to third gearshift is made, it takes even less power to accelerate the motorcycle than it did in gears one and two. Finally the bike is traveling at 45 miles per hours, fast enough to be shifted into fourth, or high gear. Notice that the gears that make up the fourth gear set are the same diameter, or a one-to-one (1:1) gear ratio. Because the transmission input and output shafts now turn at the same speed, engine torque is not multiplied as it was in the lower gears. In fact, all stock Harley-Davidson transmissions (four, five, or six speeds) all have a 1:1 high-gear ratio. In addition to torque multiplication, the gear sets inside the transmission also perform another function—dropping engine rpm each time it's shifted to a higher gear. This keeps the engine operating where it makes the best torque—between 2,000 to 4,000 rpm. The drop between each gear, or speed, on most transmissions is about 500 rpm.

OVERALL GEAR RATIO AND MPH

The final drive, or overall gear ratio, is the relationship between engine rpm, rear-wheel rpm, and whatever gear the transmission is shifted into. As we already mentioned, the top, or high gear in all stock gearboxes, is a 1:1 ratio so the transmission will not be a factor in calculating final-drive gear ratios. In this example, we'll use a 2009 Road King. We need to calculate the primary and the secondary drive ratios and multiply them together to obtain the overall gear ratio. The compensating sprocket (attached directly to the engine's crankshaft) has 34 teeth and the clutch sprocket has 46 teeth. The primary ratio is calculated by dividing 34 into 46, giving us a primary ratio of 1.35:1. To figure out secondary pulley ratio, we divide the counter pulley (32 teeth) into the

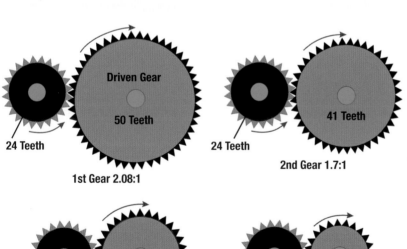

FIGURE 10 The gear sets shown represent the four speeds inside a four-speed transmission. The gears multiply engine torque and reduce engine rpm: higher gear—faster road speed—lower engine speed.

Continued

HOW TO MEASURE ENGINE PERFORMANCE

GEAR RATIOS *continued*

rear-drive pulley (68 teeth). This results in a secondary ratio of 2.125. The last step is to multiply the two ratios together—1.35 × 2.125 = 2.87:1—the overall gear ratio. This means every time the engine completes a single revolution, the rear pulley (and rear tire) will turn 2.87 times. The ratio matches the gear ratio for sixth gear, listed on Harley's website for a 2009 Road King.

Now that we know the overall gear ratio we can use some additional math to translate engine rpm into miles per hour. First we need to take into account tire size as it will figure into our overall calculations for rpm vs. miles per hour. We need to determine the diameter and radius of our tire. There are two ways to accomplish this task. One uses tire size information and lots of math and the other uses a piece of masking tape or chalk, a tape measure, and not as much math—your choice.

With the tire size information in an owners' manual or molded to the sidewall of the tire, there is enough information to calculate wheel and tire radius. We'll use the rear tire on a Road King as an example. The size on the sidewall of the tire is listed as 180/65-16. The 180 is the tire's width in millimeters, the 65 is the percentage of tire height to width (aspect ratio), and the number 16 is the diameter of the wheel. If we take the tire's width of 180 millimeters and multiply it by .65 we get 117 millimeters. We need to convert 117 millimeters into inches so we divide 117 by a 25.4 (this is the formula for converting millimeters into inches) to obtain 4.6 inches. This is the distance from the tread on the ground to the top of the sidewall of the tire. The last step is to add 4.6 inches plus one half of the wheel diameter (8 inches on our Road King) to get a combined tire-and-wheel radius of 12.6 inches. If you got a headache from reading this and trying to understand the math, this alternative method for calculating tire radius will give you some fresh air, a little exercise, and less math for your poor brain to do.

Place a piece of masking tape on the sidewall of the rear tire exactly where it touches the ground. Using some chalk, mark the pavement so that the tape and chalk mark line up. Now roll the motorcycle forward in a straight line until the rear tire completes one revolution and the masking tape is next to the ground. Use the chalk to mark this spot. The distance between the two chalk marks represents the tire's circumference and even takes into account tire air pressure as it affects diameter. If you want to be more accurate, push the motorcycle forward far enough for the tire to complete three revolutions, marking each one with chalk on the pavement. Now take the average the three distances readings. Using a calculator, you find the distance between the chalk marks in our example is 79⅛ inches. This number needs to be converted from fractions of an inch into decimals (1 divided by 8 = .125 inches). The tire's circumference of 79.125 inches is now divided by 3.14 (PI) to calculate the diameter and then divided by 2 to obtain the radius. The Road King tire's radius is 12.6 inches.

We're almost there. Now that we know the wheel and tire's radius is 12.6 inches, we can figure out miles per hour. Instead of multiplying PI times twice the radius and then converting the results from minutes and inches to miles and hours, there is a simple, straight-forward formula.

mph = (engine rpm × radius) divided by (final gear ratio × 168)

The number 168 is used to adjust for minutes, inches, and miles per hour and is a constant in this formula. Using the final drive ratio from the Road King, the math for calculating rpm to miles per hour looks like this:

3,000 rpm × 12.6 tire radius = 37,800
2.87 drive ratio × 168 constant = 482.16
37,800 / 482.16 = 78 mph

Our Road King, with its final drive ratio of 2.87:1 in high gear, will be traveling at 78 miles per hour with the engine turning 3,000 rpm. Here is an even easier way to calculate rpm and miles per hour: Type this link into your Internet browser: www.bakerdrivetrain.com/gearratios/rpmcalc.htm. This will take you to Baker Drivetrain's website and the Baker rpm vs. Speed Calculator, where you can plug in all the numbers from the primary drive sprockets, secondary drive pulleys, miles per hour, and the ratio of what gear the transmission is in. The Speed Calculator will figure out either engine rpm or miles per hour, depending on what you're looking for.

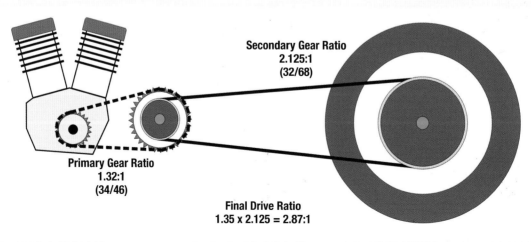

FIGURE 11   The primary gear ratio is 1.35:1 and the secondary pulley ratio is 2.125:1. When combined, the overall gear ratio is 2.87 to 1.

Primary Drive Sprockets				
1987 to 2006 Softail and 1992 to 2005 DYNA Models				
Compensating	Clutch Sprockets			
Number of Teeth	35	36	37	38
21		80P		
22	80P			82P*
23			82P*	82P
24		82P*	82P	
25		82P		
27**			84P*	84P
28**		84P*	82P	

Primary Chain Pitch Count

Primary Drive Sprockets				
1987 to 2006 FLH and FLT Models				
Compensating	Clutch Sprockets			
Number of Teeth	35	36	37	38
21	74P*	74P		
22	74P*		76P*	76P*
23			76P*	76P
24		76P*	76P	
25	76P*	76P		
27**		78P*		
28**	78P*	78P*	78P	

Primary Chain Pitch Count

FIGURE 12 These charts from Baker Drivetrain show the possibilities of regearing the primary drive on Big-Twin engines for Softail, Dyna, FLH, and FLT models. Baker offers sprockets for other models as well. *Courtesy Baker Drivetrain, www.bakerdrivetrain.com*

*This combination requires BAKER Fat Shoe. Old-style chain tensioners will need "L" bracket adjuster. **BAKER Direct Drive 6-Speed compatible only.

CHANGING YOUR GEAR RATIOS

Now that you have an understanding of how gear ratios are calculated and how to relate miles per hour to overall gear ratio, we'll take a look at how to actually change them starting with the primary drive. The primary chain transmits power from the engine to the clutch via two sprockets. Depending on what year and model of bike you have, there are several choices for changing primary gear ratio. The chart from Baker Drivetrain shows some of the possibilities for Softail, Dynas, FLH, and FLT Big Twin models. Baker Drivetrain offers clutch sprockets with different numbers of teeth and these must be used with a Baker clutch. The "P" refers to the number of links in the chain for that specific combination of sprockets.

Like the primary drive, the secondary drive ratios can be changed as well. The secondary counter pulley can be changed to modify the secondary pulley ratio using the stock rear pulley. For Big Twins up to 2006 (2005 on Dyna models), counter pulleys of 29, 30, 31, 32, 33, and 34 teeth are offered from Baker and all are available in either long-life steel or aluminum. The aluminum pulleys are only used for competition applications as they wear quickly. If you are changing the counter pulley and reducing the tooth count by more than 2 teeth, a shorter secondary drive belt is required. A general rule is that 1 tooth down on the front sprocket will move the rear axle ⅛ inch forward. If you own a Cruise Drive model (six-speed) 30- and 31-tooth pulleys are available. A 30-tooth pulley will require the use of an international drive belt that has one tooth less than stock.

CONCLUSION

The primary sprockets and secondary pulleys listed here are only a few of the options that Baker Drivetrains and other aftermarket companies offer. Changing your overall gear ratio can add significant value to an engine rebuild or power-enhancing project by letting the engine run at ideal rpm for either cruising or acceleration. Miles per hour vs. engine rpm, overall gear ratio—it's a lot to get your head around. If you have any questions or just want to find out about the possibilities for your specific model and year of Harley, give Baker a call. They have years of experience and can help you navigate the minefield of sprockets, pulleys, belts, and chains.

HOW TO MEASURE ENGINE PERFORMANCE

CORRECTION FACTORS

Air and fuel are the two ingredients that internal combustion uses to produce power, and the composition of the two is never exactly the same, especially air. This makes performance comparisons between dynamometer runs by the same motorcycle problematic and comparisons between two different bikes run on different days even worse. Variances in atmospheric pressure, temperature, and humidity need to be taken into account when measuring horsepower. All horsepower and torque numbers use some type of standard correction factor that normalizes them to sea level conditions, but the correction factors don't account for all the variables. For example, a dyno run made on a cold day indicates a corrected 100 Hp but on a hot day (same motorcycle and dyno) only produces 96 Hp. What happened to the 4 horsepower? The engine's fuel map would have to be leaned out to compensate for the hotter weather to get back the lost power. But even after changing the fuel map, the engine may still make less than 100 Hp because the hot air is less dense (less oxygen) than cold air.

The more oxygen in the air entering an engine, the more power it can potentially make. Lower altitudes have higher barometric pressure compared to higher altitudes. The closer an engine is to sea level, the more oxygen it has to make power. Quarter-mile times at a drag strip located at sea level will be faster than one at 4,000 feet in altitude, even with fuel map changes to compensate for the less dense air. Humidity or water vapor in the air also displaces oxygen and reduces power.

To compensate for these changes in weather, dynamometer correction factors take into account air temperature, barometric pressure and vapor pressure. The standard

This stack of modules for a Dynojet dynamometer includes an Atmospheric Sensing Module (fourth one down from the top) that measures absolute pressure, air temperature, and relative humidity. This information is used with software to correct power and torque measurements to standard atmospheric conditions according to SAE standard, DIN, JIS, or EEC formats. *Dynojet Performance*

correction factor used in the United States is SAE J1349 (Society of Automotive Engineers). In Europe, it's DIN 70020 (*Deutsches Institut für Normung*). JIS (Japanese Industrial Standard) is used for Japan. Most dynamometer manufacturers will print the correction factors that were used to calculate numbers for dyno runs right on the torque and horsepower graphs. Corrected numbers are helpful when comparing one motorcycle to another, or the same motorcycle to itself after engine modifications are made. In the real world, a motorcycle's horsepower is not corrected at the drag strip. Quarter-mile runs at sea level with an air temperature of 55 degrees and moderate humidity will produce faster times than runs at 3,000 feet of altitude, 80 degrees air temperature, and high humidity, no matter what changes the engine tuner makes to compensate for the different environments.

DRIVETRAIN POWER LOSS AND HORSEPOWER

All of the dynamometer types that were previously listed can be one of two configurations: an engine dynamometer where the engine is removed from the motorcycle and connected directly to the dyno; or a chassis dynamometer where the engine, transmission, final drive, and rear wheel/tire turn a large rotating drum. Most riders do not have the budget or time that professional race teams do when it comes to testing engine horsepower on an engine dynamometer. Instead, they use a chassis dyno because it's much easier, and less expensive, than removing their engine each time they want to measure power output.

Getting horsepower numbers from an engine dyno is like weighing yourself with no clothes on. In your birthday suit, your actual body weight is displayed on the bathroom scale. Testing a motorcycle on a chassis dyno is like weighing yourself with clothes on. Are you wearing tennis shoes or riding boots? Do you have a jacket on? Are the clothes wet? All these variables affect the reading on the scale, and obtaining your real weight is a guessing game. Just like your clothes cloud your actual body weight when measuring power, the transmission, drivetrain, final drive, and tires all add variables to horsepower numbers. The latest dynamometer software uses complex formulas and numerous assumptions to correlate rear-wheel horsepower numbers with engine flywheel horsepower. In the end there is no accurate method to measure, predict, or determine engine flywheel horsepower from a chassis dyno. In view of this fact, let's take a look at the power lost from the drivetrain when testing an engine on a chassis dynamometer.

It is well known that flywheel, or crankshaft, horsepower is higher than rear-wheel horsepower. If an engine makes 100 Hp at the crankshaft but only 90 at the rear wheel, then there is a 10 percent power loss between the engine and rear wheel. The Law of the Conservation of Energy states that energy can't be created or destroyed, only changed from one form to another. That 10 Hp wasn't lost, but changed from mechanical energy into heat. The heat was created by the transmission gears, chain and sprockets, belts, pulleys or driveshaft, and bevel gears all rubbing up against each other. In general, chains and sprockets have the most efficient transfer of the engine's power to the rear wheel. Belts are next, followed by shaft-drive designs.

How much do each of these designs lose in power transmission? It depends on who is asked the question. For some general numbers, chains lose about 10 percent, belts around 12 percent, and shaft drives 15 percent. One way to take an educated guess is to look at the manufacturer's crankshaft horsepower and compare that number to a stock bike that was run on a chassis dynamometer. The difference between the two readings represents the power lost through the drivetrain. This assumes that the manufacturers did not exaggerate their numbers in the first place.

Another variable that contributes to drivetrain power loss is whether the engine's power has to make a 90-degree turn to get to the rear wheel. For example, the driveshaft on a BMW Boxer twin engine or Honda Gold Wing is turning in the same plane as the engine's crankshaft, so the direction of rotation does not change through the transmission. But where the driveshaft is connected to the rear end, or final drive, power has to be transmitted through a 90-degree turn via bevel gears so that the rear wheel can drive the motorcycle forward. By contrast, a chain- or belt-drive motorcycle has the crankshaft, transmission, countersprocket, and rear sprocket all turning in the same plane. Power transmission is more direct, thus there is less power lost. Another factor in how much power is robbed from an engine is the design of the gears inside the transmission. A spur gear is commonly used in motorcycle gearboxes and is efficient at transmitting power. Some manufacturers use helical cut gears that are much quieter than spur gears, but lose efficiency in power transmission because they are subject to side loading that creates heat inside the transmission.

In addition to these variables there is problem with applying percentages of power loss to any type of drivetrain. For example, if a motorcycle is being dyno tested and the engine makes 90 Hp at the rear wheel, and we apply a 15 percent drivetrain loss because it has a shaft drive, the power would be calculated at 103.5 Hp (90 × .15 = 13.5 + 90 = 103.5). After an exhaust-system change, new camshaft, air filter, and performance dyno tuning, the engine makes 135 Hp at the rear wheel. If the same 15 percent drivetrain loss is applied, the calculated crankshaft power would now be 155.5 Hp. The problem is that the drivetrain is the same, so the actual loss of power it creates should not change between the stock and modified engines. However, applying the same 15 percent power loss to the stock engine gives 13.5 Hp, while applying it to the modified engine gives a loss of 20.3 Hp. This difference of 6.7 Hp illustrates why assigning percentages is not accurate when it comes to calculating drivetrain power losses for chassis dyno testing.

PUTTING HORSEPOWER IN PERSPECTIVE

Almost all motorcycles that are reviewed in magazines have horsepower and torque numbers listed. When riders bench race, these same numbers are thrown around with bravado as each owner brags about their engine modifications. All powersports manufacturers use the numbers to sell performance, image, and technology. After reading this chapter on measuring horsepower, it's easy to conclude that these numbers are neither easy to compare nor consistent. The same motorcycle tested on different days, measured on different chassis dynamometers, with different correction factors, tire pressures and dyno operators, will generate different numbers. So how can any horsepower and torque numbers be useful?

A horsepower reality check requires thought as to how power measurement numbers are used. Remember that when a motorcycle manufacturer uses horsepower and torque numbers, they are doing so to sell motorcycles. They test their engines under ideal conditions and measure power at the crankshaft. They can't "adjust" numbers too drastically because of legal issues with advertising claims, and most use SAE correction factors to level the playing field. Magazines are a mixed bag regarding how they get their performance numbers. The better magazines will use the same dyno and operator to get all the horsepower numbers for the bikes they test. With the correction factors applied, they are usually consistent. Comparing one magazine's numbers to another is pointless, though, because of the variables in just about everything related to testing. Bench racing horsepower numbers, whether at bike night or on the Internet, are also pointless and should not be used to provide real numbers for a particular motorcycle.

The only time horsepower and torque numbers become somewhat serious is when a rider is going to spend money. If an aftermarket exhaust system or other performance parts are going to be installed and the desired outcome is a different exhaust note and some bragging rights, then Hp and torque are immaterial. If the gain, or loss, in power is important, then measuring power output needs to be approached with some common sense.

Find a local dynamometer service and interview the operator before you make an appointment for testing. The horsepower and torque numbers you get are only as good as the operator. Ask how long he or she has operated a dyno, what types of bikes they have experience testing, what correction factors are used, what brand of dyno they have, and what charts and graphs they will provide when testing is completed. Will they take time to explain what the numbers mean so you'll understand what steps to take next? If you have read this book and the dyno operator knows less than you do, find another testing facility. An experienced dyno operator will check rear-tire air pressure (a fairly large factor in power output on a chassis dynamometer) and check to see if any emission-related components need to be removed

or disconnected before testing. For consistent testing, two to three runs should be averaged to get final numbers for performance measurements.

Know what goals you want the dyno test to gauge, based on the modifications you have made or are contemplating making. Are you looking for all-out performance, better street-riding performance, or fuel mileage? If you don't know why you want your motorcycle tested and what you hope to discover from the horsepower and torque numbers, the dynamometer operator won't either. The only numbers that really matter are the ones from your motorcycle that you trust. They can be used to see if that new exhaust system, or other component, helped or hurt your engine's power output. Resist the temptation to compare horsepower and torque numbers with friends, magazines, or other sources for bragging rights about engine power output. Instead, use the numbers you get to become educated about whether or not you're achieving your performance goals for your motorcycle.

REAL WORLD TESTING

One magazine that has years of experience producing articles that relate to increasing engine horsepower and torque using aftermarket accessories is *American Iron Magazine*. The magazine specializes in the coverage of American-made motorcycles, including Harley-Davidson, Indian, and Big Dog Motorcycles. It features articles and stories on how-to projects, motorcycle repairs, maintenance, classic bikes, events, and even has a Hog Helpline for readers' questions.

Information from *American Iron Magazine* is featured in this book because the magazine uses the best practices when it comes to measuring the results of engine modifications. These include measuring engine performance before, and after, the installation of aftermarket engine components. In addition, it uses the same dynamometer and dyno operator (Rob's Dyno Service) to test all of its project bikes. This gives the readers reliable, consistent information in knowing exactly how the addition of an exhaust system, performance air cleaner, ignition, or fuel injection controller or even a big-bore cylinder kit will affect horsepower and torque on a motorcycle.

We'll take a look at two aftermarket exhaust system installations, two air cleaner modifications, and an engine displacement increase project, all with before and after dynamometer results. While the six articles from *American Iron Magazine* represent typical modifications made to Harley-Davidson motorcycles, they will help to illustrate how the process works on other makes and models of bikes.

PERFORMANCE AIR FILTERS

We'll start out with one of the most basic types of changes a rider can make to his or her motorcycle: the aftermarket air filter. Stock air cleaners and filters on all motorcycles serve two functions: (1) filter the dust and dirt out of the air going into the engine and (2) keep intake noise to a minimum.

There is another, though it's only cosmetic, function for air cleaners, and that is one of style or looks, particularly on cruisers. Most in-line engines' air cleaners are hidden and do not factor into the overall look of the motorcycle.

Keeping dirt from entering an engine is an obvious reason for an air cleaner—after all they are called "air cleaners" or "air filters" for a reason—but reducing noise caused by air entering the engine is not as apparent. When motorcycle manufacturers have their products certified for sale in the United States, they have to meet noise restrictions. Exhaust noise is the largest contributor to the total noise or decibel output of a motorcycle, but there are other noise producers, including engine mechanical noise and air-intake noise. To make exhaust sound as pleasing to potential customers (more sound is usually desirable) other noises have to be reduced as much as possible. A quieter air-intake system, of which the filter and cleaner are a part of, means that the exhaust can be slightly louder. If an air filter design that is quiet makes slightly less engine power because it restricts airflow into the engine, that's OK because the louder exhaust is what many customers want and what sells motorcycles. The motorcycle aftermarket figured this out long ago and thus offers "Performance" air cleaner assemblies that increase engine intake airflow, resulting in engine horsepower and torque gains. These increases are usually in the range of 0 (air cleaner change made no difference in power output) to as much as 12 percent. The more restrictive the stock air-filtration system is, the more gain can be had with an aftermarket system. Wild claims of 20 percent or more power from exhaust makers is advertising hype and doesn't pan out with hard numbers on the dyno.

Following are three articles on air cleaners all courtesy of *American Iron Magazine* and written by the editor, Chris Maida. The first is the Doherty Machine PowerPACC air cleaner that was installed on a 2009 Electra Glide Standard. The engine is otherwise stock and the dyno chart illustrates the power gain. No EFI modifications were necessary as the stock EFI system was able to compensate for the slight increase in airflow provided by the new air cleaner. The next air cleaner article is the Ness Big Sucker Air Cleaner. This system fits all 2008 to 2010 FLT models. The dyno chart is a good example of where maximum horsepower and torque numbers don't tell the whole story of the results of an increase in airflow. The third air cleaner article uses the same Doherty PowerPACC air cleaner on a 2007 Road King. This installation did require EFI modification and a Rapid Bike EFI control unit was used to tune the fuel curve to the new airflow.

Only 290 Ducati 888SPOs were imported into the United States in 1993. This rare motorcycle has a four-valve motor and a second-generation Weber-Marelli P8 ECU. Ducati first used this EFI technology on the 851 and 888, and later on the 748 and 916 models (which included the Weber-Marelli 16m ECU). This early arrangement featured a single injector per cylinder. On subsequent models, Ducati first moved to a dual-injector-per-cylinder arrangement, then switched to a single-port injector (eliminating the use of two injectors per cylinder) mounted above the throttle body to serve as a shower or high-mount injector. *Stephen Snyder*

AIR FILTERS AND PERFORMANCE

One engine modification that many riders don't always associate with all-out engine performance is air filters. Your stock air filter may seem harmless enough, but how much does it affect engine horsepower? We'll take a closer look at air filter designs, how they work and what options are available when it comes time to replace your stock air filter.

When it comes to all-out engine performance we often look to the world of motorcycle racing to see what works for making horsepower. Using an air filter, or not, is only an option for road racing and at the drag strip. Choosing not to use an air filter provides the ultimate in non-restrictive air intake. Closed road courses are a relatively clean environment as are drag strips and often a simple mesh screen is used to keep out rocks and debris kicked up by other competitors. The other side of the coin is any type of off-road competition where common sense tells you an air filter is mandatory. Not using an air filter while circling a motocross track or riding across the desert will allow your engine to suck in every bug, every rock, and millions of dust particles, resulting in a destroyed engine real quick. But what about riding on the street? When you go for a ride, the air blowing past you seems fairly clean—or is it? Even small dust particles (the ones you can't see) act like sandpaper inside your engine. The abrasive mixture of air and dirt starts wearing out your engine's cylinders as it gets between piston rings and cylinder walls. From there it passes into your oiling system via the crankcase, where it can cause damage to bearing surfaces, lifters, camshafts, and so on. The end result of not using an air filter is an engine that wears out long before it's supposed to. If you ride around or near open fields and dirt roads the environment is even dirtier and engine wear is accelerated.

AIR FILTER DESIGNS

A good air filter design balances high airflow with maximum dirt filtration. In fact, an air filter's efficiency can be measured. The Society of Automotive Engineers (SAE) uses test procedure SAE J726 where air filters are measured to see how much air-borne junk they can retain. The "Course Test Dust" uses dirt particles ranging in size from 5.5 microns up to 176 microns (a human hair is about 50 microns in diameter), which are forced through the air filter being tested. Filter efficiency is measured by the percentage of test dust that is captured in the filter without passing through it. The majority of engine wear is caused by dirt and dust in the 10- to 20-micron size, smaller than you can see without the aid of magnification. A good quality air filter can retain 97 percent of these sized particles while at the same time providing good airflow.

Air filtration media refers to what the filtering element is made of, and there are three common types used on motorcycles: paper, foam, and cotton fiber. Pleated or folded paper elements are widely used in both the automotive and motorcycle industries and are the most common. Paper air filters work fairly well for street use where excessive dust and dirt are not present. Paper filter elements have fibers that are packed closely together or that are fairly thick to stop small dust particles. All the offending dirt is trapped on the surface of the paper. The downside to using paper is that once the small openings are blocked on the surface of the element the filter restricts airflow. You should inspect a paper filter at least once a year or more often if you ride in dusty conditions. By using compressed air and blowing the dirt out of the filter in the opposite direction of normal airflow you can get a paper air filter to last between 10,000 and 15,000 miles before it needs replacement. If you live in a rural area the filter will get dirty faster and you will have to replace it more often.

Off-road vehicles of all kinds have used foam filters for many years. Open cell polyurethane foam filter elements offer excellent protection from really dirty environments. The foam is soaked in oil, which helps trap dirt particles. Foam filters can hold more dirt than paper filters because the dirt penetrates the surface of the foam and is stored throughout the depth of the filter. The downside to foam filters is that they have to be fairly large to trap dirt while at the same time not becoming too restrictive to airflow. For use in normal street riding foam filters should be washed in detergent and water and re-oiled about once per riding season. UNI Air Filters offers replacement foam air filters for both street and off-road motorcycles.

Oil impregnated, pleated cotton fiber is the design used by K&N. The cotton fiber is thicker than paper and will trap more dirt. Dirt and dust particles are stopped by layers of crisscrossed, oiled cotton fibers. The particles are collected on the surface of the filter and do not block holes as they do on paper designs. Instead, they cling to the fibers and become part of the filtering media. K&N calls this "depth loading," a process it claims allows the filter to retain significantly more dirt per square inch than a paper filter. This type of design is used for both on- and off-road applications. They should be maintained once per year, and they can be washed, re-oiled and used over about 25 times—longer than most of us own a particular bike.

Which type is best: foam, cotton fiber, or paper? It's a hard call. With the high cost of some OEM paper filters you may find that a replacement filter from K&N or UNI is less expensive over time as both are re-useable. This may be an advantage if you ride where dirt and dust are abundant even on paved roads. If you don't want to go to the trouble of cleaning and re-oiling your air filter, then a replaceable paper type is a good choice. The important thing is to check your air filter every 5,000 miles or at least once each riding season.

AIR BOXES

Because air filters reduce engine noise to some extent, we couldn't leave out a discussion about air boxes. Excessive intake engine noise is a problem that manufacturers must deal with when designing an engine's air-intake system. If you were to ask the average prospective motorcycle buyer what sound he or she prefers when listening to a running motorcycle, it's the exhaust "note" every time. If intake and mechanical engine noise can be reduced, then the exhaust system can be louder. Manufacturers know this and they go to great lengths to reduce all types of engine noise. Hydraulic valve lifters, bevel-cut gears, and restricted air-intake systems reduce engine noise and make it possible to produce a "cooler" (louder) sound from the back end of a motorcycle. At the same time the air-intake system can't be too restrictive because engine power will suffer.

One way to quiet down a noisy intake system is to redirect the airflow into the engine using baffles, reduced inlet openings, and small air filters. This is done regularly to cruisers because high horsepower is not as important as on a sport bike. Manufacturers of air filters and air filter kits for these bikes make claims that their products increase engine power, and in some cases this is true. Replacing a stock air cleaner and filter will allow more air to flow into the engine, and when combined with re-jetting carburetors or re-mapping fuel injection systems, can get you more power and better overall drivability.

Sport bikes and standards are different than cruisers because for the most part they use an air box to overcome intake restrictions. The design of an air box causes the air inside it to vibrate or resonate. Air box resonance is much like blowing across the top of a bottle. When you get the airflow right, the air inside the bottle vibrates and makes a sound. On a motorcycle, air will vibrate inside the air box at some engine rpm ranges. This causes high air pressure inside the air box and acts like "ram air" when the intake valves open and forces more air into the cylinder. For an air box to work it has to be sealed from the outside atmosphere and sized correctly. In fact, air boxes are generally quite large—as big as engine displacement in some cases. Many sport bike riders have found out the hard way that removing an air box or drilling large holes in it doesn't necessarily increase airflow to the engine. In fact, many of those types of modifications have the opposite effect.

A LITTLE EXPERIMENT

Whether you ride a sport bike, standard or cruiser, here is an experiment you can try to see if an aftermarket air filter will get you more horsepower. Remove your air filter, not the air cleaner housing, on a cruiser or air box on a sport bike, and go for a ride. Depending on how restrictive your stock air filter was the engine's power may seem lazy and not pull as strongly through the gears. The most likely cause of this condition is that the engine is running lean because more air is able to get to it. By adding a jet kit or re-mapping your fuel injection system slightly richer you can get the lost power back and then some. This little experiment will not produce consistent results from bike to bike and does not always work for determining if your stock air filter is restrictive.

ADDING AN AFTERMARKET AIR FILTER

On some models of motorcycles, replacing your stock air filter is simply a matter of swapping the old one for the new. Other bikes, especially cruisers, require that air cleaner hardware be changed as well. Two quality companies that manufacture air filter kits, which include all hardware as well as the filter, are Küryakyn and Thunder Manufacturing. Both companies offer kits for domestic and metric cruisers. Their hardware comes in hundreds of styles and finishes and kits are listed for specific makes, models, and years of motorcycles. If you ride a standard or sport bike, check out K&N or UNI Air Filter's websites to see if they list a performance filter for your bike. If a manufacturer recommends modifying your fuel system when replacing your stock filter with either an air filter or complete kit it is because they know from experience that the stock filter setup was restrictive and using their products will cause it to run lean. This will be especially true if you change your stock exhaust system at the same time. Whether you choose to keep your air filter stock or opt for an aftermarket setup, the most important thing to remember is to inspect your air filter at 5,000-mile intervals.

A well-engineered aftermarket air filter can be the easiest, cheapest way to attain additional performance from an engine. *Courtesy K&N Engineering Inc.*

POWERPACC AIR CLEANER

By Chris Maida, editor of American Iron Magazine

The common rule of thumb is that it costs about $100 for every single horsepower you gain. The Doherty Machine PowerPACC (#1248) that we bolted onto a stone-stock, fly-by-wire 2009 Electra Glide Standard costs $299.95. Since it boosted the engine's power output almost 4 ponies and over 2 ft-lbs. of torque, it works out to about $75 per horsepower. Not bad! The last time we bolted on a PowerPACC, we got a 6 hp increase, but that bike also had a performance exhaust system installed, which brings us to another simple rule of making power. Changing cams, air cleaners, pipes, etc., is all about getting more air in and out of the engine. More air allows you to burn more fuel, which is what makes the wheels go round. If the exhaust system doesn't let the air out as fast as the air cleaner lets it in, it becomes a bottleneck and restricts the power that engine can make. Guess we'll have to bolt some pipes onto this bike at a later date and see what happens. And since this year's machine is equipped with O_2 sensors, we didn't bolt on a fuel adjuster this time around. However, if we do install pipes, we'll also install and dial in a fuel adjuster to see what power gains we get with the complete package. We don't need to install one, but we should reap more power since the air/fuel mixture will be set richer than the O_2 sensors' required setting of 14.5: 1.

Like the other versions of the PowerPACC, this one comes with a washable, high-volume air filter element and all the necessary mounting hardware. The PowerPACC 1240 series is made specifically for Delphi fuel injected models, as is our #1248, which is for 2008 and later touring models fitted with the cableless throttle body. Air cleaner kits are also available for Keihin CV, S&S E or G, and Mikuni (42, 45, and 48mm) carburetors, but check if an adapter kit is needed for your specific application. We went with the black powder-coated Doherty cover, but all of these cleaners will accept the stock round or oval H-D covers. That is, except the teardrop versions, which use an S&S-style teardrop cover. By the way, this installation, which is easy to do, was performed right on Rob's dyno by the man himself. Yep, Rob is a very experienced wrench and often does these upgrades right on his dyno. During our installation, the breather crossover pipe had to be bent out slightly to clear the Fat Bob tanks on our 2009 Standard Touring bike. However, this is no longer an issue on all new kits. As for the actual power curve, if you check out the accompanying dyno chart you'll see that power is increased for the entire rpm range of the engine, not just at high rpm.

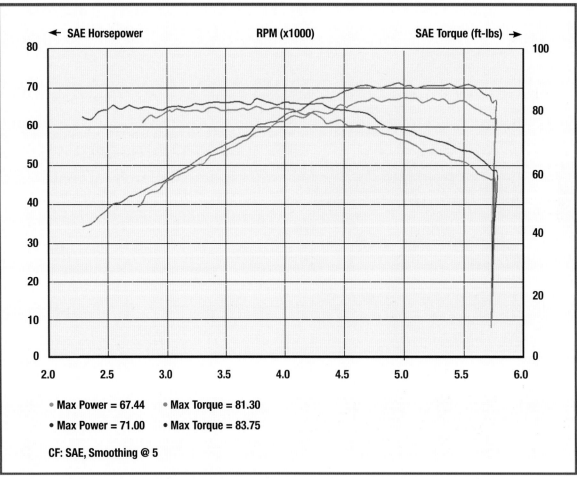

- Max Power = 67.44   • Max Torque = 81.30
- Max Power = 71.00   • Max Torque = 83.75

CF: SAE, Smoothing @ 5

FIGURE 13   This is the result of bolting on the PowerPACC air cleaner with no other modifications. SAE horsepower is on the left and engine torque on the right scale. The results are a 3.5 increase in horsepower and 2.5 increase in torque (5.1 and 3 percent, respectively). The biggest increases take place above 4,000 rpm for both torque and horsepower. *Courtesy* American Iron Magazine *and Rob's Dyno Service*

HOW TO MEASURE ENGINE PERFORMANCE

NESS BIG SUCKER AIR CLEANER

By Chris Maida, editor of American Iron Magazine

The Ness Big Sucker is a proven performer when it comes to getting more air into your V-twin, and it does so with class! We're going to show you how easy it is to bolt on an Arlen Ness Stage I Billet Sucker with chrome Smooth outer cover for 2008–10 FLT models ($214.95). And, yes, you should be able to do this job in your home garage in an hour. The Stage I kit features a Team Ness high-flow filter element that can be used with all 1993 and later H-D oval or round outer covers. You can also, as we did, order the kit with a Ness chrome steel outer cover. The Ness Stage II kit features a 20 percent larger Team Ness high-flow filter element, but you must use an 8" round Ness or OEM outer cover with this one. Big Suckers are available for all H-D Evo and Twin Cam models except factory 103" engines. However, it can be used on a 96" engine taken out to 103". The Ness Big Sucker has an all-in-one backing plate, which you can get in either a satin or chrome finish. This backing plate has a built-in carburetor/throttle body support and built-in breather tunnels for each head to help decrease crankcase pressure inside the engine. Each tunnel exits at the mount of the carburetor/throttle body to create a closed-loop system. These breathers have O-ring banjo bolt seals and a radiused intake manifold. As you will see, this Ness air cleaner setup eliminates all oil hoses, oil fittings, and oil leaks. Since 2008 and later bikes have O_2 sensors in their exhaust header pipes, the stock EFI ECM module adapts this air cleaner change. That means we don't have to do any EFI map changes after this install. Our thanks to Rob of Rob's Dyno for doing our before (baseline) and after dyno runs, so we could accurately measure just what power gains we got by doing this easy installation.

This next article revisits the effects of a Doherty Power PACC air cleaner on a 2007 Road King. After bolting on the new air cleaner, the dyno results were not optimal so another accessory was installed: the Rapid Bike EFI controller. The Rapid Bike Module System enables modification for fuel injection/ignition mapping of engines with 1 to 4 cylinders. It can operate in a range of 500 to 17,000 rpm and features original-equipment wiring harness connectors for simple installation. The control unit connects to a PC or laptop using a standard USB connection and there is even wireless/WiFi capabilities for some models. The Rapid Bike controller is a piggyback design and works like Dynojet's Power Commander. The Rapid Bike module works on many fuel-injected motorcycles, scooters, sprint cars, and snowmobiles. For more information about the product check out www.rapidbikeusa.com or call 718-468-4680.

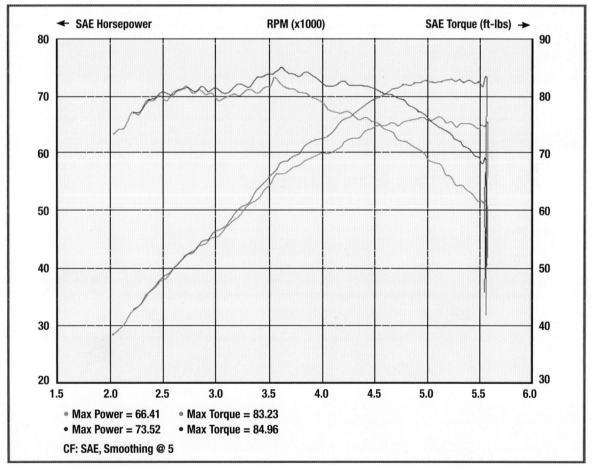

● Max Power = 66.41   ● Max Torque = 83.23
● Max Power = 73.52   ● Max Torque = 84.96
CF: SAE, Smoothing @ 5

FIGURE 14   With the installation of the Ness Big Sucker air cleaner. the increase in horsepower was 7.1, or just under 10 percent. This indicates that the stock air filter system on this motorcycle had lots of restriction. The maximum increase in torque was slightly less than 2 foot-pounds at 3,600 rpm. Notice that above 3,600 rpm the torque curve is between 5 to 8 foot-pounds above stock. Additional torque like this will be felt in seat-of-the-pants acceleration. The same is true of the horsepower curve as it shows a steady increase from 3,600 rpm to redline of 5,500 rpm. *Courtesy* American Iron Magazine *and Rob's Dyno Service*

(ft-lbs)

DOHERTY POWERPACC AIR CLEANER AND RAPID BIKE EFI CONTROLLER

By Chris Maida, editor of American Iron Magazine

To get more power from an engine, you have to get more fuel burning over the piston. And since the amount of fuel you can burn depends on how much air you have, more power comes from moving more air in and out of the cylinders. To that end, we installed one of Doherty Machine's PowerPACC 1240 series air cleaners ($270) for the first of this two-part performance install. The 1240 series cleaners are made specifically for Delphi fuel-injected bikes and come with a washable, high-volume air filter element. All of Doherty's air cleaners (except the teardrop versions) accept the stock oval or round air cleaner covers and come with all necessary mounting hardware. And if you have crankcase pressure problems with your bike, order your PowerPACC equipped with Doherty's PowerVents, which will significantly reduce the engine's crankcase pressure, preventing oil from misting out of the air cleaner.

As for who would do the deed on our 2007 Road King test bike, we went to see the good folks at New Roc Harley-Davidson/Buell. Once there, we were sent to the lift of their master of the socket drive, Dave, who wasted no time installing the PowerPACC air cleaner on the bike. However, before he did that, we had Rob of Rob's Dyno take the Road King for a few runs on his dyno to get an honest printout of what the King was putting to the rear wheel. Of course, Rob got the bike back after the install, and he again flogged the beast on the dyno to see what gains we got. As you can see on Dyno Chart I, our base run registered 76.86 hp and 92.65 ft-lbs of torque. Once the Doherty was installed, Rob ran the bike on the dyno for about 10 minutes to let the King's ECM remap itself to the new airflow. The result is also displayed on Dyno Chart I: 78.3 hp and 92.5 ft-lbs of torque. Though we got a gain, it was not what we should have achieved. Figuring it was a fuel-supply issue, we bolted on a Rapid Bike EFI adjusting unit ($400) and asked Rob to spend just a little time dialing it in to see if the numbers would come up as they should. Dyno Chart II tells the tale: 81.92 hp and 95.2 ft-lbs. of torque. Much better! That's a gain of over 5 hp and almost 3 ft-lbs of torque. Owners of pre-2007 bikes (and pre-2006 Dynos) will get even better results. The Rapid Bike module sold by TechnoResearch is an add-on control unit which allows the tuner to modify a bike's ignition timing and fuel-injection settings. This is a plug and play install, requiring no wire cutting or other changes to the bike's original wiring harness. The tuning is done via a PC connected to the unit by a USB cable.

PERFORMANCE EXHAUST SYSTEMS

Contrary to popular belief, loud pipes don't save lives, do make more exhaust noise, but don't necessarily make more horsepower. Installing an aftermarket exhaust system on a motorcycle is as much of an emotional exercise as it is a performance one. Custom looks and a better sound (which is often only in the "ears" of the owner) are often the main reasons for spending money to get rid of stock exhaust. The real performance factors that justify exhaust changes are an increase in engine power and lighter weight exhaust components. Ironically, the most popular brand of bike that has exhaust systems changed from stock to aftermarket are installed on Harley-Davidson motorcycles. The weight savings that an aftermarket exhaust offers is a moot point as even the lightest Harley weighs in at 563 pounds (the 2012 Superlow and 883 Sportster) while the larger bikes weigh in at around 889 pounds. However, there are increases to be made in the horsepower and torque departments. Because of noise restrictions, the factory systems on most motorcycles also limit the engine's performance potential. Hence, aftermarket exhaust systems are by far the most popular engine modification for all brands of motorcycles. We'll take a look at two exhaust system installs with the resulting dyno charts to show engine power increases. Just like the performance air cleaners, exhaust systems will generally show modest gains in horsepower and torque. It's always the combination of small factors that provide overall increases in power as they all add up to a better performing motorcycle when they work in harmony with each other. EFI tuning is just part of the process of matching the performance capabilities of engine modification. The first article is the installation of a Radio Flyers exhaust system on a 2011 Road Glide.

By far the most common component that owners change on their bikes is the exhaust system. Pictured is a Two Brothers M2 V.A.L.E. exhaust system for a Yamaha FJR 1300. Two Brothers makes exhaust systems for just about all motorcycles. Check out the company website for details: www.twobros.com.

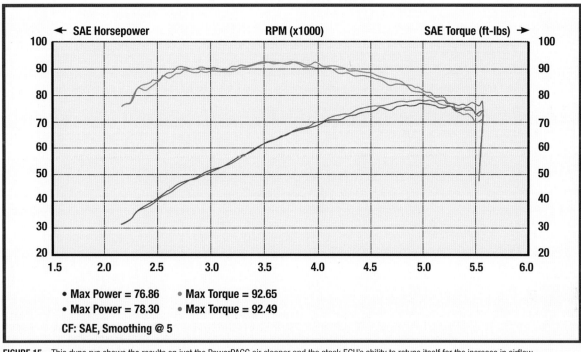

FIGURE 15 This dyno run shows the results on just the PowerPACC air cleaner and the stock ECU's ability to retune itself for the increase in airflow. A 1.4 horsepower increase and only a few 10ths increase of torque are the result. With only a .8 percent increase in horsepower and a .9 percent increase in torque, the addition of the high-flow air cleaner does not seem worth the expense. *Courtesy* American Iron Magazine *and Rob's Dyno Service*

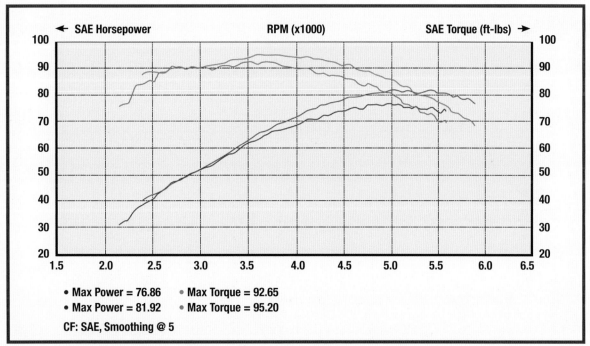

FIGURE 16 This run records the results after the addition of the Rapid Bike EFI controller. The stock ECU was unable on its own to increase or correct the fuel curve to match the increased airflow. Using the Rapid Bike controller, the fuel values were adjusted to maximize horsepower and torque. The results are an increase of 5 horsepower starting at 4,200 rpm. Maximum torque did not increase as dramatically, but torque was increased above stock from 3,600 to redline of 5,500 engine rpm. *Courtesy* American Iron Magazine *and Rob's Dyno Service*

2 8 125
(ft-lbs)

RADIO FLYERS

By Chris Maida, editor of American Iron Magazine

Exhaust sound is important to Harley people. In fact, it's equally important to the folks in Milwaukee who build our bikes, which is why, several years ago, there was a movement within the Motor Company to copyright the distinctive potato-potato-potato cadence of the most famous V-twin motorcycle engine ever produced. We all know that the copyright was denied, but that hasn't diminished our love for that most distinct sound. So when an aftermarket exhaust company sets out to develop a new muffler system for Harley-Davidson motorcycles, it does so with trepidation and care. One such company is Von Braun, makers of a wide range of quality Harley exhausts for current H-D Touring models. We put our hands on a set of VB Radio Flyers so we could mount them on a 2011 Road Glide. And though we can't reproduce on paper the sound they generate, close your eyes for a moment and imagine a pleasing baritone burble that's not offensively loud, yet is slightly deeper than the potato-potato potato rhythm you expect to hear from a stock set of cans.

Think in capital letters: Potato-Potato-Potato. And it only gets better as engine revs build. In truth, the Radio Flyers have a slightly higher volume than the stock units, but more to the point, it's their tone that makes them so appealing. And by keeping the volume within reason, they're not obtrusively loud so we can still listen to the bike's sound system while tooling down the road. Think of it as the best of both worlds: you get to enjoy your favorite tunes coming from the speakers while listening to your favorite sound of all time, that big, bad V-twin engine of yours. But we replace exhaust systems on our bikes for more than just the aural gratification they give us. We also want style and performance. While style is a subjective thing, I can't deny that the Radio Flyers clearly enhanced the look of the Road Glide that we put them on. Foremost, the Flyers' 4"-diameter muffler bodies flow smoothly into their CNC-cut end caps for a cool look, important criterion for a custom bagger. Von Braun's mufflers and end caps come in two finishes: chrome and black mufflers with either silver or black end caps, producing four variations. We selected the black mufflers with black end caps for our conversion.

That brings us to the performance aspect of why we trade out our bikes' exhaust system. The proof is in the pudding, as they say, and the place to taste the pudding is on a dynamometer. For that we went to our buddy Rob of Rob's Dyno in Gardner, Massachusetts, for a baseline run with the stock exhausts, and the real deal with the Von Braun pipes. We had the benefit of making the muffler swap while the bike remained on the dyno, which also gave us the opportunity to test the systems back to back on the same day. As you can see from the accompanying dyno sheets, there's more to the Radio Flyers than just a pleasing sound.

HOW TO MEASURE ENGINE PERFORMANCE

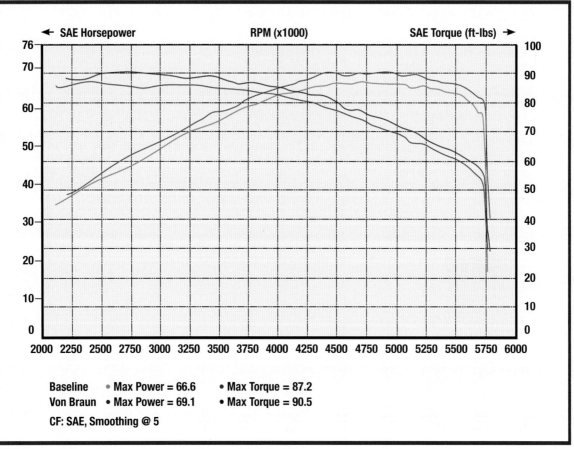

Baseline • Max Power = 66.6 • Max Torque = 87.2
Von Braun • Max Power = 69.1 • Max Torque = 90.5
CF: SAE, Smoothing @ 5

FIGURE 17 The Radio Flyer's exhaust system produced an increase in both horsepower and torque throughout the engine's rpm range. Though power gains are modest (2.5 horsepower and 3.3 foot-pounds of torque) the combination of custom looks, a better sound, and slight increase in engine performance are probably worth it to many owners. *Courtesy* American Iron Magazine *and Rob's Dyno Service*

TAILGUNNER MACH II CLASSICS EXHAUST

By Chris Maida, editor of American Iron Magazine

It's no news that exhaust system upgrades are the most often made modification to a new Harley-Davidson, be it a Sportster, Touring, or any model in between. In fact, new pipes and/or mufflers are usually the first mod made by an owner. That's because though H-D's new exhaust systems are pretty good at flowing air right from the factory, there's always room for improvement, especially in the rumble department. To that end, we got our hands on a set of Tailgunner Mach II Classic mufflers and bolted them onto a spanking-new 2009 Electra Glide Standard to see just what kind of gains in sound and performance we would get for one hour of work. Tailgunner's Mach II Classics have CNC-machined nacelles that come in either a hardened, anodized Stealth Black finish or polished aluminum. You can also choose between removable 16" Power-Baffles for quieter rides or the louder 10" Power-Baffle. All Tailgunner mufflers are made in America using 16-gauge steel that's covered in an excellent chrome finish. The Mach II Classics are available for all 1986–2010 H-D baggers. However, true dual header pipes need to be installed on 2010 models. To do the deed, we asked our buddy and longtime dyno guy Rob of Rob's Dyno to do the installation. Rob strapped the bike down with the stock pipes and did his runs. Then he changed the muffler with the bike still on the dyno. The accompanying dyno sheet tells the tale. What you can't see there is that the bike had a nice low rumble to it with the Mach IIs fitted with the 16" Power-Baffles. The owner told us it's just what he wanted: a bit more sound, but not enough to piss off the neighbors when he rolls in late at night.

This final article is the most involved regarding engine modifications. In addition to the displacement increase from 96 cubic inches to 103 cubic inches, the cylinder heads were ported, forged pistons were added, an over-sized (50-millimeter) throttle body is used, an aftermarket camshaft and exhaust system was installed, and a Harley-Davidson Race Tuner EFI controller was used to match fueling requirements with all this engine work. The dynamometer results are dramatic with an increase in horsepower of 34.7 and 24.3 for torque. That works out to around $114 per horsepower over the stock motor and is close to the $100 per added horsepower rule-of-thumb.

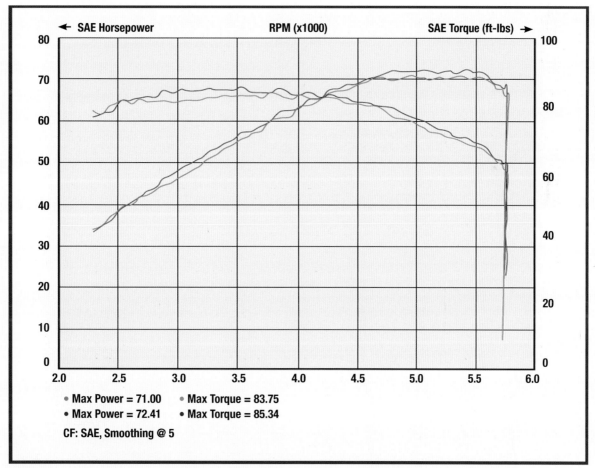

- Max Power = 71.00   • Max Torque = 83.75
- Max Power = 72.41   • Max Torque = 85.34

CF: SAE, Smoothing @ 5

HOW TO MEASURE ENGINE PERFORMANCE

FIGURE 18   This is the same bike that had the Doherty PowerPACC installed but did not have any EFI mapping done as the stock computer was able to compensate for the increased airflow from the nonstock air cleaner. This dyno run adds the Tailgunner exhaust to the mix. There were only slight gains over the air cleaner installation, but overall the combination of both air cleaner and exhaust made a substantial difference from stock. From the factory the bike made 67.44 horsepower and 81.3 foot-pounds of torque. Now it outputs 72.4 horsepower (up 7 percent from stock) and 85.3 foot-pounds of torque (up 5 percent from stock). *Courtesy* American Iron Magazine *and Rob's Dyno Service*

HEMI 96" TO 103"

By Chris Maida, editor of American Iron Magazine

PART 1

Mention the word *hemi* to an old motorhead, and visions of Shovels, Pans, Knuckles, Ironhead Sportsters, and, if he's also a car freak, Chrysler muscle cars will instantly come to mind. But this version of a hemi motor is not one of those old designs. No sir! This hemi is very much a modern engine. We've worked with the guys at Hemi Performance in the past, so when they gave me a call and wanted us to test their newly designed kit, which punches a stock 96" Big Twin out to 103", it was a no-brainer. Once I found out what they had in mind, a call was placed to our buddy Mark Fabrizi at Marquee Customs, and a bike was lined up. When the kit arrived, Mark and I gave it the once over, and plainly saw that this was going to be an easy, high-quality installation. Hemi uses lots of Screamin' Eagle parts, so local shops and Harley–Davidson dealers alike should have no problems or qualms about the installation. Of course, Hemi works a bit of its own magic to the ports on the SE heads, so they flow more cfm than the out-of-the-box ones.

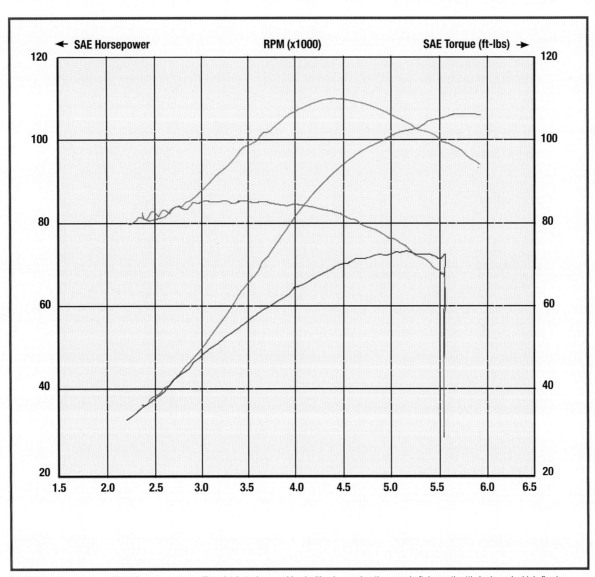

FIGURE 19 Seven more cubic inches may not seem like a lot, but when combined with a longer duration camshaft, larger throttle body, and a high-flowing exhaust—all tuned to work together—the results speak for themselves. Thirty-four more horsepower and 24 more foot-pounds of torque over the stock motor can definitely be felt when going for a ride. Looking at the chart you can see that the engine starts running out of air at around 4,500 rpm as the torque peak starts to drop. Horsepower keeps climbing until the engine rpm limit is reached at 5,800 rpm. *Courtesy* American Iron Magazine *and Rob's Dyno Service*

HOW TO MEASURE ENGINE PERFORMANCE

(ft-lbs)

PART 2

It's time to give you some info about the Hemi Performance kit we're installing onto a stock 2007 Softail Deluxe. According to Ron at Hemi, this kit was designed to give Twin Cam owners an economical way to boost their 96-inchers' power output into the 105–108-hp range, with comparable torque numbers. As you can see by the accompanying dyno chart, Ron hit his goal on this build! As for cost, Ron keeps this in check by using Screamin' Eagle components and doing his own machine work. Ron either reworks your stock heads and cylinders, or does a swap out with you, which is why this kit should cost an owner only about $3,885 installed. You say you want more power? Ron and crew can handle that, too. Hemi Performance is a full-service shop equipped to do engine-machining and blueprinting, as well as being an authorized dyno tuning center.

Now that you know a little about the shop, let's go over the parts used. The heads are the stock 96" castings that were ported by Ron so they flow another 20 cfm. The stock valve springs were swapped out for SE beehives, but the stock valves are reused, since they are large enough to feed a 103" engine. The cylinders are also reworked stock units. (However, Ron will soon be offering 4.250"-bore cylinders that look just like a stock 88" or 96" cylinder from the outside.) The cylinders are precision-bored to achieve the required 103" displacement, exactly like the old 88" to 95" conversion.

Rob Swartz has been working on and riding motorcycles since he was 16 years old. With his years of experience as a professional technician, Rob found that many shops relied on his diagnostic abilities to help them with motorcycles that had complex fuel and ignition problems. He has been certified as a Dynojet operator and Power Commander tuner. In addition, he has certifications from Victory, Kawasaki, S&S, Rapid bike, and Direct Link tuning software. He started Rob's Dyno Service and has found that having a portable dynamometer makes it possible to bring his tuning skills and experience directly to the customer. He performs tuning and diagnostic work for a number of motorcycle dealerships and supports aftermarket manufacturers in the development of new products. In addition, he is involved in supporting racing efforts of several top teams and assisted many racers to championship seasons. More than just running a business, Rob receives a great deal of satisfaction from his work. "I have found when I tune a bike correctly, and I make it run the way the customer wants it to, they fall in love with their bike all over again," he says. More information on Rob's Dyno Service can be found in the Sources section at the end of this book or online at www.robsdyno.com.

Ron does this on a CNC turning center in a special fixture he designed, which locates the bore of the cylinder directly in the center of the head's combustion chamber. He does this extra work because he's seen cylinder bores that were 0.020" out of sync with the mating head.

The cylinder is then placed in torque plates, so it can be honed to fit the new pistons. Those pistons are forged 10.5:1 compression CP units. Ron prefers CP pistons, since the skirts are barrel-ground and not cam-ground with a taper. Ron states that this allows the piston to roll on its dwell (axis), rather than slam over when the piston changes direction. When it came to cam selection, we had the option of going with either Screamin' Eagle 258 camshafts or an SE257 kit. Both make nice power (one more torque, the other more horsepower), but are not too aggressive, so they are easy on the valvetrain. Both of these grinds also bleed off some compression at low rpm, so the engine is easier to start, especially when hot. The engine will also run a bit cooler at slow speeds and will be less prone to detonation. These cams are able to work well with a variety of different performance exhausts. As per Ron's request, we went with a D&D Fat Cat Big Boar system. We've used D&D exhaust setups on a number of high power builds, and they have always given us excellent performance. As for the other components of the Hemi Performance kit, they include a number of SE components, such as a Race tuner, cylinder stud kit, Quick Install pushrods, and a 50mm throttle body, which comes completely assembled and ready to install. The larger throttle body is needed to let in enough air to fill those bigger cylinders. Also included is a complete James Gasket kit. As for who would do the build, our buddy Mark Fabrizi at Marquee Customs, veteran of many an *American Iron* tech article, did the wrench spinning. Since we also needed a pro to dial in the EFI maps and get our dyno numbers, we called another buddy, Rob of Rob's Dyno, to spin the drum for us. Rob has worked with us on a number of performance builds, and he always does an excellent job, as quickly as possible. His years on the dyno really come into play in reducing the number of runs needed to get everything adjusted correctly with solid power numbers as the result.

DYNO RESULTS

As you can see, the power output is the same in the low-rpm range, but quickly increases as soon as the engine gets to 3,000 rpm, which is just outside the engine's cruising rpm range. This will keep fuel mileage high while still giving you plenty of power on tap once you open the throttle. It also keeps the bike's riding characteristics the same during low-power operation, meaning no abrupt power peaks when starting from a stop and so on. Torque output peaks at 109 foot-pounds at about 4,000 rpm, well below what anyone would consider high rpm. That gives you plenty of truck-passing juice right where you want it. Horsepower, however, continues to climb in a strong arc right up to the 6,000 rpm cutoff point, in case you do want to stay on the throttle. Nothing like having plenty of *go* ready at the flick of your wrist!

HOW TO MEASURE ENGINE PERFORMANCE

Chapter 5
How to Tune EFI Systems

This 2004 Kawasaki race bike was prepared by Attack Performance, located in Huntington Beach, California (www.attackperformance.com). Attack Performance offers a variety of services, including Dynojet Power Commander installation and tuning, race prep, scheduled maintenance, and more. *Attack Performance*

There are two generic approaches to tuning an EFI system: (1) The motorcycle is strapped down to a chassis dyno and the dynamometer operator does the tuning for whatever controller is installed, using the appropriate software, or (2) the owner does the tuning using seat-of-the-riding-pants as a performance measurement tool or a data logger like the Veypor tool.

We'll start with the seat-of-the-pants approach. A rider can feel the difference if engine performance is better or worse when performance modifications, such as an aftermarket exhaust system and air filter, are added to his or her motorcycle. But this performance increase will only take place if EFI fueling is tuned to match the increased airflow through the engine that these components potentially offer.

It is possible to tune fuel requirements to engine modifications and determine the results simply by riding because it's easy to know when the fuel mixture is way too lean (not enough fuel) or way too rich (too much fuel). What one can't determine accurately is when the AFR is close to ideal, but in general "close" is good enough for tuning EFI systems by feel alone, especially for street-riding purposes.

The first step is to follow the directions for whatever aftermarket EFI controller has been installed on the motorcycle. If the controller comes with a fuel map (like Dynojet's Power Commander or the ThunderMax controller by Zipper's Performance), make sure that the map loaded into the controller is the correct one for the bike's year, make, model, and aftermarket components. If there isn't a map available for the exact combination of bike and aftermarket components, select a map that is close. If the controller uses the factory fuel map as a baseline for setting AFR, follow the procedure to set the buttons on the controller to their suggested positions for your motorcycle.

EFI controller companies set up their products to work on many popular brands of motorcycles with specific exhaust systems and other engine modifications. The recommended base map or button settings for a particular controller should be in the ballpark regarding air-fuel ratios, providing a good starting point for further tuning.

LOW-TECH FUEL MAPPING

In Chapter 3, Catalytic Converters, Air-fuel Ratios, and Oxygen Sensors, AFRs were discussed at length. Having fuel delivery that correctly matches the flow of air into the engine and out the exhaust is the key to getting the most

out of the modifications made to an engine. Extensive engine modifications can include a big-bore kit for more engine displacement, non-stock connecting rods for a longer stroke, aftermarket camshafts, ported cylinder head(s), full exhaust system or mufflers, and high-flow air cleaner or filter element. All of these modifications will require changes to the EFI system's fuel map in order to match fuel delivery to airflow through the engine.

The consequences of not re-mapping the fuel system can include rough idle, hesitation upon acceleration, surging at part throttle, fouled spark plugs, poor fuel mileage, and less overall engine power than the stock motorcycle. While running an engine a little too rich or lean at part throttle can cause these problems, operating an engine too lean at wide open throttle (at any rpm) can cause far worse things to happen. Lean conditions when the engine is trying to make maximum power can cause detonation, or engine knock. This, in turn, can melt the tops of aluminum pistons, causing severe engine damage. The bottom line is that AFR mistakes (either rich or lean) can be tolerated at part throttle, but a lean condition at full throttle is bad news.

The following is a procedure for determining if an engine is running rich or lean without using high-tech tools like a five-gas analyzer or wideband oxygen sensor. This method of determining AFR requires some high-tech supplies—masking tape, a felt marker, magnifying glass, small flashlight, and two or three sets of spark plugs and the tools to change them. The first step is to mark the throttle so throttle position can be seen when riding the motorcycle. Place a strip of masking tape around the throttle sleeve and another smaller piece of tap on the switch housing. With the

These spark plugs show three mixture conditions: overly rich (sooty black plug at right), close to ideal (light gray or tan at center), and too lean (white plug at left). For this much "color" to show, all of these plugs must have well over 1,000 miles on them. Plugs that have only been run for a few miles will probably not show any color, or if they do it will be where the insulator meats the metal shell and will be difficult to see without magnification. When the fuel mixture is correct, most spark plugs will look like the center plug. Although it appears similar to the center plug, the telling sign on the left plug that the mixture is too lean is that the center electrode is starting to melt and has a rounded tip. *Battley Cycles*

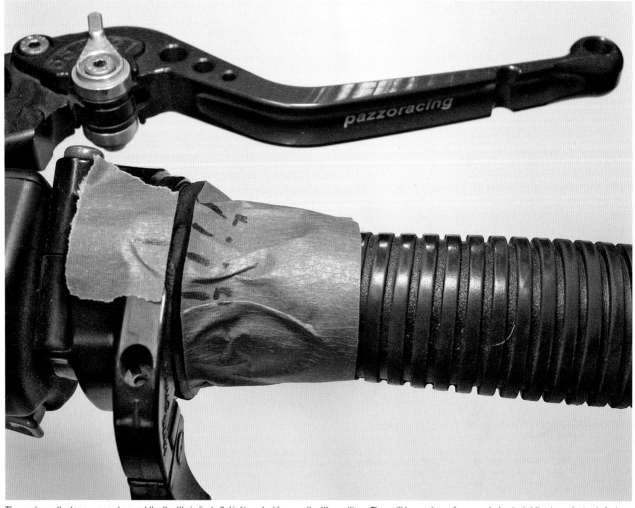

The marks on the tape wrapped around the throttle indicate 0, ¼, ½, and wide-open throttle positions. They will be used as references during test riding to evaluate air-fuel mixture at different engine rpm and throttle openings.

throttle closed, write "0" on the throttle and mark a witness line on the tape on the switch housing. Open the throttle all the way and make another mark for full throttle. Now place the throttle halfway between the two marks and mark that position as half throttle. Place two other marks at the quarter and three-quarter positions. Start the engine and take a short ride to bring it up to normal operating temperature. Shut the engine off and install a fresh set of spark plugs in preparation for the next step in the process.

Note: On some motorcycles, changing spark plugs can be challenging because access is difficult. Bodywork, frame rails, fuel tank, and airbox may all be in the way of getting a wrench on the spark plugs. Several plug changes will be required during testing, and if this work can't be accomplished by the side of the road without bringing an entire toolbox, one may want to consider having AFR tuning done at a shop that has a dyno and wideband oxygen sensor or other AFR measuring method.

The next step is to start the engine and go for a ride for at least 10 miles at one-quarter throttle, or as close to that setting as possible. Then it's time to read the spark plugs for fuel mixture. This next step is a bit tricky, because the engine needs to be turned off without letting it return to idle speed. While at one-quarter throttle, pull in the clutch, close the throttle and shut the engine off using the kill switch. This will retain whatever color is on the spark plugs without the influence of the fuel mixture at idle. Safely coast to the side of the road, watching for any traffic. Remove the spark plugs to determine if the engine is running rich, lean, or just right.

Using the magnifying glass and flashlight, look into the spark plug where the porcelain insulator comes out of the metal base. This area around the insulator base is where the combustion process fuel mixture can be read. If the AFR is too rich, the base of the insulator will be dry-looking sooty black. Sometimes the black ring will extend up the insulator toward the tip. If the mixture is too lean, there will be no soot around the insulator, and the color will be white. If the mixture is close to correct, the base of the insulator will be light tan, light gray, or chocolate brown. Riding only 10 miles is not usually enough time to color the entire insulator, and even if the engine is too rich, the insulator color may still be white. Label and save the spark plugs for later reference. Adjust the EFI controller either richer or leaner for the rpm range that affects throttle operation.

Note: Leaded fuel will produce only slight changes in spark plug color, and determining the fuel mixture accurately is difficult at best. Just looking at the insulator, without the aid of a magnifying glass and strong light, will not provide enough information to judge AFR.

Use the same procedure for a half-throttle operation. This is more difficult, because speeds will be increased. Again, the throttle must be chopped and the engine immediately shut down without idling. Remove and read the plugs to determine if the AFR is rich or lean. Make the appropriate adjustments to the EFI controller for half-throttle operation.

Install new plugs and go through the same procedure at full throttle. The wide-open throttle test should be done at a racetrack or drag strip for safety and legal reasons, as the posted speed limit will be exceeded during the test. It's best to shift the transmission into fourth gear and start from an engine speed below where it normally makes power. This will help keep speed to a reasonable level. Hold the throttle open until engine speed reaches redline. Chop the throttle as in the previous steps. Using the spark plugs as a reference, make the EFI controller adjustments to get the AFR closer to the ideal mixture.

An additional quick test for full-throttle AFR is to ride the motorcycle in fourth or fifth gear at an rpm just below where the engine starts to make power. Open the throttle all the way and immediately close the throttle down about one-eighth of a turn. If the engine slows down as expected, the AFR is close to being correct. If the engine picks up speed (even a few hundred rpm), the full-throttle mixture is too lean, and more fuel needs to be added. If the engine hesitates or stumbles, the full-throttle mixture is too rich, and fuel should be subtracted from the fuel map.

If the motorcycle uses a Power Commander PCIII or Dobeck GEN3 controller, the buttons that change fueling can be used as diagnostic tools for determining if the AFR is rich or lean. If the engine has a performance issue at part throttle, try pushing the button to add fuel that affects midrange fueling. If the problem becomes better, the fuel mixture was lean. If the problem becomes worse, the fuel mixture was already rich and adding fuel just made it even richer. If a PC-V is used, bringing a laptop along for the ride will allow changes to the fuel map to determine "rich" or "lean" conditions.

Once the fuel mapping is close, based on spark plug readings, the motorcycle should be ridden for at least 100 miles. If the engine pings or knocks when the throttle is suddenly opened, or the acceleration is not what it should be, an overall lean condition is indicated. If black smoke comes from the exhaust when accelerating (have another rider follow the bike to observe this), or the plugs appear black and sooty, the AFR is too rich. If engine performance is good for all throttle positions and the plug insulators are tan to chocolate brown in color, the fuel map is set as close as is possible without several runs on a dynamometer using more accurate methods of determining AFR.

Leaded gasoline makes reading spark plugs for fuel mixture difficult. Leaded gasoline will leave a trace of color on spark plugs, but to actually see it requires a strong magnifying glass and light. The mixture ring that results from the fuel-to-air ratio is located at the base of the insulator and may only become visible after a number of miles are ridden.

Some EFI controllers, like Dynojet's PC-V and Zipper's Performance ThunderMax, allow users to modify ignition timing. But what exactly should be changed and why? Those questions, not to mention the potential dangers of making changes, are often a mystery to many motorcycle enthusiasts. Can an adjustable ignition system work for producing both maximum power and fuel economy? Do really bad things happen to good engines if ignition timing is set incorrectly? We'll try to answer all these questions, but first let's take a look at what ignition advance is, and how it affects engine performance.

THREE STAGES OF COMBUSTION

Before we discuss ignition advance, the process of how air and fuel are burned inside the combustion chamber needs to be understood. Combustion takes place when hydrogen and carbon (gasoline) are rapidly combined with oxygen (air) to produce heat.

Combustion is a three-step process. A small blue-colored ball of flame, called the nucleus, is formed when a spark from the ignition system jumps the air gap on the cylinder's spark plug. This takes place before the piston has reached the top of its stroke. The hatching out stage is next, as the nucleus is torn apart and fingers of flame reach out into the combustion chamber. At this point in the combustion process, there is a relatively small amount of heat (about 1,000 degrees F) generated from the air and fuel starting to burn. Propagation is the last stage of combustion, in which a fireball is created. The edge of the fireball is called the "flame front," and as it advances across the combustion chamber, a serious rise in temperature takes place. This last stage takes place as the piston reaches the top of its stroke, also known as top dead center. The temperature will peak as high as 5,500 degrees F, causing a pressure increase inside the cylinder of several tons.

All this force has to go somewhere, and the only moveable component inside the cylinder is the piston. As the piston is pushed down, its motion creates torque at the crankshaft, which eventually turns the rear tire. This is the engine's power stroke.

At the beginning of the power stroke, peak, or maximum combustion temperature and pressure must be reached when the piston is at the top of its stroke. For this to take place, combustion needs to be started before the piston reaches top dead center (TDC) of its upward movement. After peak combustion, the air-fuel mixture will continue to burn after the piston moves past top dead center—called ATDC (after top dead center). The entire combustion process must be complete by 30 degrees of crankshaft rotation through the power stroke for maximum "push" on the top of the piston. When the fireball burns out, nitrogen, carbon dioxide, and water vapor are mostly what is left inside the cylinder. These gases will continue to expand and push the piston down until about 70 degrees ATDC.

As the crankshaft continues to rotate, and the piston moves down the cylinder, the volume of the cylinder increases faster than that of the expanding gases. There is little force left to push down on the piston and the power stroke is effectively over. The combustion process must be completed by 30 degrees ATDC in order for the piston to exert maximum torque to the engine's crankshaft. At 5,000 rpm, a V-twin engine will burn the air-fuel mixture 41.6 times per second in each cylinder. A liter class sportbike running at 12,000 rpm will ignite the air-fuel mixture in its cylinders 100 times each second.

Although combustion happens at a rapid pace, it still takes a somewhat fixed amount of time for the process to take place. When you have the throttle wide open and the engine is turning 2,000 rpm, it takes about 2 milliseconds (2/1,000ths of a second) for the entire air-fuel mixture to burn. Accelerate to 12,000 rpm and the burn time is still about 2 milliseconds, but now there is less time to get the job done because the engine is turning faster.

To completely burn the air and fuel at an engine speed of 2,000 rpm, ignition must begin at 20 degrees before top dead center (BTDC) to allow combustion to be complete by 30 degrees ATDC. As engine speed increases, less time is available to burn the mixture, so the spark needs to take place even earlier. At 4,000 rpm the spark will have to start at 36 degrees BTDC for combustion to be finished by 30 degrees ATDC. By changing the point at which spark starts and combustion begins, we can ensure that we will extract the maximum amount of heat from the air-fuel mixture and produce the most power for any given throttle setting. As we stated earlier, the rate of combustion is relatively the same at different engines speeds, given similar operating conditions. This is why the air-fuel ignition process needs a head start, or what is referred to as ignition advance.

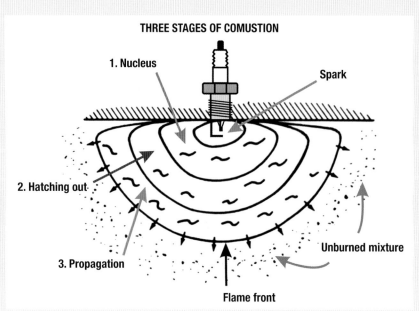

THREE STAGES OF COMUSTION

1. Nucleus

Spark

2. Hatching out

3. Propagation

Unburned mixture

Flame front

FIGURE 1 The initiation of combustion is a three-step process that starts with spark from the spark plug. Step 1 is the nucleus with the initial spark at its center. Step 2 is called "hatching out." Step 3 is combustion flame propagation. This sequence of events can be photographed using a high-speed camera and a special test engine with a glass window into the combustion chamber.

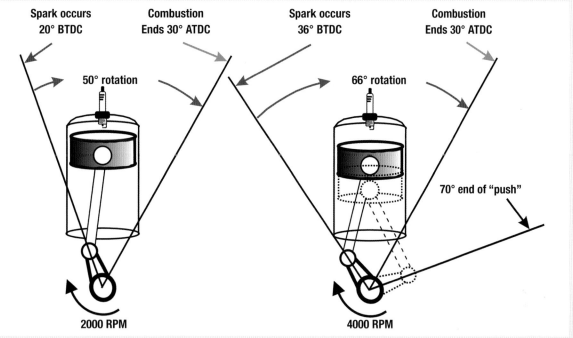

FIGURE 2 Because gasoline and air burn at about the same rate of speed at low and high rpm, the ignition spark must be given more of a head start when the engine is turning faster. For example, a V-twin burns its air-fuel mixture 41.6 times each second when running at 5,000 rpm. A sportbike engine running at 12,000 rpm will ignite its air-fuel mixture hundreds of times each second. With less time available, the high rpm engine must have more time to complete the combustion. In this illustration, the engine at left is turning 2,000 rpm and ignition starts at 20 degrees BTDC. The engine at right is turning at 4,000 rpm, and its ignition timing is advanced to 36 degrees BTDC. This gives extra time (in crankshaft degrees) for the combustion process to be complete by 30 degrees after top dead center (ATDC).

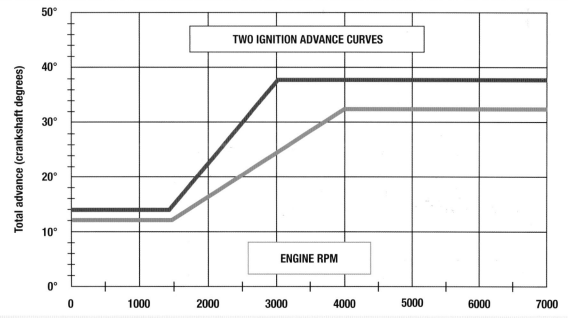

FIGURE 3 This graph shows degrees of ignition advance vs. engine rpm. The curve in red is more aggressive than the blue curve. The red curve adds advance ignition timing at a faster rate than the blue curve, and it has more total advance. Providing the engine does not detonate during the power stroke, the red advance curve will make more power than the slower, less-aggressive blue curve.

Continued

ADVANCED THEORY

As mentioned before, maximum cylinder pressure will in turn produce the most torque and horsepower at wide-open throttle. Fuel consumption goes up during this condition, as a rich air-fuel mixture is also required to make the most power. Depending on engine design, ignition spark at wide-open throttle should occur between 28 and 36 degrees BTDC of crankshaft revolution. Contrary to what some sportbike riders may tell you, however, most street riding is done at part throttle.

Part throttle operation produces a different set of conditions inside the combustion chamber, and ignition timing must be changed to make everything work smoothly. Amounts of both air and fuel flowing into the engine are greatly reduced at part throttle. This condition results in reduced cylinder pressure and a leaner air-fuel ratio inside the combustion chamber at the time of ignition. Because the molecules of fuel are spaced farther apart in a lean air-fuel mixture, they burn much more slowly than they would in a rich air-fuel ratio where fuel and air molecules are closer together. This slower burn rate requires more ignition advance at part throttle than at wide open throttle. Depending on the engine design, ignition timing may start as much as 30 to more than 45 degrees BTDC at part throttle. Advanced ignition timing serves two purposes: (1) to maximize cylinder pressure at TDC and (2) to keep the spark plugs from fuel fouling. The end result of part-throttle ignition advance is greater fuel economy, as the early ignition timing takes advantage of the lean mixtures during steady state cruising.

Changing when the spark starts and combustion begins allows you to extract the maximum amount of heat from the air-fuel mixture, producing the most power for any given throttle setting. Due to the mechanics of leverage, the time to complete combustion may remain more or less constant at 30 degrees ATDC, but engine speed and how far you twist your wrist is a moving target.

Another factor that determines ignition-timing parameters is combustion chamber design. Many modern engines use four valves and may even have two spark plugs. The shape of the combustion chamber and piston crown also promote rapid burning of the air-fuel mixture. Ignition spark must take place at different times, depending on engine-operating conditions.

Ignition timing on vintage motorcycles is changed for different engine rpm ranges via weights and springs that move a plate where the ignition points are mounted. This advance unit is usually found on the end of the camshaft. As engine speed increases, the weights pull against the springs, mechanically

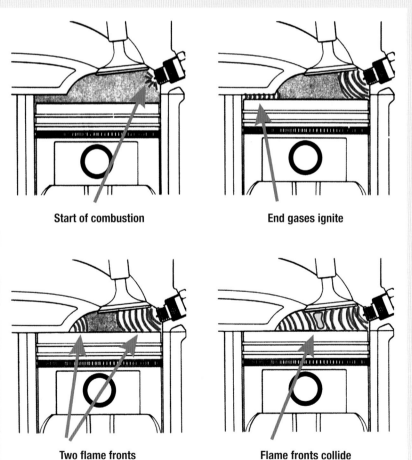

Start of combustion

End gases ignite

Two flame fronts

Flame fronts collide

FIGURE 4 This simplified drawing shows what happens inside the combustion chamber when engine ping or knock occurs. A second flame front ignites the end gases of the combustion chamber away from the spark plug. Starting at left, the progression of the flame is shown. As the two flame fronts approach each other, the pressure inside the cylinder spikes, causing a knocking sound. This pressure spike will also create a thermal shock that can melt a hole in the piston if left unchecked.

advancing the ignition timing. Modern motorcycles use an engine-management computer to control ignition timing, which takes into account engine rpm, throttle position, engine load, engine and air temperature, and barometric pressure. This is one reason that fuel-injected engines produce good power while at the same time are capable of getting high fuel economy.

How much ignition timing advance does your engine need? Each engine is different and requires spark timing to be optimized for each throttle setting and rpm plus other factors mentioned previously. The only way to accurately determine total spark advance and plot an advance curve is by measuring torque at each engine-operating condition on a dyno. Fortunately, this work has been done at the factory. However, if you purchase an aftermarket controller that allows changes to the ignition advance curve on your bike, beware of having too much advance for wide-open throttle conditions. With the engine attempting to make maximum power, the great limiting factor regarding ignition advance is detonation or knock. If the combustion process experiences detonation at wide-open throttle, the piston may become damaged—and it doesn't take but a few seconds for this to take place.

I HEAR YOU KNOCKING

Any discussion about spark advance would be incomplete without talking about detonation, knock, or ping. These terms are used interchangeably, but for the purposes of our discussion, they all have the same meaning.

If ignition timing takes place too early during the compression cycle, the piston will not be far enough up the cylinder to build sufficient compression (cylinder pressure) to rapidly burn the air and fuel. Instead, the air-fuel mixture could ignite, but burn too slowly due to the low compression at that point in the compression stroke. As the mixture burns, heat and pressure start to rise in the cylinder, until the point at which the end gases (air and fuel that is farthest from the spark plug) spontaneously ignite. This creates two flame fronts (one from the spark plug, the other from the end gases) burning simultaneously. The two flame fronts move toward each other and eventually collide, producing a knocking sound.

Pre-ignition is different from detonation and is caused by fuel igniting before a spark is sent to the spark plug. You may have heard this sound on an older car when the engine refused to shut off, even after the key was removed from the ignition.

Detonation that causes engine damage generally occurs at three-quarter throttle openings and above. Too much total spark advance, or an advance curve that comes in too early at low rpm, can cause detonation. In addition to overly advanced ignition timing, other factors can contribute to engine knock. High-intake air temperatures, an overheated engine, low octane fuel, too much compression, and carbon buildup inside the combustion chamber can all lead to detonation.

If an aftermarket EFI controller is used to change ignition timing, follow the manual's instruction guide carefully. Most controllers limit how far timing can be changed at specific rpm. In fact, most EFI-controller manufacturers provide warnings either in their written instructions or in the software that caution the user about changing ignition timing. Owners who do not have experience in this area should leave the stock timing alone. Small changes in timing may work for all-out racing, where maximum horsepower is a tuning goal, but on the street they won't be felt when riding and may even lead to engine damage. If you hear your engine ping or knock and continue to ride around at wide open throttle, try to head in the direction of your nearest motorcycle dealer, where you may end up having your engine rebuilt—so don't forget to bring your wallet.

DICTIONARY OF IGNITION TERMS

TDC, BTDC, and ATDC: Top dead center, before top dead center, and after top dead center all relate to the piston position in relationship to crankshaft rotation.

Advance curve: The rate at which ignition timing is advanced BTDC throughout the rpm range.

Cranking advance: Ignition timing when the starter is cranking the engine measured in degrees. Usually different than ignition timing at idle on electronic ignitions.

Initial advance: The advance measured in degrees with the engine at idle. On older systems, initial and cranking advance are the same.

Total advance: Sometimes called total ignition timing. This is the maximum amount of ignition timing. Additional timing past this point can result in engine damage, not more power.

Static timing: Ignition timing set with the engine not running. This can be accomplished using a voltmeter, a test light on older points-type ignition systems.

Dynamic timing: Timing is set using a timing light with the motor running. This method is more accurate than static timing, because lash between the cam and crankshaft are eliminated.

Advanced timing: Ignition timing that takes place before the piston reaches top dead center of its stroke. Usually referred to as timing BTDC.

Retarded timing: Ignition timing is related to advance timing but takes place closer to TDC.

Detonation, knock, or ping: The sound produced either by pre-ignition or uncontrolled burning of the air-fuel mixture. While not a problem at part throttle, at full throttle it can burn a hole in the top of a piston. Can be caused by hot outside air temperature, low-octane gas, too much ignition timing, too lean a fuel mixture, and too much compression.

VEYPOR MOTORCYCLE INTELLIGENCE DATA LOGGER
Installation

In Chapter 4, How to Measure Engine Performance, the Veypor Motorcycle Intelligence data logger was introduced and its general capabilities were discussed. The Veypor offers an alternative to traditional dyno testing and is a cost-effective way for motorcyclists to evaluate the effectiveness of modifications made to their motorcycles. Here is a step-by-step installation of the Veypor on a 2005 Yamaha FJR 1300. Installation on other motorcycles will be similar and moving it between different bikes is fairly easy. In fact, the Veypor works on cars and trucks as well. Following the installation, we'll discuss the Veypor VAS software and how it can be used to evaluate engine-performance modifications.

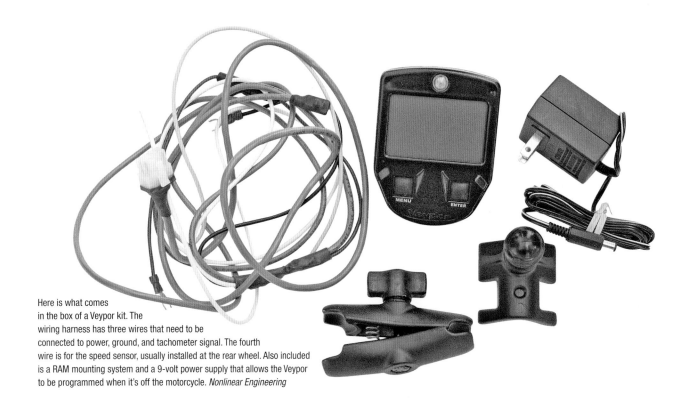

Here is what comes in the box of a Veypor kit. The wiring harness has three wires that need to be connected to power, ground, and tachometer signal. The fourth wire is for the speed sensor, usually installed at the rear wheel. Also included is a RAM mounting system and a 9-volt power supply that allows the Veypor to be programmed when it's off the motorcycle. *Nonlinear Engineering*

We used the existing RAM ball on the FJR, but a handlebar RAM mount is provided with the Veypor. Lots of other accessories can be used with this mounting system, including GPS, satellite radio, cell phone, or CB radio. Check out www.ram-mount.com for details. *Nonlinear Engineering*

The Veypor can be mounted at an angle easily visible to the rider and has a quick-disconnect plug to make it easy to remove from the motorcycle when parking. *Nonlinear Engineering*

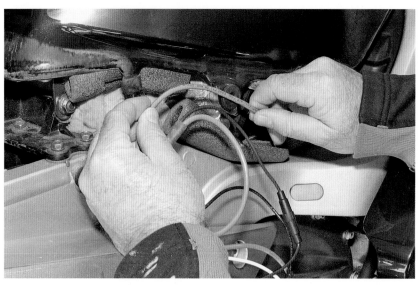

We ran the wiring harness under and along the side of the fuel tank. The wiring harness is long enough for all motorcycles and can reach up to the bars, under the seat, and back to the rear wheel for the speed sensor. *Nonlinear Engineering*

We had an existing power and ground panel to which the Veypor's wiring harness connects. It can also be connected directly to the battery. A switchable power wire is ideal if you want to permanently install the Veypor on a motorcycle. This type of connection will allow the unit to only operate when the ignition key is in the on position. *Nonlinear Engineering*

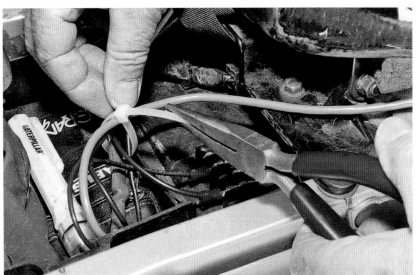

We used nylon tie wraps to keep the wiring neat and out of the way. If the Veypor is to be moved to another motorcycle, the tie wraps can be easily cut for another installation. *Nonlinear Engineering*

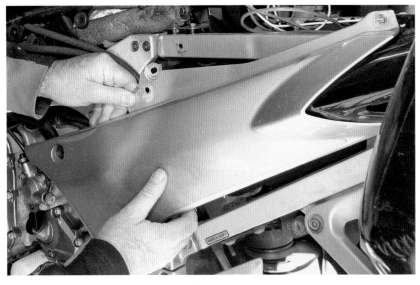

The Veypor needs to be connected to the engine's negative ignition coil wire to receive an rpm signal. Most motorcycles have their ECU located under the seat, and, rather than remove lots of body panels to get to the ignition coils, we used the FJR's wiring diagram and found the same wire at the ECU connector. *Nonlinear Engineering*

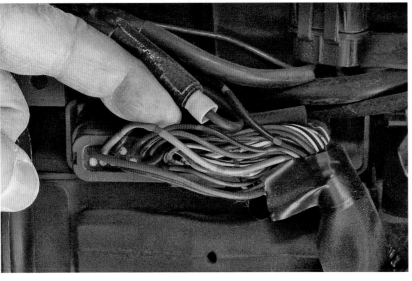

The Veypor can be connected to any ignition coil (the FJR has two). The Veypor's smart software recognizes the tachometer signal and displays an accurate rpm reading on the screen. The unit's software also has the capability to file the tachometer signal if the rpm readings are not accurate. The orange wire at the ECU is the one we connected to for the tack input. *Nonlinear Engineering*

We chose to solder the tack wire to the ECU coil wire. The Veypor comes with wire splice terminals if you want another way to connect them. *Nonlinear Engineering*

Here is a close-up of the magnet-and-wheel speed sensor. These can be attached with super glue (provided in the kit) or weatherproof tape. The sensor can be mounted on the front or rear wheel. *Nonlinear Engineering*

Here is the magnet stuck to the rear brake rotor. Some epoxy will keep it in place. Moving it close to the center of the wheel will not affect wheel balance as the magnet is very lightweight. *Nonlinear Engineering*

Here is the sensor installed. We used the ABS wheel-sensor housing, but other locations will work as well. The magnet has to be within 8/10ths of an inch from the sensor to work, allowing flexibility for mounting options. *Nonlinear Engineering*

The Veypor in driving mode. Display includes gear selection, rpm, mph, G force, time since start, and miles traveled since start. There are five other driving mode screens to choose from. *Nonlinear Engineering*

Performance Measurement

Performance-run data recorded on the Veypor can be displayed onscreen in the graphing mode. These screens will provide quick results of quarter-mile or roll-on timing runs and can be displayed instantly. Data can be stored from multiple runs and are saved in the Veypor's memory, even if it is disconnected from its power supply and removed from the motorcycle. In the run timing mode, the Veypor measures roll-on timing, ¼-mile runs, auto 0–60 runs, and braking runs.

The roll-on timing mode records data between two programmable speed set points. By performing roll-ons in different gears over a wide range of speeds, an accurate performance map for a motorcycle can be obtained. Information that is captured for roll-on runs includes maximum horsepower/rpm, max torque/rpm, run time, run distance, and max speed. Similar to the roll-on mode is the dynamometer mode that records data between programmable rpm points. Information for either mode is useful for setting up an ECU fuel map or for selecting gear ratios (sprocket sizes) for a racetrack.

The Veypor automatically backlights its display for night riding. This screen shows its capability to perform braking runs. After accelerating to just over 60 miles per hour, the brakes are applied and the distance in feet that it took the motorcycle to decelerate from 60 to 0 miles per hour is displayed. The top of the screen shows a progress bar when accelerating to 60 miles per hour. *Nonlinear Engineering*

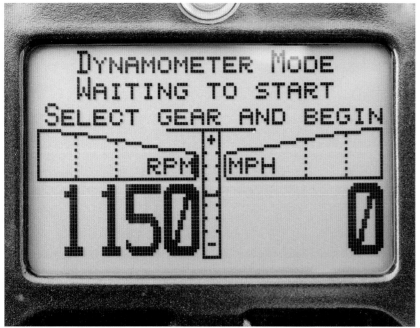

In the dynamometer mode, performance is measured between a start-and-stop rpm. In third or fourth gear, the rider opens the throttle below the start rpm and closes it after passing the stop rpm. The Veypor starts logging data automatically. After the run, the unit enters the graphing mode and the screen displays horsepower, torque, and rpm, plus many other performance parameters. *Nonlinear Engineering*

To effectively measure performance in either roll-on or dynamometer mode, select the start and stop motorcycle speed (roll-on mode) or engine rpm (dyno mode) set points.

For roll-on mode, shift into the desired gear and run the motorcycle at just below the start set point. Open the throttle all the way and accelerate until the stop point has been reached. The Veypor will automatically start recording data when the start speed is reached and stop recording when the stop point speed is achieved.

For measuring performance in the dynamometer mode, a different procedure is used. Fourth, fifth, or sixth gear should be used at relatively low engine rpm to start the run. With the bike running at just below the start rpm point, open the throttle and hold it wide open until the stop rpm set point is reached. Don't shift into a higher gear during the run, as this will cause erratic acceleration peaks in the performance graphs.

Horsepower measured by a Veypor system is the net power at the rear wheel, not flywheel horsepower. Real-world

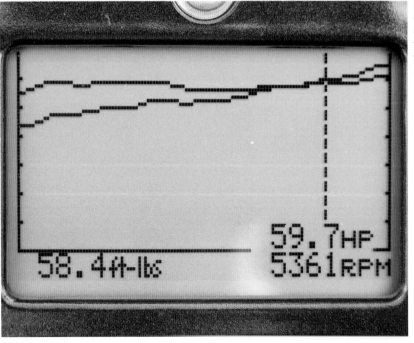

This is the graph analysis main screen that contains a summary of the current run. Horsepower and torque are displayed at specific engine rpm at the top. On the right the display shows that 252 feet were traveled in 3.10 seconds and the maximum speed (Vel) was 71.5 miles per hour. On the left are the graphing options. *Nonlinear Engineering*

conditions are measured, including aerodynamic drag, rolling resistance from the tire, and drag from the ram-air induction system from the air moving around an accelerating motorcycle (something a chassis dynamometer cannot measure). In general, Veypor numbers will be somewhat lower than dyno numbers due to aerodynamic drag. More important than comparing Veypor horsepower and torque numbers to those obtained from dyno runs is that Veypor numbers be compared to each other for the purpose of determining if engine modifications make more, or less, power.

Horsepower and torque are plotted on the graph. The dashed, vertical line is a cursor that can be placed anywhere on the graph to read horsepower and torque at specific engine rpm. This graph is indicating that at 5,361 rpm, the rear wheel was producing 58.4 foot-pounds of torque and 59.7 horsepower. *Nonlinear Engineering*

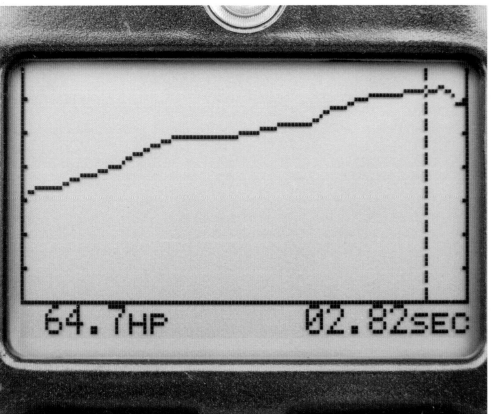

This graph shows horsepower vs. time in seconds: 2.82 seconds into the run, the rear wheel was making 64.7 horsepower. As in the previous graph, the cursor (dashed line) can be moved to see different time vs. horsepower readings. *Nonlinear Engineering*

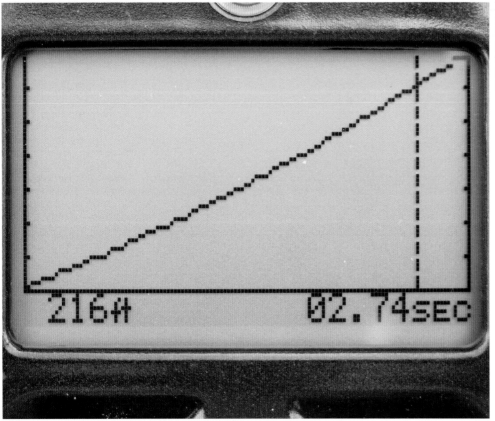

This graph measures acceleration in feet vs. time: 216 feet were traveled in 2.74 seconds. This, and the other graphs, can be used to measure the differences between fuel map changes from one run to another. *Nonlinear Engineering*

A similar graph shows speed vs. time. From the start of the run, it took 2.70 seconds to reach 68.6 miles per hour. Like the other graphs, this can be used to evaluate exhaust system performance, fuel mapping, or other modifications. *Nonlinear Engineering*

68.6MPH   02.70SEC

PLOTTING VEYPOR DATA ON A COMPUTER

Veypor Analysis Software (VAS) is downloadable from the company's website. VAS can display run data, lap times, and data-logging information. The software can overlay up to seven types of graphs for analyzing engine-performance changes. Users can select specific ranges, for plotting horsepower and torque curves in individual gears. Performance details like 60-foot, 330-foot, ⅛-mile, and ¼-mile times can be displayed or plotted. Up to four runs can be compared at a time for extensive analysis. Here are just some of the numerous screens that VAS can display.

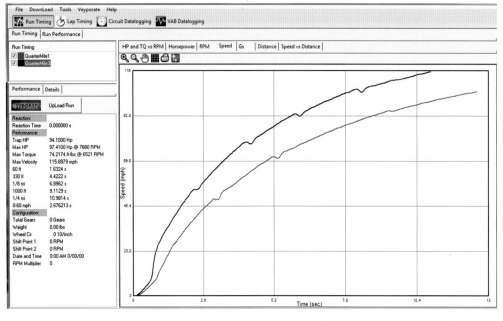

FIGURE 5 This is the VAS Run Timing screen. Two runs are being compared (QuarterMile1 and QuarterMile2, top left) for speed vs. distance. Run 1 (red line) was slower than run 2 (black line). The small dips in each plot represent shift points for each gear. Run 2 hits 92.8 miles per hour at about 5.6 seconds compared to run 1, which takes longer to reach the same speed at about 9.4 seconds. *Nonlinear Engineering*

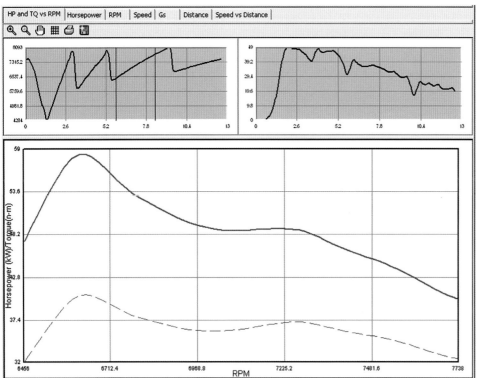

FIGURE 6 This plots torque and horsepower versus rpm, similar to a dynamometer graph. Torque is the solid line, and the dashed line is horsepower. The smaller plot on the top left shows the exact rpm range over which the dyno plot was made (indicated by to dark vertical lines). The large plot is expanded so the data fills the screen. The plot on the top right is horsepower vs. time. *Nonlinear Engineering*

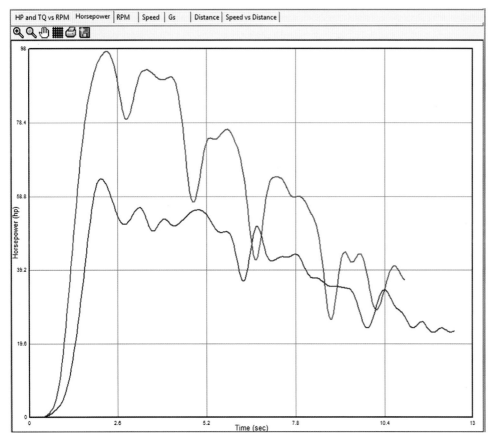

FIGURE 7 This graph shows horsepower vs. time for overlaid runs. The dips in each plot are shift points. Notice that as the gears are shifted up, horsepower drops in each successive gear. This is because torque multiplication is greatest in the lower gears. Peak horsepower is produced in first gear for both runs and diminishes from there. *Nonlinear Engineering*

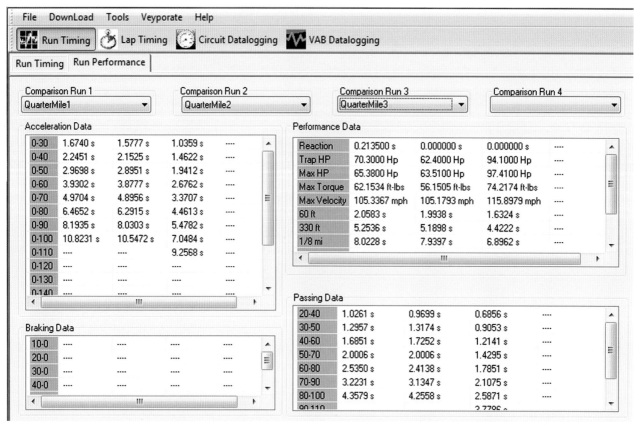

File   DownLoad   Tools   Veyporate   Help

Run Timing   Lap Timing   Circuit Datalogging   VAB Datalogging

Run Timing | Run Performance

Comparison Run 1	Comparison Run 2	Comparison Run 3	Comparison Run 4
QuarterMile1	QuarterMile2	QuarterMile3	

Acceleration Data

0-30	1.6740 s	1.5777 s	1.0359 s	.....
0-40	2.2451 s	2.1525 s	1.4622 s	.....
0-50	2.9698 s	2.8951 s	1.9412 s	.....
0-60	3.9302 s	3.8777 s	2.6762 s	.....
0-70	4.9704 s	4.8956 s	3.3707 s	.....
0-80	6.4652 s	6.2915 s	4.4613 s	.....
0-90	8.1935 s	8.0303 s	5.4782 s	.....
0-100	10.8231 s	10.5472 s	7.0484 s	.....
0-110	.....	.....	9.2568 s	
0-120	.....	.....	.....	
0-130	.....	.....	.....	
0-140	.....	.....	.....	

Performance Data

Reaction	0.213500 s	0.000000 s	0.000000 s	.....
Trap HP	70.3000 Hp	62.4000 Hp	94.1000 Hp	.....
Max HP	65.3800 Hp	63.5100 Hp	97.4100 Hp	.....
Max Torque	62.1534 ft-lbs	56.1505 ft-lbs	74.2174 ft-lbs	.....
Max Velocity	105.3367 mph	105.1793 mph	115.8979 mph	.....
60 ft	2.0583 s	1.9938 s	1.6324 s	.....
330 ft	5.2536 s	5.1898 s	4.4222 s	.....
1/8 mi	8.0228 s	7.9397 s	6.8962 s	.....

Braking Data

10-0	.....	.....	.....	.....
20-0	.....	.....	.....	.....
30-0	.....	.....	.....	.....
40-0	.....	.....	.....	.....

Passing Data

20-40	1.0261 s	0.9699 s	0.6856 s	.....
30-50	1.2957 s	1.3174 s	0.9053 s	.....
40-60	1.6851 s	1.7252 s	1.2141 s	.....
50-70	2.0006 s	2.0006 s	1.4295 s	.....
60-80	2.5350 s	2.4138 s	1.7851 s	.....
70-90	3.2231 s	3.1347 s	2.1075 s	.....
80-100	4.3579 s	4.2558 s	2.5871 s	.....
90-110			2.7796 s	

FIGURE 8   The VAS run performance comparison screen shows data for up to four runs. Acceleration data shows distance vs. speed. Performance data shows max horsepower, torque, speed, and run intervals (60 feet, 330 feet, ⅛, and ¼ mile). Passing data shows time between speeds. *Nonlinear Engineering*

DOBECK GEN3 CONTROLLER INSTALLATION

Dobeck controllers were discussed in Chapter 2. Here we'll go through a typical installation of a Battley Cycles GEN 3 Dobeck controller for a 2009 Ducati Hypermotard. In stock form, the motorcycle exhibits several flat spots when accelerating and does not have especially quick throttle response when revving the engine. Adding the Dobeck controller addresses all these problems and makes the motorcycle easier to control and ride. After installation we'll go through the steps for tuning the controller. Dobeck controllers sold by other companies use the same procedure. The only real difference between controllers is the programming code for specific motorcycle applications. Here are the steps for a typical GEN 3 controller installation.

Now that the Battley GEN3 controller is installed, we'll adjust the fuel curve. The controller's programming takes into account the specific motorcycle for which it was designed and any existing engine modifications. If the owner wants to add an aftermarket exhaust later, or change to a different exhaust, the controller allows for this adjustment. In the following example, the motorcycle was in stock configuration when the controller was installed. The owner

has added an exhaust system and performance air filter and needs to adjust AFR to compensate for the engine's newfound ability to breathe.

1. **Warm-Up** The first step is to take the motorcycle for a short ride to fully warm the engine to normal operating temperature.

2. **Drive-Cycle Evaluation** The controller controls three driving cycles or zones: cruise, acceleration, and full throttle. Each zone can add fuel to the pre-programmed fuel curve using the three buttons located on the faceplate of the controller. Before adjusting any of these zones, engine-performance problems must be identified.

   A. Ride the motorcycle at part throttle (green zone). Note any hesitation from off-idle acceleration, surging at steady throttle operation, hesitation when gently accelerating from part throttle, or popping from the exhaust when decelerating. If any of these problems are detected, try to duplicate them several times. Write down the results for reference.

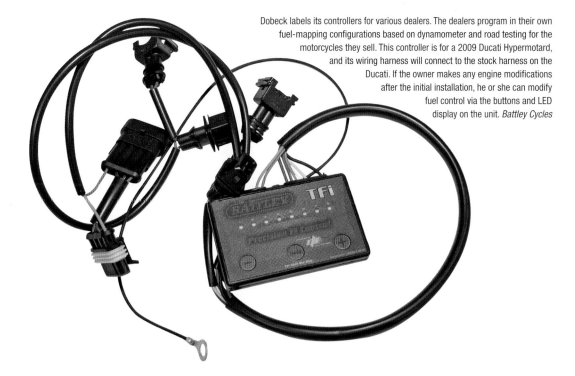

Dobeck labels its controllers for various dealers. The dealers program in their own fuel-mapping configurations based on dynamometer and road testing for the motorcycles they sell. This controller is for a 2009 Ducati Hypermotard, and its wiring harness will connect to the stock harness on the Ducati. If the owner makes any engine modifications after the initial installation, he or she can modify fuel control via the buttons and LED display on the unit. *Battley Cycles*

Pictured is the integrated circuit board inside the Dobeck GEN 3 controller. It measures around 4 × 3 inches and, despite its small size, a lot of digital engineering went into its functionality to modify the stock ECU's injector pulse width signal. *Battley Cycles*

The seat needs to be removed on the Hypermotard to gain access to the wiring harness. The 1,100-cc twin-cylinder engine makes 90 horsepower at 7,750 rpm and 76 foot-pounds of torque at 4,750 rpm. The motorcycle weighs in at only 390 pounds dry—can you say *fun*? *Battley Cycles*

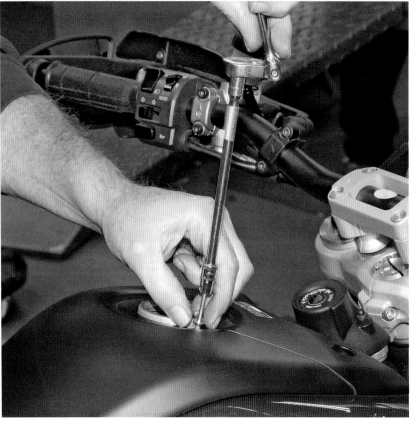

The tank panel needs to be removed so the side panels can come off. The main ECU wiring harness is located in the right side panel. *Battley Cycles*

With the tank panel removed, the fuel-sending unit can be seen just behind the fuel filler. *Battley Cycles*

A side panel is being removed. Be careful when removing body panels. They are fragile and expensive to replace. *Battley Cycles*

HOW TO TUNE EFI SYSTEMS

127

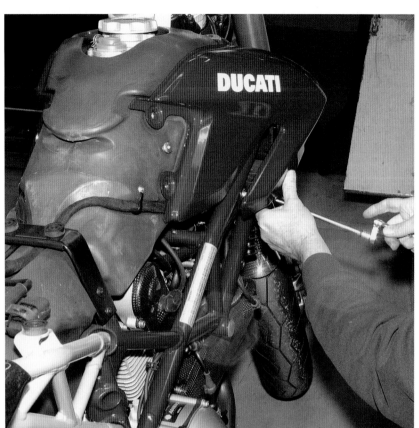

The right side panel is being removed by Chris Sanders of Battley Cycles. Sanders is the dealership's brains when it comes to fuel-map tuning, and he programs the Battley branded Dobeck GEN 3 controllers for each motorcycle application. *Battley Cycles*

The Ducati Hypermotard's ECU is attached to the frame underneath the right tank panel. Note the large electrical ground connector located on the lower ECU mounting screw. The ground wire for the controller will be connected here, so the unit has a true ground in relationship to the bike's ECU. This ground connection is a better ground than the battery negative terminal, engine, or chassis. *Battley Cycles*

The controller is placed next to the ECU until the wiring harness from each injector is connected. The controller will be tucked in behind the ECU and is easily accessible for future fuel control tuning. *Battley Cycles*

One of the fuel injector connectors is shown. This connector will plug into the controller, and the controller's injector harness will now connect directly to the fuel injector. The GEN 3 controller intercepts the pulse-width signal from the stock ECU and modifies it according to its program. *Battley Cycles*

Sanders completes the injector harness connections to the controller. The entire installation took about half an hour. *Battley Cycles*

The programming code, developed by Chris Sanders at Battley Cycles, is uploaded into the GEN3 unit from a laptop. The code, or program, is specific to the Ducati Hypermotard with the stock exhaust system. If the owner changes to an aftermarket exhaust later, he or she can modify the controller's program using the unit's buttons and LED display. *Battley Cycles*

HOW TO TUNE EFI SYSTEMS

The GEN3 controller's LED display goes through a self-diagnostic sequence when the engine is first started to verify that everything's connected correctly. If there is a poor connection to one of the injectors, the LEDs will identify which one has the problem. *Battley Cycles*

The Battley GEN3 controller comes pre-programmed for a specific motorcycle equipped with aftermarket exhaust. It is user-adjustable via the three buttons and a series of eight LED lights on the faceplate. *Battley Cycles*

B. Accelerate the motorcycle hard (yellow zone) from several different rpm settings in third or fourth gear. The controller's yellow acceleration zone affects moderate to hard acceleration. Problems to look for include a lack of normal power, hesitation, ping or knock, and exhaust backfire. If the engine pings, or knocks, back off the throttle immediately and do not repeat this part of the evaluation until the fuel curve's yellow zone has been richened up. Write down the results for reference.

C. The red zone controls fuel at wide-open throttle. Shift into fifth gear and run the engine to the rpm where it usually starts to make power. Then hold the throttle open and accelerate to redline. Listen for detonation in the form of engine ping or knock. If either of these is present, back off the throttle and stop this part of the evaluation. If no knocking is present, evaluate whether the engine's power feels normal or as if it's running out of fuel. Write down your results.

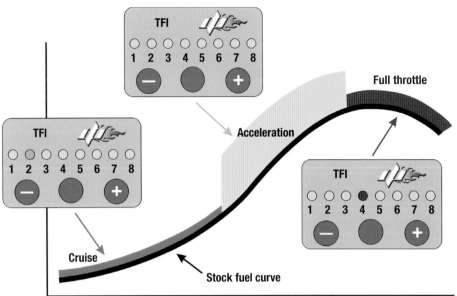

FIGURE 9 A graphic display of what's going on inside the GEN3 controller can help make clear the effect of adjusting the fuel curve via the mode, minus, and plus buttons. The black line represents the stock ECU fuel curve. The green line is for cruise, yellow for acceleration, and red for full-throttle operation. The LEDs for each zone correspond with the level of fuel added to the stock fuel curve. For example, the red zone lights up the fourth LED, the yellow zone is at 7, and green zone is set to level 2. In this drawing, the level of fuel corrections have been exaggerated to show how the buttons operate. A typical fuel curve uses more subtle additions. During actual programming, the LEDs flash to indicate zone fuel correction. *Dobeck Performance*

3. **Adjusting the Fuel Curve** The problems encountered during each of the three drive zones can be addressed by adding or subtracting fuel from each zone. To enter the adjusting mode, press the center, or mode, button. A green LED will flash, indicating that the controller is in the green cruising zone. The number of the LED will indicate how much fuel correction is currently set for that zone. In Figure 9, the number 2 LED is flashing. Pressing the mode button again will light a yellow LED, indicating the yellow acceleration zone. In Figure 9 the number 7 LED is flashing, showing that the zone is set almost to its maximum setting. To enter the red

full-throttle zone, press the mode button again. In our example, the number 4 LED flashes, indicating the amount of fuel added for the red zone.

Just riding a motorcycle with newly installed pipes, it's difficult to tell if the AFR is too rich or lean, especially if the mixture is close. For each zone that exhibited a problem during the drive-cycle evaluation, try adding one or two LED lights to change the fuel curve. Fuel increases can be made in .5 increments from 1 to 8 (1, 1.5, 2, 2.5, 3, and so on). Two side-by-side LEDs will flash to indicate a half of a whole number.

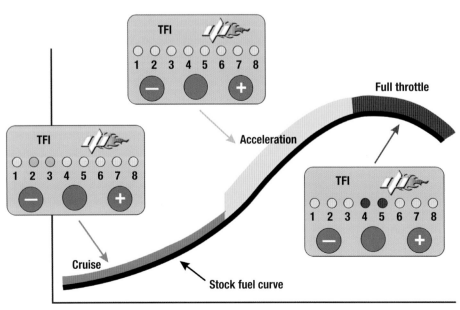

FIGURE 10 In this graphic, the zone settings have all been changed. Note the amount of fuel correction (indicated by the thickness of the colored lines) corresponds to the controller's LED display. The green cruise zone has been changed from 2 (Figure 9) to 2.5, as indicated by the number 2 and 3 LED flashing together. Fuel in the yellow acceleration zone has been reduced from LED number 7 to 4, and fuel in the red full-throttle zone has been increased slightly from 4 to 4.5. *Dobeck Performance*

If the problem for a particular zone is better on a second test ride (and fuel was added), then the AFR was too lean and correcting the fuel curve increased performance. Conversely, if adding fuel to a particular zone makes a problem worse, then the mixture was already too rich and the next adjustment should subtract fuel to correct the AFR.

Saving the LED settings is simple. Don't press any buttons for a few seconds, and the LED fuel correction levels will automatically be saved in the controller. There are also other light modes used for diagnostics; these are explained in the installation instructions. Button adjustments can be made by the side of the road (locate a safe place and pull completely off the road) when performing the low-tech fuel-mapping tests outlined earlier in this chapter. Keep in mind that if a motorcycle engine has problems in addition to lean or rich fuel mixtures, no EFI controller can fix them. For example, if the throttle bodies are out of synchronization, no amount of button pushing will fix the problem. Bad rings, low compression, fouled spark plugs, bad gas, dirty air filter—these all affect engine performance and should be addressed before EFI tuning. If the engine has performance problems, and the controller is suspected, disconnect the fuel injector wiring harness and connect it back to the stock ECU. If the problems are still present, the controller is not at fault. Any issues should be repaired before reinstalling the controller.

DYNOJET POWER COMMANDER PCIII AND PC-V

Dynojet's Power Commander PCIII and PC-V were discussed at length in Chapter 2, Aftermarket EFI Controllers. Installation for both the PCIII and PC-V is simple and straightforward. Each Power Commander comes with a custom wiring harness made specifically for installation on a particular motorcycle. Written instructions with photos are included with each unit. The example that follows is for installation on a 2005 Yamaha FJR1300.

The PCIII and PC-V are similar in that, when purchased, they are supplied with base maps that have been developed

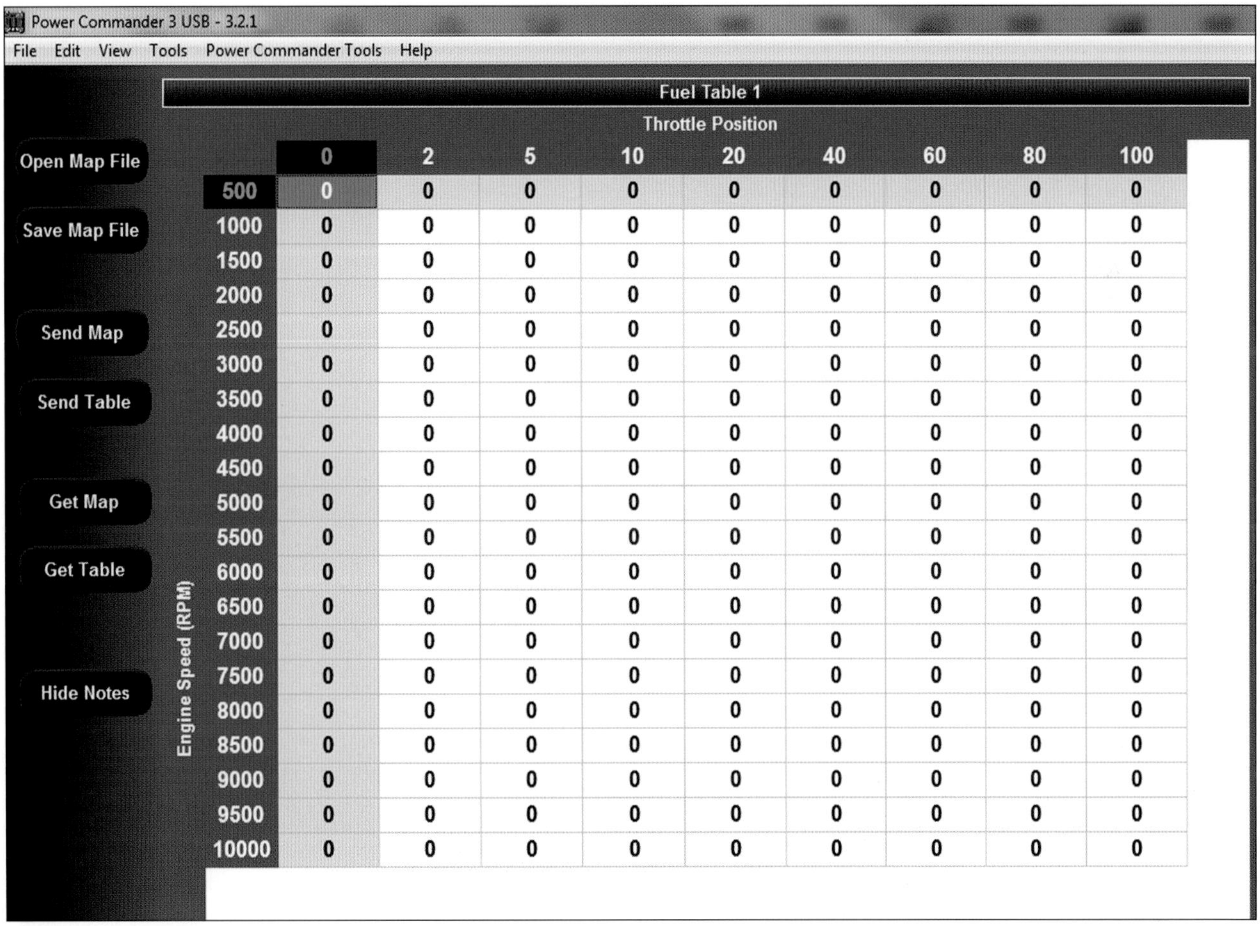

	0	2	5	10	20	40	60	80	100
500	0	0	0	0	0	0	0	0	0
1000	0	0	0	0	0	0	0	0	0
1500	0	0	0	0	0	0	0	0	0
2000	0	0	0	0	0	0	0	0	0
2500	0	0	0	0	0	0	0	0	0
3000	0	0	0	0	0	0	0	0	0
3500	0	0	0	0	0	0	0	0	0
4000	0	0	0	0	0	0	0	0	0
4500	0	0	0	0	0	0	0	0	0
5000	0	0	0	0	0	0	0	0	0
5500	0	0	0	0	0	0	0	0	0
6000	0	0	0	0	0	0	0	0	0
6500	0	0	0	0	0	0	0	0	0
7000	0	0	0	0	0	0	0	0	0
7500	0	0	0	0	0	0	0	0	0
8000	0	0	0	0	0	0	0	0	0
8500	0	0	0	0	0	0	0	0	0
9000	0	0	0	0	0	0	0	0	0
9500	0	0	0	0	0	0	0	0	0
10000	0	0	0	0	0	0	0	0	0

FIGURE 11 The Power Commander PCIII zero fuel map has all 0s entered into the fuel table. The value of "0" means that the PCIII is making no fuel corrections to the stock fuel map. Throttle position is laid out across the top and engine rpm is on the left side of the fuel table. *Dynojet Research*

The PCIII for this installation has four connectors that will plug into the stock fuel injector wiring harness. The connectors are color-coded (black and white) and correspond with the colors of the stock connectors. The only other wire is a ground wire that needs to be connected directly to the battery's negative terminal. *Dynojet Research*

The PCIII will fit under the seat, and the wiring harness must be threaded around and through the subframe of the motorcycle. Tie wraps are used to secure the wiring harness in place. *Dynojet Research*

The two pairs of connectors are plugged into the stock wiring harness. Contact cleaner should be used to remove dirt and corrosion from the connectors before plugging them together. The wiring all tucks in behind the fuel rail and is held in place with tie wraps. *Dynojet Research*

to provide improvement over the stock ECU's map for many combinations of engine modifications. A zero map is provided, too, which is basically all zeros entered into the fuel table with no fuel corrections provided over stock settings. With the zero map loaded into the PCIII or PC-V, the Power Commander essentially does nothing regarding fuel correction. The zero map is a good diagnostic tool and can be used to determine if the stock ECU is causing an AFR-related problem or if they are in the controller's fuel map.

In addition to the zero map, a fuel map for the stock exhaust system and stock or aftermarket air filter is provided with each Power Commander. Depending on the motorcycle's manufacturer, stock ECU maps are optimized for 60 to 70 percent of potential engine performance. With a motorcycle completely stock, a Power Commander base map will increase performance levels to around 85 to 95 percent of potential engine performance.

Once aftermarket parts are added to a motorcycle, alternate maps may be found on either the CD that came with the controller or on Dynojet's website. Dynojet is constantly updating its map database for specific motorcycles, and it is not unusual to find maps for specific exhaust systems. The differences between Brand A exhaust and Brand B may be small; however, these differences will increase engine-performance optimization beyond the stock motorcycle's factory equipment. For example, listed are the maps for a 2009–2010 Suzuki SV650 and SV650S:

- Zero Map
- Stock Exhaust, Stock or Aftermarket Air Filter
- Arata Full Exhaust, Stock or Aftermarket Air Filter
- Leo Vince High Mount Full Exhaust, Stock or Aftermarket Air Filter
- M4 High Mount Slip-On, K&N Air Filter, Airbox Snorkel Removed
- Two Brothers Slip-On, Stock or Aftermarket Air Filter

The more popular the motorcycle, the more fuel maps are available for specific years and models. For example, more than 136 maps are listed for 2009 Harley-Davidson FL touring models. These fuel maps encompass complete exhaust systems, slip-on mufflers, camshafts, air filters, big-bore kits, cylinder-head modifications—the list is almost endless.

Another source for fuel maps is the Internet, particularly motorcycle forums. No matter the motorcycle's make, model, or year, there is probably an online forum comprised of members with the same, or similar, bike. In addition to providing brand/model-specific camaraderie, swapping lies about who is the fastest, and information about parts, accessories, and riding gear, a great deal of technical information is usually available, including members' custom Dynojet fuel maps. Forum members have spent thousands of dollars and many hours having their bikes tuned on dynamometers. If the forum community is large enough, chances are that a custom map exists that fits the combination of parts or modifications one is looking for. If asked nicely, most forum members willingly share their fuel maps with other members. A good example of map-sharing is the Smoothness Map available on www.fjrforum.com for all years of Yamaha FRJ 1300s. This example is for a PCIII, but it also applies to a PC-V Power Commander.

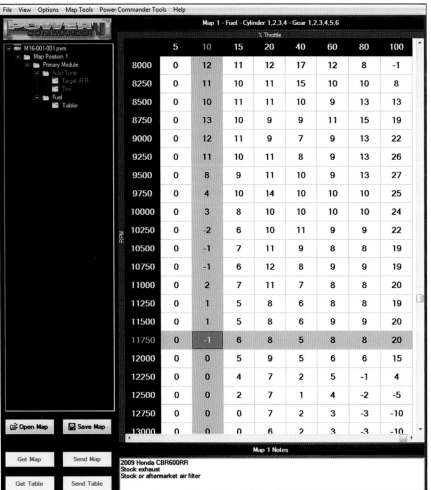

FIGURE 12 This is the PC-V base map for a stock 2009–10 Honda CBR 600 RR sport bike. The numbers in the cells represent the percentage of change from 0 (no fuel correction) to either a positive number (more fuel added) or a negative number (less fuel than stock). The only way to develop a fuel table like the one shown is by using a wideband oxygen sensor and dynamometer testing. *Dynojet Research*

Map 1 - Fuel - Cylinder 1,2,3,4 - Gear 1,2,3,4,5,6

RPM \ % Throttle	5	10	15	20	40	60	80	100
8000	0	12	11	12	17	12	8	-1
8250	0	11	10	11	15	10	10	8
8500	0	10	11	11	10	9	13	13
8750	0	13	10	9	9	11	15	19
9000	0	12	11	9	7	9	13	22
9250	0	11	10	11	8	9	13	26
9500	0	8	9	11	10	9	13	27
9750	0	4	10	14	10	10	10	25
10000	0	3	8	10	10	10	10	24
10250	0	-2	6	10	11	9	9	22
10500	0	-1	7	11	9	8	8	19
10750	0	-1	6	12	8	9	9	19
11000	0	2	7	11	7	8	8	20
11250	0	1	5	8	6	8	8	19
11500	0	1	5	8	6	9	9	20
11750	0	-1	6	8	5	8	8	20
12000	0	0	5	9	5	6	6	15
12250	0	0	4	7	2	5	-1	4
12500	0	0	2	7	1	4	-2	-5
12750	0	0	0	7	2	3	-3	-10
13000	0	0	0	6	2	3	-3	-10

Map 1 Notes

2009 Honda CBR600RR
Stock exhaust
Stock or aftermarket air filter

Open Map Save Map
Get Map Send Map
Get Table Send Table

FIGURE 13 This is the Dynojet base map that came with the Power Commander for a 2005 Yamaha FJR 1300. The rpm resolution is set to show 500 rpm intervals (at left). The highlighted area illustrates where on the fuel table that the majority of the fuel additions were required to the stock map. All of these values are positive, indicating the stock map was too lean for best performance. When developing the map, Dynojet targeted air-fuel ratios at around 13.4:1 to maximize engine performance. *Dynojet Research*

Fuel Table 1

Engine Speed (RPM) \ Throttle Position	0	2	5	10	20	40	60	80	100
500	0	0	0	0	0	0	0	0	0
1000	0	0	-4	0	0	0	0	0	0
1500	0	9	0	0	0	-5	0	-1	1
2000	0	10	12	-4	-7	-11	-9	-2	-1
2500	0	11	15	6	-3	-4	-3	-1	-1
3000	0	7	10	7	-2	-7	-6	-4	-3
3500	0	3	14	16	7	-5	-5	-2	0
4000	0	5	16	19	15	0	-5	-4	-6
4500	0	5	12	13	17	0	-8	-8	-9
5000	0	5	10	20	26	0	-8	-4	-2
5500	0	5	10	21	23	-1	-6	-7	-7
6000	0	5	10	20	24	4	-7	-5	-5
6500	0	0	0	26	25	8	-5	-2	-3
7000	0	0	0	24	25	12	-3	-2	-3
7500	0	0	0	19	23	13	1	-4	-3
8000	0	0	0	16	27	17	6	-1	-5
8500	0	0	0	15	22	20	9	-2	-4
9000	0	0	0	15	20	22	14	-2	-4
9500	0	0	0	0	21	23	14	1	-3
10000	0	0	0	0	0	0	0	0	0

Open Map File
Save Map File
Send Map
Send Table
Get Map
Get Table
Hide Notes

2005 Yamaha FJR1300
Stock exhaust
Stock air filter
Stock O2 sensor disconnected

Power Commander 3 USB - 3.2.1

File   Edit   View   Tools   Power Commander Tools   Help

| | Fuel Table 1 | | | | | | | | |
| | Throttle Position | | | | | | | | |
Engine Speed (RPM)	0	2	5	10	20	40	60	80	100
1000	0	0	0	0	0	0	0	0	0
1250	0	5	7	-5	-2	0	0	0	0
1500	0	10	15	-10	-5	-1	0	0	0
1750	0	12	14	-8	-4	-5	-5	-4	-8
2000	0	14	13	-7	-3	-10	-11	-9	-16
2250	0	14	15	1	-6	-11	-11	-9	-12
2500	0	15	17	9	-10	-13	-11	-10	-8
2750	0	7	17	15	-3	-13	-12	-11	-7
3000	0	0	17	21	3	-13	-14	-13	-6
3250	0	0	16	21	6	-6	-6	-6	-4
3500	0	0	15	22	10	1	1	1	-2
3750	0	0	15	24	15	0	-2	-2	-3
4000	0	0	15	27	21	-2	-6	-6	-4
4250	0	0	7	21	19	-3	-8	-8	-4
4500	0	0	0	16	18	-5	-11	-11	-4
4750	0	0	0	18	21	-3	-9	-9	-3
5000	0	0	0	21	25	-2	-8	-8	-2
5250	0	0	0	21	25	-1	-7	-8	-5
5500	0	0	0	21	25	-1	-7	-9	-8
5750	0	0	0	18	25	1	-7	-9	-7
6000	0	0	0	16	25	4	-8	-9	-7
6250	0	0	0	18	25	5	-8	-8	-6
6500	0	0	0	21	26	7	-8	-8	-6
6750	0	0	0	10	24	9	-6	-7	-7
7000	0	0	0	0	23	11	-5	-7	-8
7250	0	0	0	0	23	12	-3	-8	-8
7500	0	0	0	0	23	14	-2	-9	-9
7750	0	0	0	0	24	15	0	-8	-7
8000	0	0	0	0	25	16	2	-7	-5
8250	0	0	0	0	23	16	3	-7	-5

Open Map File
Save Map File
Send Map
Send Table
Get Map
Get Table
Hide Notes

Custom map; no O2 Sensor; 500 rpm increments; 13.2 - 13.5 range; 4/24/04

FIGURE 14 This fuel map was downloaded from www.FJRForum.com. With close to 4,000 members worldwide, more than a few forum members have had Dynojet Power Commander fuel maps developed on a dyno and are willing to share the benefits of their efforts. This fuel table has values for 250 rpm intervals instead of every 500, as shown on the previous table. The map was developed by a member named "Wally" to smooth out engine performance above the PCIII base map and was named the "Smoothness" map. The values in the cells for fuel correction represent a great many hours of dynamometer testing, and the performance results on a bike with stock exhaust are outstanding. *FRJ Forum*

The stock fuel map for 2003 to 2005 Yamaha FJR1300s meets EPA emissions requirements but at the expense of poor throttle response and surging at steady highway cruising speeds, typically between 60 and 75 miles per hour in fifth gear. The Smoothness map was developed to eliminate part-throttle surging at cruise speeds, to smooth out overall acceleration, and to reduce engine vibration. The map uses an AFR of 13.2:1 to 13.5:1 from 5 percent at 1,500 rpm to 80 percent of throttle opening at 6,000 rpm. Above 6,000 rpm, the Dynojet base map was left intact.

While receiving great reviews from FJR forum members for good street manners and flawless acceleration, the Smoothness map suffered from one problem—a drop in fuel mileage. Many riders who used to get around 42 to 48 miles per gallon were now only getting 36 to 39 miles per gallon. Most of them just accepted this as a small price to pay for superior engine performance; however, there was a solution.

The decrease in fuel mileage is due to too much fuel at part throttle. By locating the fuel cells in the table that control the air-fuel ratios at cruising highway speeds and reducing their values, gas mileage should be restored (theoretically at least).

The first step in this process is to be able to identify what rpm and throttle opening the FJR's engine is running between 60 and 85 miles per hour in fifth gear (FJR's do not have a sixth gear). Figuring out rpm vs. mph is easy, as the rider can simply look at the tachometer and speedometer at these speeds and write down the numbers.

Determining throttle position is not as obvious. Here's how to determine exactly where the throttle position is for the cruising speeds that most affect fuel mileage. Connect a laptop to the PCIII and go to the Power Commander Control Center Tools drop-down menu and select Set Throttle Position. Wrap a strip of masking tape around the throttle and place another piece on the switch housing.

With the Throttle Calibration page displayed, open the throttle to 5 percent. Place a witness mark on switch housing masking tape and another on the throttle sleeve tape. Write 5 percent next to the mark on the throttle. Do the same for 10- and 20-percent throttle opening positions, using the laptop to verify each position. Now go for a ride on a flat section of road and note the throttle position and engine rpm for 60 miles per hour (in fifth gear on the FJR or sixth gear on other motorcycles). Do the same for 65, 70, 75, 80, and

HOW TO TUNE EFI SYSTEMS

137

The marks on the duct tape indicate 5, 10, and 20 percent of throttle opening in the Power Commander Control Center software. By looking at how the marks line up on the throttle and the motorcycle's tachometer, rpm and throttle position can be determined for fuel mileage tuning purposes.

Fuel Table 1

Buttons: Open Map File, Save Map File, Send Map, Send Table, Get Map, Get Table, Hide Notes

Engine Speed (RPM)	0	2	5	10	20	40	60	80	100
500	0	0	0	0	0	0	0	0	0
750	0	0	0	0	0	0	0	0	0
1000	0	0	0	0	0	0	0	0	0
1250	0	5	7	-5	-2	0	0	0	0
1500	0	10	15	-10	-5	-1	0	0	0
1750	0	12	14	-8	-4	-5	-5	-4	-8
2000	0	14	13	-7				-9	-16
2250	0	14	15	1				-9	-12
2500	0	15	17	9				-10	-8
2750	0	7	15	12				-11	-7
3000	0	0	13	16				-13	-6
3250	0	0	12	16				-6	-4
3500	0	0	12	16				1	-2
3750	0	0	12	18				-2	-3
4000	0	0	12	21				-6	-4
4250	0	0	6	17	14	-3	-8	-8	-4
4500	0	0	0	13	13	-5	-11	-11	-4
4750	0	0	0	15	19	-3	-9	-9	-3
5000	0	0	0	17	23	-2	-8	-8	-2

Set Throttle Position — Closed 5248 < Current 1512 > Open 25344 — Reset / OK / Cancel

Custom map; no O2 Sensor; 250 rpm increments; 13.2 - 13.5 range; 7-8-2006
Measured throttle position in 5th at: (used PC to confirm % of opening vs. throttle grip)
4000 = 9% about 70mph
4300 = 13% about 75mph
4500 = 15% about 80mph
Change fuel @ 5% from 3750 to 4250, 10% from 3750 to 4250 about 1 number richer to try an eliminate surge between 4000 and

FIGURE 15 Once the Power Commander PCIII is installed, throttle position needs to be calibrated. This information is used by the PCIII to correctly calculate which fuel cell on the table to use for any given throttle position. If idle speed is changed at a later time, the throttle calibration should be performed again. *Dynojet Research*

FIGURE 16 The fuel table cells highlighted in the red box represent fuel control for part throttle at cruising speeds between 60 to 85 miles per hour. To increase fuel mileage, these numbers will be reduced by subtracting fuel from the map until the point at which fuel mileage is increased without affecting acceleration performance. *Dynojet Research*

Fuel Table 1						
Engine Speed (RPM) \ Throttle Position	0	2	5	10	20	40
500	0	0	0	0	0	0
750	0	0	0	0	0	0
1000	0	0	0	0	0	0
1250	0	5	7	-5	-2	0
1500	0	10	15	-10	-5	-1
1750	0	12	14	-8	-4	-5
2000	0	14	13	-7	-3	-10
2250	0	14	15	1	-6	-11
2500	0	15	17	9	-10	-13
2750	0	7	17	15	-3	-13
3000	0	0	17	21	3	-13
3250	0	0	16	21	6	-6
3500	0	0	15	22	10	1
3750	0	0	15	24	15	0
4000	0	0	15	27	21	-2
4250	0	0	7	21	19	-3
4500	0	0	0	16	18	-5
4750	0	0	0	18	21	-3
5000	0	0	0	21	25	-2
5250	0	0	0	21	25	-1
5500	0	0	0	21	25	-1

85 miles per hour. Pull off the highway and write down the numbers for later reference. Back in the garage, reconnect the laptop to the PCIII. With the fuel table displayed and the numbers that were collected during testing, it's easy to see what fuel cells are controlling AFR for cruising speeds in high gear. Figure 16 shows the results.

All the values in the highlighted areas are positive, indicating that fuel has been added to the stock ECU's fuel table. Remember that "0" indicates no change to AFR from stock settings. These values need to be reduced to increase fuel mileage. A 10 percent reduction for each cell is a good starting point. The PCIII's fuel table shows fuel correction values in each cell in terms of a percentage of the stock setting. For example, if the number 17 is displayed then 17 percent more fuel has been added over the stock value of 0 for that throttle position and engine rpm. We want to reduce the 17 percent increase by 10 percent of 17 percent, or 1.7 percent; 17 minus 1.7 is 15.3, so we want to change the number in

the cell to 15.3. Since the Power Commander will not accept decimals, round up if the target number ends in a decimal of .5 or higher; round down if less than .5. In our example, we would enter 15 in the cell.

Subtracting 10 percent for each number makes the assumption that the air-fuel ratio is the same for each cell. Even if this is not entirely the case, the 10 percent reduction is still a good place to start. Because the goal of reducing these numbers is to increase fuel mileage, and the numbers occur at part throttle, the potential for leaning out the fuel mixture too much will not cause engine damage. This would not be true if the fuel table numbers were reduced at higher throttle openings (more than 50 percent).

The next step in this process is to go for a test ride to evaluate the results of subtracting fuel at part throttle. The rider should pay close attention to how the engine feels at a steady throttle at specific road speeds, engine rpm, and throttle positions (looking at the marks on the masking tape).

Fuel Table 1

Throttle Position

Engine Speed (RPM)	0	2	5	10	20	40
500	0	0	0	0	0	0
750	0	0	0	0	0	0
1000	0	0	0	0	0	0
1250	0	5	7	-5	-2	0
1500	0	10	15	-10	-5	-1
1750	0	12	14	-8	-4	-5
2000	0	14	13	-7	-3	-10
2250	0	14	15	1	-6	-11
2500	0	15	17	9	-10	-13
2750	0	7	15	12	-3	-13
3000	0	0	13	16	3	-13
3250	0	0	12	16	5	-6
3500	0	0	12	16	8	1
3750	0	0	12	18	12	0
4000	0	0	12	21	16	-2
4250	0	0	6	17	14	-3
4500	0	0	0	13	13	-5
4750	0	0	0	15	19	-3
5000	0	0	0	17	23	-2
5250	0	0	0	19	24	-1
5500	0	0	0	21	25	-1

FIGURE 17 Here are the results of reducing all the part throttle numbers (inside green box) by 10 percent from our original fuel table. The rpm is highlighted at the left of the table. *Dynojet Research*

FIGURE 18 This is the Power Commander software's map-compare utility, where fuel table values from two maps can be compared side by side. The two maps (smoothness map.djm and 07-08-2006fuel.djm) are listed at the upper left. The table highlights the cells that are different between the two maps in red. In addition to the numbers, a graph at the top shows a curve in different colors between the two maps. *Dynojet Research*

If the engine surges at a steady throttle, or if it hesitates when gently accelerating from one cruising speed to a higher speed, too much fuel has been taken away from the cell(s) that affect that section of the fuel table. Fuel needs to be added back into these cells to eliminate the problem. Conversely, some rpm and throttle settings will not show any issues and can be leaned out more by a few numbers. The whole process will take several test runs and some hours to refine part-throttle fuel mixture.

Once the fuel table numbers have been reduced to the point that there are no engine-performance problems, fill up the tank and start keeping track of fuel mileage with the revised settings. In our example, the motorcycle's mpg went from a low of 36 miles per gallon back up to an average of 43 miles per gallon—similar to the stock settings but with superior/ smoother acceleration and overall engine performance due to the use of the Smoothness map.

Fuel Table 1									
Throttle Position									
Engine Speed (RPM)	0	2	5	10	20	40	60	80	100
500	0	0	0	0	0	0	0	0	0
750	0	0	0	0	0	0	0	0	0
1000	0	0	0	0	0	0	0	0	0
1250	0	5	7	-5	-2	0	0	0	0
1500	0	10	15	-10	-5	-1	0	0	0
1750	0	12	14	-8	-4	-5	-5	-4	-8
2000	0	14	13	-7	-3	-10	-11	-9	-16
2250	0	14	15	1	-6	-11	-11	-9	-12
2500	0	15	17	9	-10	-13	-11	-10	-8
2750	0	7	15	12	-3	-13	-12	-11	-7
3000	0	0	13	16	3	-13	-14	-13	-6
3250	0	0	12	16	5	-6	-6	-6	-4
3500	0	0	12	16	8	1	1	1	-2
3750	0	0	12	18	12	0	-2	-2	-3
4000	0	0	12	21	16	-2	-6	-6	-4
4250	0	0	6	17	14	-3	-8	-8	-4
4500	0	0	0	13	13	-5	-11	-11	-4
4750	0	0	0	15	19	-3	-9	-9	-3
5000	0	0	0	17	23	-2	-8	-8	-2
5250	0	0	0	19	24	-1	-7	-8	-5
5500	0	0	0	21	25	-1	-7	-9	-8
5750	0	0	0	18	25	1	-7	-9	-7
6000	0	0	0	16	25	4	-8	-9	-7
6250	0	0	0	18	25	5	-8	-8	-6
6500	0	0	0	21	26	7	-8	-8	-6
6750	0	0	0	10	24	9	-6	-7	-7
7000	0	0	0	0	23	11	-5	-7	-8
7250	0	0	0	0	23	12	-3	-8	-8
7500	0	0	0	0	23	14	-2	-9	-9
7750	0	0	0	0	24	15	0	-8	-7

FIGURE 19 With the PCII connected to a computer, pushing the three-range buttons will highlight the cells in the fuel table over which the button has control. The mid-button has been pressed, and the yellow cells show what cells are affected. *Dynojet Research*

| Fuel Table 1 | | | | | | | | | |
| Throttle Position | | | | | | | | | |
	0	2	5	10	20	40	60	80	100
2250	0	14	15	1	-6	-11	-11	-9	-12
2500	0	15	17	9	-10	-13	-11	-10	-8
2750	0	7	15	12	-3	-13	-12	-11	-7
3000	0	0	13	16	3	-13	-14	-13	-6
3250	0	0	12	16	5	-6	-6	-6	-4
3500	0	0	12	16	8	1	1	1	-2
3750	0	0	12	18	12	0	-2	-2	-3
4000	0	0	12	21	16	-2	-6	-6	-4
4250	0	0	6	17	14	-3	-8	-8	-4
4500	0	0	0	13	13	-5	-11	-11	-4
4750	0	0	0	15	19	-3	-9	-9	-3
5000	0	0	0	17	23	-2	-8	-8	-2
5250	0	0	0	19	24	-1	-7	-8	-5
5500	0	0	0	21	25	-1	-7	-9	-8
5750	0	0	0	18	25	1	-7	-9	-7
6000	0	0	0	16	25	4	-8	-9	-7
6250	0	0	0	18	25	5	-8	-8	-6
6500	0	0	0	21	26	7	-8	-8	-6
6750	0	0	0	10	24	9	-6	-7	-7
7000	0	0	0	0	23	11	-5	-7	-8
7250	0	0	0	0	23	12	-3	-8	-8
7500	0	0	0	0	23	14	-2	-9	-9
7750	0	0	0	0	24	15	0	-8	-7
8000	0	0	0	0	25	16	2	-7	-5
8250	0	0	0	0	23	16	3	-7	-5
8500	0	0	0	0	22	16	4	-7	-5
8750	0	0	0	0	18	18	5	-7	-5
9000	0	0	0	0	15	21	7	-7	-5
9250	0	0	0	0	7	10	3	-3	-2
9500	0	0	0	0	0	0	0	0	0

(Engine Speed (RPM) — left axis label)

FIGURE 20 The high button has been pushed, highlighting the cells that it can modify. Every time the button is pressed while in the adjustment mode, each cell is changed 2 percent (5 percent on Harley-Davidson installations) up or down. *Dynojet Research*

PCIII BUTTON ADJUSTMENT

The PCIII provides the option of adjusting the installed fuel map by using buttons on the faceplate of the unit. The buttons divide the rpm range into thirds and cover all throttle positions within their specified rpm range. The rpm range can be verified by connecting the PCIII to a computer and powering up the PCIII (either with the 9-volt power adapter or by turning the motorcycle's ignition on). While the unit is communicating with the software, push the "low" button. The map will be highlighted in the area affected by the low button. Repeat this for the mid and high buttons to verify their ranges.

Note: The buttons alone will not act as a substitute for a base map, as the adjustments control fuel table cells that cross throttle position and rpm ranges. Button adjustments should be used as a diagnostic tool, or tuning aid, instead of a method for producing a map. For example, if a motorcycle has a weak, worn-out fuel pump, and the engine seems to have lost power at wide-open throttle, pushing the "high" button to richen up the fuel table for the high rpm settings should minimize the performance problem, compensating for the weak fuel pump. Of course, compensating for a problem is not the same as fixing it. Verifying a bad pump is done by checking fuel pressure.

To adjust the buttons, first make sure that the kill switch is in the run position, then turn the ignition switch to the on position. Within 5 seconds of turning on the ignition switch, press all three buttons simultaneously. Select the range you wish to adjust—low, mid, or high—by pushing the corresponding button once. To decrease fuel to the map, hold the button down and watch the LED light bar, on the left side of the PCIII, move downward. When the two center lights are illuminated, the adjustment is at the "0" setting (no fuel correction to the map). To increase fuel, press the button repeatedly to move the lights upward. Each light bar is a 2 percent (5 percent on Harley-Davidson models) fuel change over the existing map in the Power Commander.

After making adjustments, wait 20 seconds before starting the engine or turning off the ignition switch. This will allow the button settings to be saved to the PCIII's memory. To verify that the settings have been saved, twist the throttle and watch to see if the lights move up and down the light bar. If they do, the settings are saved and the engine can be started or the ignition can be turned off. With the engine running, the light bar does not indicate either rich or lean conditions but does show throttle position with the exception of full throttle that will not light the top of the light bar.

The mid-button is pressed to increase the percentage of fuel to 4 percent over the values in the base map. Each LED on the light bar (at left) represents 2 percent. Two bars up from 0 is illuminated, indicating 4 percent additional fuel correction to the midfuel range on the map. *Dynojet Research*

With the two center LEDs illuminated, zero fuel correction has been made to the base map. The lightbar's LEDs will go up, indicating more fuel, or down, for less fuel correction. *Dynojet Research*

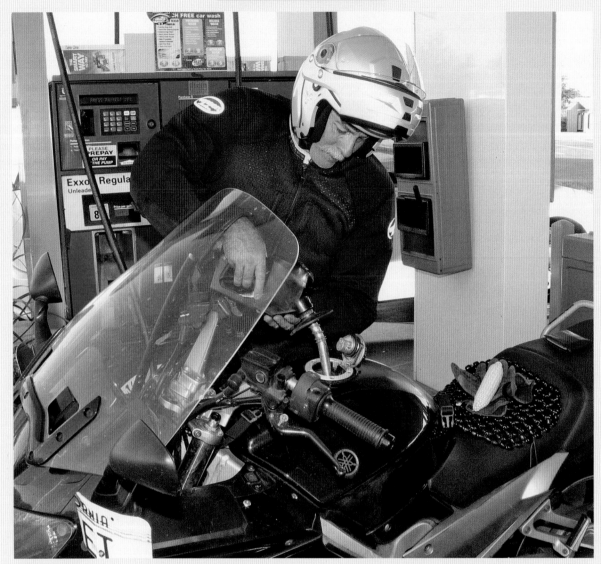

While the fuel tank on this Yamaha FJR 1300 only holds a little more than 6 gallons, nationwide, motorcycles and other powersport vehicles use about 2.6 billion gallons each year.

We like our "juice." Each year U.S. consumers purchase 130 billion gallons of gasoline. Now granted, most of that is for fueling cars and trucks, but about 2 percent of that total gets pumped into motorcycles—about 2.6 billion gallons. Most motorcyclists know the basics of how internal combustion engines and gasoline relate: Fuel and air are burned in the engine, which produces heat that is turned into power that drives the rear wheel. What is less known is how gasoline actually produces energy or how it's designed and manufactured by the bighearted (insert sarcasm here) oil companies that keep the pumps flowing.

Of special concern to the owners of vintage motorcycles is the current trend to add, or blend, up to 10 percent of ethanol, also known as ethyl alcohol or grain alcohol, into gasoline. The question is, are these blends harmful to older engine technology? Do they affect the engine power or fuel mileage of modern powerplants? We will explore these and other questions by taking a closer look at exactly what you are putting in your fuel tank.

ENERGY

It takes energy for a motorcycle to get from point A to B, and gasoline is simply a convenient way to store the energy required to get us to our destination. Let's put the amount of energy stored in gasoline into perspective. A common way to measure how much energy is contained in any type of fuel is the Btu, or British Thermal Unit. The definition of a Btu is really simple. It's the amount of heat energy that it takes to raise the temperature of a pound of water by 1 degree Fahrenheit. For example, if a wooden match is struck and burns completely, it would produce about 1 Btu. A gallon of gasoline contains around 118,000 Btus.

Energy works in mysterious ways: a gallon of gasoline's Btu heat energy, the calories in a cheeseburger, or the kilowatts of electrical power, it's all the same thing—stored energy.

Another way to measure the amount of energy stored in a gallon of gasoline is how much electricity it could produce in kilowatts, and it turns out a gallon is the equivalent of around 36 kilowatt hours (kW-h). If you left a 1,000-watt space heater on continuously for 36 hours, it would consume about the same amount of energy found in a gallon of fuel.

Calories, yes the same ones we eat, are another way to measure the amount of energy stored in gasoline. If you were to stop at McDonald's for lunch and manage to eat 114 hamburgers, you would be consuming 31,000 calories—approximately the same amount of energy found in a gallon of gasoline. But all gasoline is not created equal and there are other properties besides energy storage to consider when filling up the tank between your legs. To begin with, riders are faced with a choice of what octane number is the best for their motorcycle at every gas station stop.

OCTANE

Most riders are familiar with the term *octane* because every time they buy gas a choice must be made between at least two, or as many as five, octane ratings (87, 88, 89, 90, and 92), depending on what part of the country you're filling up in. Basically the octane rating refers to how much the fuel can be compressed inside the engine before it spontaneously ignites. The higher the octane rating, the higher compression ratio the engine can use and not

Does a gas station really have four underground storage tanks, one for each fuel? Probably not. The different octane-rated fuels are blended at the pump from only two underground tanks—one with 87 octane and the other with 93 octane. The formula "(R + M) / 2 Method" on each of these octane ratings is the equation for the average of the "Research" and "Motor" test methods of determining a fuel's octane rating.

Continued

ALL ABOUT FUEL *continued*

Nationally branded gasoline stations can be found more often than regional brands of fuel. Generally, the larger oil companies are a little more consistent in the quality of the products they sell but not always.

One of the reasons we ride motorcycles—fuel prices. The prices shown are from August 2011 on the East Coast.

Don't let the eco-friendly BP logo fool you into thinking that the use of gasoline is environmentally friendly. The widespread, worldwide use of hydrocarbon-based fuels for more than 100 years has lead to global warming, the more serious effects of which have yet to be felt.

experience engine knock or ping under hard acceleration. Higher octane fuel by itself does not cause an engine to make additional horsepower but only gives it the potential to use higher compression ratios or a more aggressive ignition advance curve—both of which will make more power. So what is octane and where does it come from?

In the gasoline refining process, crude oil is sent into a cracking unit that separates the different fuels contained in the oil. For example, methane, propane, and butane are all produced from crude oil. Because oil from the ground is made up of hydrocarbons (dead dinosaurs, plants, and so on), when the fuels are distilled they all contain different numbers of hydrocarbon atoms, also known as hydrocarbon chains. For example, methane has a single carbon atom while propane has three carbon atoms chained together. Butane has four carbon atoms, pentane has five, hexane has six, N-heptane has seven, and iso-octane contains eight carbon atoms. Octane is used as a reference standard in the petroleum industry to describe the threshold of gasoline to self-ignite (knock) during ignition.

The good news is that of all these fuels, octane has the most resistance to spontaneously igniting and therefore is the ideal fuel choice to use in cars and motorcycles. The bad news is that less octane is produced from crude oil than other fuels, making it more costly to refine. To keep the cost down, octane is mixed with heptanes to produce different octane ratings. When you fill up with 87 octane, the fuel contains 87 percent octane and 13 percent heptane (or other fuels). That's why the greater the percentage of octane, the more the fuel costs at the pump. The octane rating does not relate to the energy content of the fuel but is a measure of the fuel's tendency to burn in a controlled manner, rather than exploding and causing engine knock.

The octane rating of gasoline is measured in a test engine that has a dynamic variable compression ratio. The compression ratio can be increased or decreased as the engine is running. The compression ratio is increased until knock is detected, thus setting a baseline for measuring other fuels. When an oil refiner wants to rate a particular fuel, it would run the fuel in the test engine under tightly controlled conditions, increasing the engine's compression ratio until knock is present and then assigning an octane number to the fuel being tested.

The test engine is first run with a blend of fuel that has a known octane rating. For example a blend of 90 percent octane and 10 percent heptanes would have an octane rating of 90. If 100 percent octane is used, the octane rating would be 100. Because some fuels are more knock-resistant than unblended iso-octane, the definition for octane rating has been extended to allow for octane numbers higher than 100. Racing and aviation fuel have octane numbers of 110 plus, and there are fuel additives, "octane boosters" that use MTBE, ETBE, isooctane, and toluene that also can increase a fuel's octane rating.

The General Electric CFR F1/F2 engine combines both globally accepted methods for octane determination in one reconfigurable system. The CFR F1/F2 can be set up for either the Standard Test Method for Research Octane Number (RON) or for the Motor Octane Number (MON) method. *Courtesy General Electric*

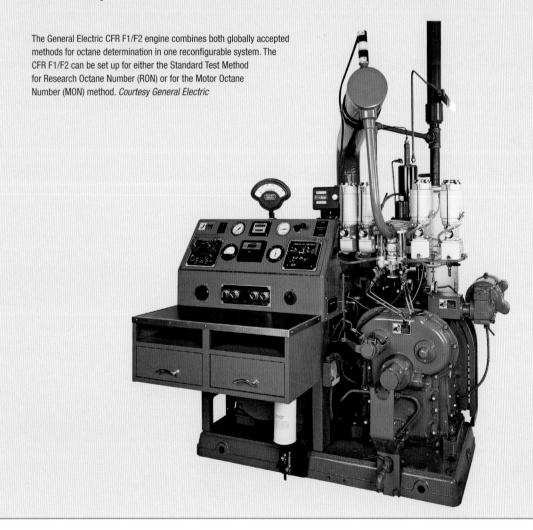

Continued

ALL ABOUT FUEL *continued*

G. A. Hope, left, of Socony Vacuum Oil Co. and A.C. Rodgers of the National Bureau of Standards operate a Cooperative Fuels Research (CFR) unit during the early 1930s in a CFR Committee evaluation program. *Courtesy John Runyard, www.runyard.org*

CFR TEST ENGINE

When gasoline engines first came into being at the turn of the last century (early 1900s), compression ratios were on the order of 4-to-1 with high-compression engines having a ratio of up to 6-to-1. Metallurgy in those days was primitive and trying to produce engines with higher compression ratios resulted in a lot of broken pistons, connecting rods, cylinder heads, and so on. As engine component materials became stronger and compression ratios increased, the need for fuel that would not pre-ignite, or knock, also increased.

Determining a fuel's resistance to self-ignite in the early 1920s was difficult, so a simpler method of rating fuel had to be devised. In fact, with more than 200 hydrocarbon compounds used in what we commonly refer to as "gasoline" today, chemical analysis still is problematic. In the early 1920s, oil companies and the automotive industry formed the Cooperative Fuels Research (CFR) committee to design and develop test engines that could measure a fuel's ability to resist pre-ignition. The first of these test engines was built by the Waukesha Engine Company in 1928 and the basic design is still in use today but with computerized controls and data-capturing capabilities.

The current CFR engines for measuring gasoline octane ratings are single-cylinder, 600cc four-stroke designs. They have an adjustable compression ratio that can be changed from 4-to-1 to up to 18-to-1 while the engine is running. Ironically, a carburetor is used to control fuel mixture, instead of electronic fuel injection, however, it is a laboratory-grade device not found in any car or motorcycle. This special carburetor has multiple float chambers, so several fuels can be tested with the turn of a valve. Intake air and fuel temperature are tightly controlled, as well as ignition timing. Before the 1970s, mechanical gauges were used to monitor engine parameters. Modern CFR engines now use a computer to both monitor and record test results. A modern CFR engine costs around $120,000, and there are several versions of the engine. CFR engines that test fuel for small planes are supercharged, and there are CFR engines for testing the combustion quality of diesel fuels or its Centane rating.

TESTING FOR OCTANE RATINGS

One of the early tests developed to measure a fuel's resistance to knock and assign it an octane rating is called the Motor Octane Number, or MON test. During this test, the CFR engine is operated at 900 rpm and the engine is placed under a high-load open-throttle condition. The temperature of the fuel is controlled and kept to 302 degrees Fahrenheit (150 Celsius). Engine intake air temperature is kept at a consistent 100.4 degrees Fahrenheit (38 Celsius). Ignition timing is varied during testing along with the compression ratio. The fuel being tested and its detonation or knock characteristics at different compression ratios are recorded. These test results are compared to test results using the baseline fuel of a mixture of iso-octane and N-heptane. Iso-octane has an octane number of 100 and N-heptane has an octane number of 0. By changing the blend of these two test fuels, measuring octane numbers between 1 and 100 are achieved. When the fuel being tested is compared to a blend of the two baseline fuels, an octane number can be assigned.

The MON test was used for a time, but it was discovered that under some part-throttle conditions automobiles would still knock even though the fuel did not have knock issues during MON testing. Another test had to be developed. It's called the Research Octane Number, or RON. During this test the CFR engine runs at 600 rpm, 300 less rpm than the MON test, and intake air temperature is matched to barometric pressure. The ignition timing is fixed, but the compression ratio is still varied during testing. The RON test is a better simulation of an automobile engine running at part throttle and RON octane numbers are usually higher than those from MON tests. As engine compression ratios continued to increase, both of these tests needed to be updated because they did not properly represent the high-compression engines of the 1960s. Because there was a fairly large difference in octane numbers between the MON and RON test methods, the AKI, or Anti-Knock Index method was adopted next. AKI is the average of RON and MON. Today in the United States, the advertised pump octane is listed as "(R + M) / 2 METHOD." Other countries use AKI but may list octane ratings as RON or even PON (Pump Octane Number).

FILLING UP

Most gas stations only have two underground fuel tanks but may offer two, three, four, or even five different octane-rated fuel choices. Fuels at these stations are blended right at the pump, and all of the octane fuels come from the two tanks. One has the highest octane-rated fuel and the other the lowest. For example, if a station offers 87, 89, 92, and 93 octane fuels, the 89 and 92 fuels are a mixture, or blend, of the 87 and 93 fuels. The 89 octane would have more fuel from the 87 tank and less from the 93 tank. Because the high-octane fuels contain more iso-octane, which is more costly to refine from crude oil, it costs more at the pump.

In addition to octane ratings, gasoline in the U.S. can either be a "Summer" or "Winter" blend depending on the season. During summer months air pollution is a problem in large metropolitan areas often causing smog. Keeping fuel from excessively evaporating in the fuel tanks of cars and motorcycles is the goal of the EPA (Environmental Protection Agency), so they require oil refiners to adhere to the Seasonal Fuel Program; hence the summer and winter fuels.

Three grades of gasoline but only two underground fuel tanks. The middle grade is blended right at the pump and draws from both the low- and high-octane storage tanks.

Continued

ALL ABOUT FUEL *continued*

The difference between the two blends of seasonal fuels is a characteristic called Reid Vapor Pressure, or RVP. RVP is the vapor pressure of gasoline measured at 100 degrees F. Fuels with a higher RVP evaporate more easily than those with a lower RVP. Gasoline must have an RVP of less than 14.7 pounds per square inch or excess pressure would build up in gas tanks causing fuel evaporation and thus air pollution. Winter fuels may have an RVP of 9.0 psi while summer fuels have a lower RVP of around 7.8. The lower RVP for summer fuels keeps evaporation to a minimum. Oil companies switch from winter to summer blends around April to June and by June 1 gas stations must start selling summer-grade gasoline. They switch back from summer to winter fuels in the middle of September. This switching back and forth may cause some performance problems in motorcycles. For example, if one fills up with a summer blend and then rides on a colder-than-usual day, the engine may exhibit some performance problems. Poor performance can happen in the fall when a tank full of "summer" fuel is used on an especially cold day of riding. Generally these performance issues go away when several tanks of fuel are used during the transition season for fuel blends.

You can make your own or buy octane boosters at the local auto parts store. Hard to say which brand is better, but one thing is consistent: eye-catching packaging. *Courtesy Advance Auto Parts*

Mix Your Own Octane Booster

Chemical Additive	Octane (R+M)/2	Cost per Gallon	Mixed with 92 Octane Premium		
			10%	20%	30%
1. Toluene	114	$18.00	94.2	96.4	98.6
2. Xylene	117	$19.00	94.5	97.0	99.5
3. Methyl-Tertiary-Butyl-Ether (MTBE)	118	Not Legal	94.6	97.2	99.8
4. Methanol	101	$18.00	94.3	Don't	Don't
5. Ethanol	101	$3.50	94.7	Don't	Don't
6. Isopropyl or Tertiary Butyl Alcohol	101	$20.00	94.5	Don't	Don't

Mix your own octane booster brew. The chart lists six alternatives to purchasing ready-made octane booster. Following are some notes about each chemical additive: 1. Toluene is a common ingredient in octane boosters that come in a can. 2. Xylene is similar to toluene and often mixed with it and sold as "race formula" gas. 3. Methyl-tertiary-butyl-ether (MTBE) is common in octane booster products and has a lower Btu value than either toluene or xylene but oxygenates fuel for better combustion. MTBE is not legal for sale, but with some effort you can make your own. 4 and 5. Methanol or ethanol, either is a primary ingredient in "dry gas." Don't mix them in ratios of more than 10 percent as it can cause corrosion of metal parts and breakdown of rubber gaskets. 6. Isopropyl/tertiary butyl alcohol is similar to both methanol/ethanol. Isopropyl alcohol is ordinary rubbing alcohol. Costs and octane numbers in the chart are approximate. For more information, check out this very cool website: www.runyard.org. *Courtesy John Runyard*

FUEL ADDITIVES

If you have made high-performance modifications to your engine (high compression heads or long duration camshafts), you may have to run fuel with an octane rating higher than the 93, which is currently available at many filling stations. To increase a fuel's octane rating, octane boosters can be added. These are available from STP, Torco, Lucas Oil Company, and others. The Lucas additive is one of the most concentrated. Mixing one bottle with 93-octane fuel will produce 10 gallons of 96.6-octane gasoline.

If you don't like the high cost of commercial octane boosters, you can mix your own. Just adding 10 percent methanol to 92-octane-rated gasoline will increase its rating to 94.3 octane. Mixing more than 10 percent is not a good idea and will cause problems with engine performance and fuel storage. Methanol is available for about $18 per gallon. Another homemade brew uses toluene to boost octane. When added to 92-octane fuel, a mixture of 10 percent produces 94.2 octane, 20 percent gets you up to 96.4, and if you add 30 percent the result is 98.6 octane. Toluene can be purchased at chemical supply or paint stores for about $18 per gallon.

Other alternatives include racing fuel, which can have octane ratings from 100 to 114 and aviation gasoline (avgas), which is rated up to 145 octane. These fuels often contain lead. Using them will plug a catalytic converter in short order. Besides being expensive, they are illegal to use on public highways. In fact, there are substantial fines for purchasing or selling avgas if you get caught.

If you have a vintage motorcycle that has not had hardened valve seats installed, you may want to consider a lead substitute additive to minimize valve seat wear. Red Line and Gunk both make lead substitutes that allow older engines to use unleaded gasoline without damaging valve seats. Lead substitutes are legal for off-road use only, so make sure your vintage motorcycle is only ridden on trails or across sand dunes—never on the highway!

LEAD

Because octane is expensive, oil companies began using other chemicals to boost octane ratings in their fuel. In the early 1940s, it was discovered that the addition of tetraethyl lead improved octane ratings and leaded gasoline came into being. Having all this lead burning in cars, trucks, and motorcycles is not healthy for the environment. In the mid-1970s, the Environmental Protection Agency (EPA) started limiting the use of lead in gasoline and banned it completely in 1996. Besides being bad for the environment, lead is not compatible with catalytic converters or oxygen sensors. With the ban on lead, other more expensive additives were used to boost octane ratings and the price of gas went up. Leaded fuel is still available but only for filling up piston-engine aircraft at the local airport. Also, the removal of lead created an unforeseen problem with engine valve seats. The lead used in fuel helped lubricate them and without lead older, softer valve seats wore out quickly. The leaded fuel and valve seat problem has not been an issue for at least 20 years. Many vintage motors have had their valve seats replaced with harder materials.

MTBE

With lead being phased out of gasoline, oil companies had to find an alternative for boosting octane. Methyl tertiary-butyl ether, commonly called MTBE, was introduced in 1979 to replace lead and increase fuel octane ratings. MTBE use expanded dramatically in the mid-1990s with the implementation of the Clean Air Act Amendments of 1990, which mandated efforts to reduce carbon monoxide emissions, as well as ozone levels in urban air. The use of this "oxygenated" fuel allowed more complete combustion of gasoline hydrocarbons. Gasoline was blended with up to 15 percent of MTBE. Unfortunately, its use reduced fuel economy by around 10 percent. In 2000, CBS News' *60 Minutes* reported on concerns about MTBE contaminating the water in 49 states. As *60 Minutes* reported, MTBE is highly water-soluble, slow to degrade, carcinogenic (causes cancer), and has become a contaminant in 20 percent of the nation's urban wells due to leaking of underground petroleum storage tanks.

Despite the disturbing fact that MTBE found in drinking water supplies had the potential to cause cancer, it took almost six years for the oil companies to finally remove it from gasoline. The mounting pressure of litigation, state bans on the additive, bad publicity, and the petroleum industry's heartfelt concern for public health (insert more sarcasm here) were the motivating factors. Cancer was not the only problem caused by MTBE. Harley-Davidson issued a recall in 1996 affecting many 1994 to 1997 models that used a vacuum-operated gas petcock/fuel valve. The rubber diaphragm inside the petcock would turn to mush when in contact with MTBE, which in turn could cause the engine to stop running due to fuel starvation—a potentially deadly problem when accelerating on to a busy highway.

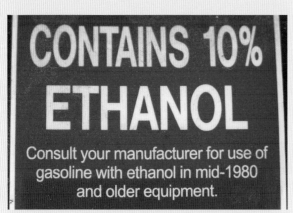

This ethanol pump label is warning owners of mid-1980 and older vehicles (including motorcycles) that the 10 percent blend may cause problems.

ETHANOL

With MTBE potentially causing cancer, the oil companies turned to other chemicals to improve octane, lower exhaust emissions, and reduce the overall consumption of crude oil and our dependence on foreign countries to supply it. The use of ethanol or ethyl alcohol (sometimes called grain alcohol) is becoming widely used across the country. Ethanol increases fuel octane and adds oxygen to fuel for lower emissions. No doubt many of you have seen the labels on some gas pumps advising that the fuel contains 10 percent ethanol or "E10" on the pump. The use of ethanol is not a new idea. Henry Ford designed his first car, the 1896 Quadricycle (a bicycle with four wheels and an engine) to run on pure ethanol. In fact, the Ford Model T could be fueled with gasoline, ethanol, or a mixture of both.

Ethanol, sometimes called bioethanol, is unlike petroleum in that it's a form of renewable energy that can be grown instead of pumped out of the ground. Corn is the most common crop in the United States for producing

Continued

You'd think that running out of gas next to a cornfield would not be a problem, but try as he might, that ear of corn is never going to fit past the fuel filler. Fortunately the local station a few miles away has "processed" corn in the form of 10 percent ethanol blended with hydrocarbons.

liquid ethanol, but potatoes and sugar cane are used too. If you have ever driven through Nebraska or Iowa, you know that lots of corn is planted, all with the potential of making its way into your motorcycle's gas tank. The rub is that if most of the corn is used for making ethanol to reduce our dependence on foreign oil, food production will decrease and case high food prices and shortages.

Separating fact from myth when it comes to the use of ethanol blended with gasoline is not easy to do. Currently, there are two ethanol blends: E10 (10 percent ethanol, 90 percent gasoline) and E85 (85 percent ethanol, 15 percent gas). Gas stations that dispense E10 will become common in the near future. E85 is reserved for flex-fuel cars that are specifically designed to run on 85 percent ethanol. E85 can also be used on cars or motorcycles that have had an E85 conversion kit installed.

According to Harley-Davidson, "We test, develop, and validate all engines to run with E-10 to ensure they will run on all fuels we expect our customers to encounter. The EFI system on current Harley-Davidson engines self-calibrates to accommodate the fuel being used. There may be a decrease in performance and economy when E-10 is in the tank, but it will be so slight that most riders will not notice a difference." Other motorcycle manufactures also calibrate their EFI systems to accommodate the use of E10. Parts used in carburetors since the mid-1980s should be compatible with the use of ethanol. For vintage motorcycles, carburetors should be rebuilt using a modern rebuild kit. All carburetor-rebuild kits sold at Harley-Davidson dealers are compatible with the use of ethanol. Check for compatibility of carburetor kits and ethanol for other brands of motorcycles.

ETHANOL VS. PARTS

Because gasoline has been around for such a long time, components in fuel systems that come in contact with it usually perform without problems. Fuel systems and ethanol are a different story. Ethanol blends can have a corrosive effect on metal parts used in your bike's fuel system, especially vintage motorcycles. Refiners mix additives into E10 to help prevent corrosion. Also fuel tank sealants made in the United States should not have problems with corrosion, but it's still a problem. However, there are materials used on older bikes that may not be compatible with ethanol, including zinc, brass, copper, lead-coated steel, cork, shellac, nylon, rubber gaskets, and hoses. Newer rubber materials are designed for contact with ethanol. In fact, most fuel hoses made after 1984 and marked with SAE J1527 are designed to withstand the use of ethanol.

Not all filling stations sell ethanol-blended fuel, but the number is growing each year. As of 2009, ethanol is sold in all 50 states in the country.

If it doesn't fit in the tank, I'll take it home and roast it. Silver Queen corn, whose sweet white kernels are a real treat in Maryland, can be found at roadside stands and sometimes even in local supermarkets.

Before ethanol was around, overlooking fuel hoses, carburetor floats, needle valves, rubber gaskets, or parts used in carburetors did not cause problems. These items deteriorated slowly, requiring only periodic maintenance. Neglect them today and lack of maintenance can cause fuel leaks and the potential for a fire. Fuel systems that use carburetors should be inspected frequently and rubber parts that appear swollen or mushy should be replaced. Another issue with the use of ethanol is that over time fuel systems tend to accumulate deposits in crevices and corners, including sediments, gums, rust, lacquer, and other materials. Ethanol will act as a solvent and loosen these types of materials, which will often plug up carburetor jets, air bleeds, and other passageways.

Storing motorcycles for long periods of time, including over the winter months, can be an issue using E10. Ethanol is hygroscopic, meaning it will absorb water vapor that forms inside a fuel tank. The water will dilute the fuel and may cause separation of the ethanol and gasoline blend. Water mixed with gas causes rough running, stalling, and a general lack of power. If you are going to store your bike for more than three months, use a fuel stabilizer to minimize the absorption of water into the fuel.

ETHANOL PERFORMANCE

A motor designed to run on 100 percent ethanol will make more power than the same size motor on gasoline. Because ethanol has an octane rating of 114, an ethanol-only engine could run compression ratios above 13 to 1 to take advantage of the high octane. However, ethanol has about two-thirds the potential energy as gasoline (76,000 Btus vs. 118,000 Btus). You would need to use more ethanol to get the same power you get from gasoline, so the potential extra horsepower would come at the cost of poor fuel economy.

The use of E10 (10 percent ethanol, 90 percent gasoline) will make slightly less power and deliver lower fuel economy than 100 percent gasoline—about 1 to 3 percent, depending on vehicle weight and size. For example, an SUV weighing 4,500 pounds and running E10 will get poorer fuel mileage than a 2,500-pound sports car (relatively speaking). Using E10 in an 800-pound motorcycle will have less effect on fuel economy because of the lower vehicle weight. Most riders will not be able to feel a power loss of 1 or 2 percent. One last issue with the use of E10 is that some motorcycles may be slightly harder to start in extreme cold weather, usually below 30 degrees F. If you plan to take your motorcycle for dyno tuning, consider which fuel is in the tank during the dyno runs. Consider what type of fuel you'll be running most of the time and what fuels are available in the area where you fill up the tank.

THE FUTURE OF ETHANOL

In 2007, Portland, Oregon, became the first U.S. city to require that all gasoline sold within city limits contain at least 10 percent ethanol, or E10. As of January 2008, some cities in Hawaii, Missouri, and Minnesota have similar requirements. The role of ethanol in the U.S. gasoline supply has grown from just more than 1 percent in the year 2000 to 7 percent in 2008. Ethanol production has nearly tripled, from 3.4 billion gallons in 2004 to more than 9 billion gallons in 2009. E10 and other blends of ethanol are sold in all 50 states and about half the U.S. gasoline supply contains some ethanol. The bottom line is E10 is not going away anytime soon. Like it or not, you will probably have to use it to power your motorcycle now and in the future. The good news is that for every gallon of ethanol used, it's one less gallon of foreign oil that we have to depend on, and that dependency has, and apparently will, continue to cost us dearly.

Chapter 6
EFI Troubleshooting and Maintenance

Diagnosing an EFI problem on this Harley-Davidson is not as hard as many riders think, once the basics of these systems are understood. In addition, it's important to practice testing procedures on a bike that doesn't have a problem. Then, when you're faced with a real EFI issue, you'll be ready to take it on. *Harley-Davidson of Frederick*

In the good (or bad, depending on your perspective) old days, diagnosing fuel delivery problems was simple and straightforward. A clogged fuel petcock, plugged carburetor jet(s), broken diaphragm in a CV carburetor, or empty fuel tank were the common causes of a nonstarting engine. The same was true regarding ignition systems of the time. A sticky set of ignition points, out-of-adjustment timing, or a fouled spark plug were pretty straightforward problems to diagnose. With many, if not the majority, of motorcycles now being equipped with electronic engine-management systems (controlling both fuel delivery and ignition spark), the only commonality between then and now for diagnosing engine-performance problems is the possibility of an empty gas tank. Everything else has changed—and so must we, if the do-it-yourself spirit in motorcycling is to be kept alive.

In this chapter about EFI troubleshooting, we're going to take a decidedly hands-on approach to diagnosis. When reading through this chapter, if you find yourself a little short on the "how-it-works" aspect of EFI systems, consider re-reading Chapter 1, Introduction to Electronic Fuel Injection. In addition, there are numerous sources of fuel injection information on the Internet that should fill in any gaps. Before continuing on to the tools and testing procedures we'll use, a discussion of scan tools and trouble codes will put EFI diagnostics in perspective.

The Hexcode GS-911 is a scan tool/laptop or PC interface that connects to the diagnostic connector on many BMW motorcycles. Through the scan tool, live engine-management data can be displayed or recorded. In addition, trouble codes can be read and erased. Unfortunately, the GS-911 only works for BMW bikes. As EFI systems become more widespread, other aftermarket scan tool manufacturers will produce products for other brands. The GS-911 is available from Hexcode (www.hexcode.co.za) and costs around $300 for the do-it-yourself model. *HexCode*

FIGURE 1 The GS-911 uses a Windows interface to display all ECU and CAN-BUS systems on this 2010 BMW F 800 R motorcycle. The diagnostic software can display ECU Info, read and clear fault codes, display real-time values (pictured), perform actuator output tests and idle actuator calibration, and reset maintenance internal reminders. *HexCode*

Navigation

Select a function to perform.

ECU Info

Read fault codes

Clear fault codes

Realtime values

Output tests

Adaptation

Idle actuator calibration

Distance to valve check

Realtime data

Log to CSV   Plot O2

Input signals:

Speed	0.0 miles/h
RPM	1274
Intake air temperature	67.1 °F
Engine temperature	163.0 °F
Throttle valve position (TPS)	0.00 %
Engine load	11.82 %
Battery voltage	14.39 V
Knock sensor 1	11.91 V
Knock sensor 2	4.43 V
Front wheel speed	0.0 miles/h
Rear wheel speed	0.0 miles/h
Fuel pressure	4526.20 mbar
Ambient air pressure	1003.92 mbar
Lambda sensor voltage	39.06 mV
Gear position	N

Output signals:

Injection time	1.82 ms
Lambda control factor	1.05
Ignition angle	14.25 °KW
Ignition dwell time	2.31 ms
Idle actuator position	41 steps

Digital outputs:

Tank venting valve (US only)	Off
Secondary air valve	On
Engine over-temperature light	Off
Actuation of starter relay	Off
Lambda sensor heating	On
Fuel pump	On
Fan motor	Off
Engine safety cut-out (of BMSK)	Off

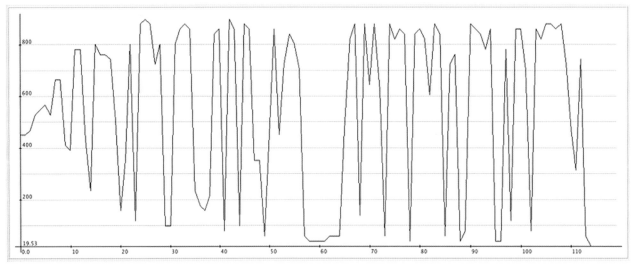

FIGURE 2   The GS-911 can display ECU engine data numerically or graphically. Pictured is the voltage output of one of two oxygen sensors on a late-model BMW motorcycle. The oxygen sensor is operating correctly, as voltage switches between 0.2 and 0.9 volts about once per second. Often, graphic displays will uncover sensor problems that are difficult to see with just numbers alone. *HexCode*

SCAN TOOLS, TROUBLE CODES?

Many riders think that to work on their motorcycle's EFI system they need the (ECU) diagnostic codes and other information that can only be obtained via a scan tool. While the use of scan tools can make troubleshooting easier and faster, they are not necessary good for basic diagnostics. Because dealers work on so many bikes, they have OEM scanners from the motorcycle manufacturers, and even independent dealers can purchase high-tech scan tools at a cost of around $3,000. The Motorscan 5650 and K&L's Scan 727 are but two examples of what's available.

Examples of more enthusiast-friendly scan tools are the Hex Code GS-911 and the Technoresearch VDST. The GS-911 is a BMW-only laptop interface that connects to the data link on many BMW EFI-equipped motorcycles. The GS-911 displays the ECU data stream and codes via software installed on a laptop. The GS-911 costs around $300 and works with Windows software. In fact, the GS-911 is a far superior interface to the factory BMW scanner software and costs thousands of dollars less. The VDST (also around $300) is also a laptop interface and can be used on some European and Harley-Davidson EFI models. The VDST must be ordered for a specific model of motorcycle.

It should be noted that not all brands of motorcycles allow the use of aftermarket scanners, and in many cases the factory's dealer-only tool is the only option for code retrieval and ECU data. Some EFI systems can display trouble codes on the bike's instrument panel or by flashing a check engine light, but most systems require a digital interface (scan tool) to see what's going on inside the ECU. Scanners and code readers aside, the tools we will use are easy to obtain, inexpensive, and simple to use. Before we get to the specific

tools, here is a word about how EFI problems are diagnosed at a dealership level.

Because time is money in the service department, time-consuming diagnostic procedures are used as a last resort toward solving EFI problems. In many dealerships, reading trouble codes and swapping parts takes place before any real diagnostic effort. Dealers also have the advantage of working on the same models, systems, years, and makes of motorcycle over and over, acquiring knowledge that owners don't have. For example, if the last five motorcycles of a particular make and model year all had an engine-performance problem, and replacing the ECU fixed it, the technician working on the next identical bike with the same symptoms is going to go to the parts counter and get an ECU, plug it into the motorcycle, and see if the problem goes away. Independent dealers (and the rest of us) don't have that luxury, as electronic parts are not returnable. Replacing an $1,800 ECU on your Honda or Ducati, only to find out that it wasn't the problem, is not going to be a good "do-it-yourself" day.

DIAGNOSTIC TOOLS

Most of the tools we will use for EFI testing can be purchased online or at local retail stores. In fact, everything except the logic probe and fuel-pressure test gauge can be purchased at Sears—and no, the author doesn't own stock in the company, but there's one near you and they're open on Sunday. If you purchase all the tools, the cost adds up to between $125 and $175, depending on how much you spent on the voltmeter. Less expensive versions of all these tools will work just as well as higher priced equipment; however, you do get what you pay for in quality.

In the service department, time and money determine how much real diagnostic time a technician will put into a work order. If quickly changing an ECU solves a complex problem, that's what takes place. The ability to swap electrical parts is a real advantage that a dealership has over the home technician. *Battley Cycles*

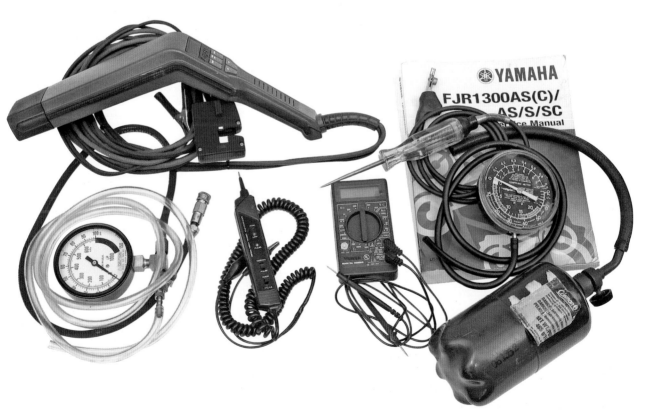

The low-buck EFI diagnostic tool selection. From top left: inductive timing light, service manual, 12-volt test light, vacuum gauge, fuel-pressure test gauge (bottom left), logic probe, digital multimeter, and propane bottle and hose. The service manual is the most expensive tool in the bunch, sometimes costing more than $100, but worth every penny.

The one tool not included in this cost is the manufacturer's service manual. If one is at all serious about diagnosing EFI problems (or any problem), the service manual is the most indispensible tool in any toolbox. Wiring diagrams, component locations, fuel-pressure specifications, and other information will greatly assist in saving time and successfully diagnosing problems. In no particular order, here are the tools used for basic EFI troubleshooting.

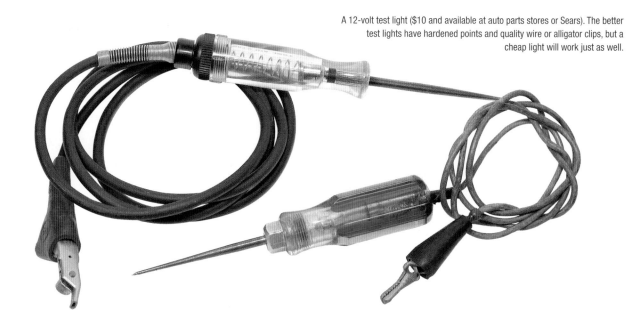

A 12-volt test light ($10 and available at auto parts stores or Sears). The better test lights have hardened points and quality wire or alligator clips, but a cheap light will work just as well.

Logic probe ($25 or more and available on the Internet). This tester is your new best friend for EFI diagnosis. The tool pictured on the right is from Radio Shack (part number 22-303, about $16). In addition to flashing its LEDs, it also emits sounds for various functions. The automotive specific unit on the left is sometimes called a red and green test light and is a more heavy-duty version of the logic probe.

Digital volt ohm meter or DVOM (between $20 to $100 and available at auto parts stores, on the Internet, or at Sears). Sears has many models to choose from that offer a lot of features for less than $100.

Propane torch ($20 and available at hardware stores or Sears). All that is needed for testing is the propane bottle, valve, and a 2-foot length of rubber hose that fits over the end of the torch.

Inductive timing light ($20 or more and available at auto parts stores or Sears). A less-expensive light will work for EFI testing. Timing lights with an ignition advance function are not necessary. The timing light is somewhat optional, as it serves a similar function to the logic probe.

EFI Fuel Pressure Test Gauge ($30 to $50 and available on the Internet). Purchase a kit instead of just a gauge, because more than one fitting or hose connection may be needed for a specific motorcycle. Also, a gauge that has a bypass hose (yellow hose in image) for checking fuel volume is useful as well.

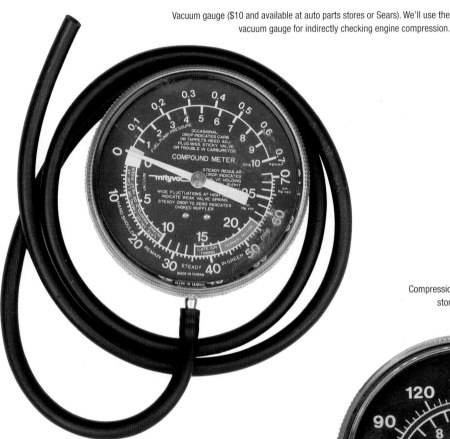

Vacuum gauge ($10 and available at auto parts stores or Sears). We'll use the vacuum gauge for indirectly checking engine compression.

Compression tester ($20 or more and available at auto parts stores or Sears). Purchase a compression tester that has several smaller spark plug adaptors for use on motorcycles.

PRACTICE

Many home technicians (and even some professionals) are baffled when it comes to diagnosing complex systems like EFI. With so many things to go wrong and lots of different directions to go when diagnosing an EFI problem, it seems overwhelming. But it's not so hard if you know the secret, and the secret is practice.

Most people understand the need for practice, especially when it comes to sports. Playing baseball, riding motorcycles, shooting pool, bowling—anything requiring a specific skill set goes a lot smoother with some experience. If you haven't picked up a baseball bat in a year and it's your turn at home plate, there's a good chance you'll strike out. As everyone knows, a little practice before the game goes a long way toward success.

Likewise, the day your EFI-equipped motorcycle fails to start shouldn't also be the first time you switch on your new digital voltmeter or take your fuel-pressure gauge out of the toolbox. Taking the time to practice using the tools in this chapter on a correctly operating fuel-injection system gives you a better than average chance of hitting the ball (diagnostically speaking) the first time up when something does go wrong with your bike. And it's easier than you think.

Don't assume that a few ounces of fuel are enough to get an EFI-fueled engine started. Some EFI systems may need as much as three-quarters of a gallon of fuel to start and run.

EFI ENGINE NO-START

The start button is pressed, the engine cranks over normally, but the EFI system is not doing its job and the engine won't start. EFI systems are mostly reliable, but, when they misbehave, a no-start condition can be a common problem, so we'll take a look at this issue first. Checking the obvious as a first step would seem to be the most logical way to diagnose a no-start condition, but you would be surprised at how many owners (and even technicians) skip the logic part of testing.

All internal combustion engines need four things to run: fuel, air, spark, and compression. With an engine that won't start, it's just a matter of finding out what's missing. To accomplish this task, we'll start with testing procedures that reveal the most information and are the easiest to perform. With that in mind, first check to see if there is fuel in the tank. Some bikes need as much as three-quarters of a gallon of fuel for the fuel pump to prime the EFI system, so make sure there is enough gas in the tank.

Our first test is a simple method to bypass the EFI system, test if there is spark at the spark plugs, and verify engine compression—all at one time. We're going to add a little propane into the engine's intake while cranking it over. The propane takes the place of fuel from the fuel injectors. If the engine starts and runs (even for a few seconds), it can be assumed that the ignition system is working (there is spark at the plugs), and that the engine has compression. Here's how to perform the test.

Gain access to the intake airbox, remove the air filter and snake a hose inside the airbox. Connect the other end of the hose to a propane torch. The use of propane will completely bypass the EFI system for fuel delivery. When the engine is turned over, the propane will be drawn into the cylinders. If a spark is present, and the engine has sufficient compression, it should start and run for a few seconds proving that the nonstarting engine has a fuel-delivery problem. On with the test: Crack open the valve on the propane bottle and crank the engine to see if it starts and runs. If the engine does

Injecting some propane into the engine's airbox will temporarily bypass the EFI fuel system. If the engine starts or runs, that proves that the ignition system is working.

not start, take a closer look at the ignition system (check for spark) or at mechanical engine issues (compression or cam timing) as potential causes for the no-start. If the engine *does* start, the ignition system and mechanical parts of the engine are working and further testing efforts can be focus on the EFI system.

Safety note: Working with propane (or gasoline) is dangerous and a fire hazard. Any raw fuel should be handled with care and a healthy dose of common sense. The EFI tests in this chapter that use propane are safe provided that there is no operator error or brain farts. Don't smoke or have other sources of ignition near you when performing these tests.

CHECKING FUEL PRESSURE

Checking fuel pump operation and fuel pressure are the next steps. On many (but not all) motorcycles, the pump operates for a few seconds when the key is first turned on. With an ear next to the tank, you should hear it run when the key is

What's one of the first things to get checked when you visit the doctor? Your blood pressure. Checking fuel pressure on an EFI system serves a similar function. If it's too low, or there is no pressure, nothing else works.

first turned to the on position. If the fuel pump works, the fuel pump relay is also operating, as it provides power to the fuel pump. If the fuel-pump relay works, you can assume that the ECU has power, since it triggers the fuel pump relay. If the pump doesn't run, check the service manual to make sure that it is supposed to do this with the key on. If there is no fuel pump operation, even though there's supposed to be, use a wiring diagram to trace power and ground wires going to and from the fuel pump to find the reason it doesn't run.

The next three tests for fuel pressure and volume are used to diagnose no-start and poor engine-performance conditions. The fuel-pump relay will need to be triggered or bypassed to keep the pump running for both pressure and volume testing. To accomplish this, unplug the relay and jump the two large terminals together; another way to trigger the fuel pump relay is to disconnect the wiring harness from the ECU and ground the fuel pump pin on the ECU connector (see the service manual to find correct wire).

Here's how to do the tests:

Connect a fuel-pressure gauge to the pump output line. Use the service manual to look up the correct fuel pressure (around 40 psi on many motorcycles) and compare it to the pressure gauge reading. If pressure is low, check voltage at the pump (there should be at least 12 volts). If voltage is good, the fuel pump needs to be replaced. Changing the fuel filter will not affect fuel pump pressure, only pump volume.

Deadhead pressure (line pressure directly from the fuel pump with no fuel return to the tank) should be checked as well. Deadhead pressure checks the pump's ability to produce enough pressure to run the engine at full throttle and should be around 60 to 100 psi (check the service manual for specific pressures and procedures). Deadhead pressure should be checked quickly, as blocking off the fuel pressure return line for too long could rupture a hose or damage the fuel pump. If fuel pressure is low, it could be a tired fuel pump or a poor electrical connection causing low amperage to the pump.

Checking fuel volume is next. This can be checked by connecting a hose to the fuel pump using it to fill a container with fuel as the pump runs (some fuel pressure gauges have a bypass hose for this purpose). Look up the acceptable pump discharge volume in the service manual. As a general rule, the pump should produce about half a quart in 25 seconds or less.

ARE THE ECU AND FUEL INJECTORS DOING ANYTHING?

If you added propane to your nonstarting engine and it ran, it can be assumed that the engine has spark and compression. The propane test, and a running engine, indicates that the ECU is not capable of providing fuel delivery to the engine via the fuel injectors. An engine that runs on propane does indicate that the EFI's cam and crank sensors are working, because their operation is required to trigger the ignition coils that produce spark at the plugs. If the engine did not run on propane, then further testing is needed to check the cam and crank sensors.

At this point in our diagnosis, we don't know if the ECU is supplying a triggering signal, or pulse, to the fuel injectors, so our next step is to verify this signal. The service department at a dealership may tell you that the only way to check basic ECU operation is to use a factory scanner or recording digital lab scope, but there are other methods. We will use several tests more friendly to the do-it-yourselfer, starting with a $10 12-volt test light.

There are several ways to check for an ECU pulse to a fuel injector. Unplug one of the injectors and connect a test light between the two wires at the injector connector. Crank the engine while watching the test light. A flashing or flickering test light verifies that the ECU is sending a pulse to the fuel injector. This test also verifies the operation of the cam and crank sensors, as they are responsible for triggering the ECU injector pulse.

Another tool that can be used for testing injector pulse is a logic probe. Connect a logic probe to the motorcycle's battery, using its (the logic probe) power and ground wires. Touch the probe to one of the injector wires (the injector can be left plugged into its connector). Crank the engine and watch the LED on the logic probe. If it flashes or pulses, the ECU is sending an injector pulse signal.

As an alternative to the logic probe, an inductive ignition timing light can be used to verify injector pulse. Clamp the timing light's probe around *one* of the wires going

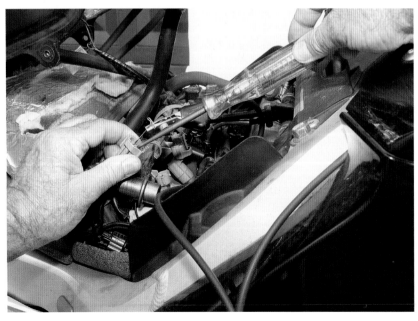

A test light connected to the fuel-injector connector from the ECU takes the place of the injector. When the ECU sends a pulse along the injector wire, the test light will flash or flicker.

Just like a test light, a logic probe can confirm the presence of an injector pulse from the ECU. Automotive versions of this tool are sometimes called red and green test lights.

Clamping the inductive probe around one of the fuel injector wires will cause the timing light to flash each time the ECU pulses that injector.

Using a screwdriver to transmit the clicking sound from an operational fuel injector is another low-tech method to verify injector pulse from the ECU.

to the injector (leave the connector plugged in). Crank the engine and watch the timing light to see if it flashes—a flashing light provides confirmation that the ECU is sending an injector pulse.

For an even lower-tech method, simply take a long screwdriver and touch the end to the fuel injector and stick the other end in your ear (no kidding!). Crank the engine and listen for a steady clicking from the injector. This may be difficult to hear over starter motor operation on some motorcycles.

If you discover that there is no injector pulse from the ECU, check for the pulse signal on more than one cylinder. Perhaps the one that was checked had no pulse but the other cylinders do. Check for pulse right at the ECU instead of at the fuel injector. If the wiring harness is damaged, the pulse may not be reaching the fuel injectors. Also, check for power

to the injectors while the engine is cranking. Use a DVOM, set to volts, or a test light to check for power to the injectors. Power to operate the fuel injectors is almost always supplied separately from power to the ECU, usually through a relay. Use the wiring diagram in the service manual to trace the 12-volt source that provides fuel injector power.

At this juncture in our diagnosis, we have either found the problem or eliminated several possibilities that could cause a no-start condition. As discussed, pressure testing the fuel pump and verifying that the pump has power will either confirm or eliminate it as a problem. We have checked for injector pulse using several methods. If no pulse was present with the engine cranking over, no power to the injectors was verified. If the injectors have power but aren't delivering fuel, then the next steps are diagnosis of the ECU and its sensors.

If no injector pulse is present from the ECU, there may be no power going to the injector. A voltmeter can be used to check for battery voltage at the injector. If no voltage is present, use the service manual to trace the power source to the fuel injectors.

Working on EFI systems doesn't have to be a dealer-only proposition. A basic understanding of what EFI components to test and how to do it could save money in the long run. The layout of this BMW Boxer engine makes getting to some EFI components easy. *Bob's BMW*

IS THE ECU DEAD?

The testing and diagnosis of this hypothetical no-start EFI motorcycle has reached the point where a dead ECU could be a possible reason why the fuel injectors aren't getting a pulse. If this problem was being worked on at a dealership, they would have already switched out ECUs to see if a new one fixed the problem. But as do-it-yourselfers we do not have the luxury of swapping electronic parts as a method of diagnosing a malfunctioning ECU. With prices ranging from $500 on eBay to well over $1,500 at a dealer, motorcycle fuel-injection computers are expensive—and not returnable. Therefore, replacing one should always be considered a last resort when diagnosing EFI problems.

There is no specific test for a bad ECU, and even when a factory scan tool displays "Replace ECU," it's only an educated guess. So how are we to know with any certainty if the ECU is junk? We'll look at what the independent automotive repair industry does for some help. After all, they have been dealing with on-board computer replacement in cars for more than 30 years.

To determine if an ECU is working or not, simple logic needs to be applied. All EFI systems and ECUs operate on the principal of information in, information processed, and command outputs generated. More specifically, the computer sensors in an EFI system send electrical signals to the ECU, which processes them and calculates how long to "fire" the injectors for fuel delivery and when to trigger the ignition coils to produce a spark. On many bikes, there are other ECU output signals besides spark and fuel, including idle control, exhaust-valve control, engine rpm, check-engine light operation, and subthrottle valve actuation.

The only ECU outputs we are concerned with are fuel and spark. The logic path for ECU diagnosis goes something like this: If the ECU has everything it needs (inputs) to produce injector and ignition pulse signals (outputs), and there are no spark or injector output signals, then the ECU must be bad. The basic inputs to any ECU are a signal from the crank sensor for engine rpm, a signal from the cam sensor for crankshaft position (not used on all EFI systems), and power and ground from the battery.

We'll start with the most common inputs that trigger fuel and ignition operation: the cam and crank sensors. There are three flavors of these sensors: AC pickup coil, Hall effect switch, and optical. The first two are by far the most common, so we'll test these first. Hall effect switches have three wires, and AC pickup coils have two. To identify an optical sensor, a service manual wiring diagram must be used, but look for more than three wires as a general guide. Because many times these sensors are buried inside the engine or behind bodywork, all of our testing will be performed at the ECU connector, which is usually located under the seat.

Looking at the backside of the ECU connector with it plugged into the ECU, we will need to determine which wires go to these sensors. Some service manuals have an ECU "pin-out" chart that lists the function of each wire at the ECU. If there is no pin-out, you can make your own by tracing wires (using a wiring diagram) from the ECU to everything that it's connected to and writing down a list of ECU pin numbers and wire colors. This information is handy to have, as it will be used for much of our testing.

Caution: A digital voltmeter or logic probe is to be used for all testing at the ECU connector. Do *not* use a 12-volt test light. If a test light is used, it could electrically fry the ECU or some of its sensors. Other words of common sense: The testing procedures in this chapter are generic in nature and will work on many brands, years, and models of EFI-equipped motorcycles. The service manual should also be used, however. It will provide specific testing methods and specifications for sensor testing.

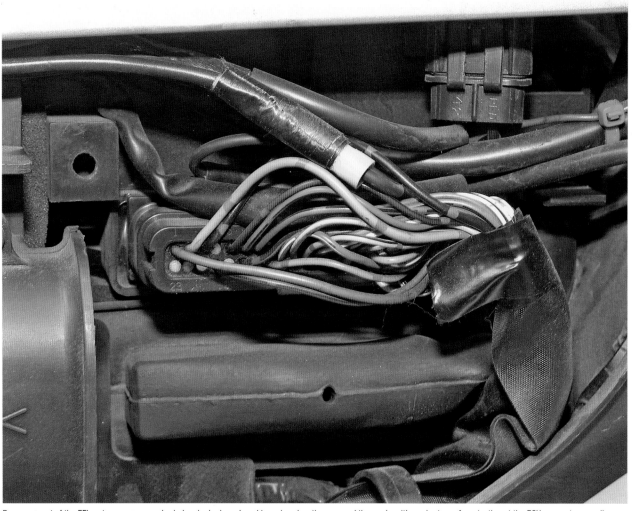

Because most of the EFI system sensors are buried under bodywork and in various locations around the engine, it's easier to perform testing at the ECU connector, usually located under the seat.

Pictured are Harley-Davidson cam and crank sensors. The cam sensor (right) is a Hall-effect switch, and the crank sensor (left) is an AC pickup coil. Both can be tested using a logic probe or digital voltmeter. *Harley-Davidson of Frederick*

HALL-EFFECT SWITCH TESTING

On many motorcycles, the cam or crank sensors are Hall-effect switches. Testing is the same for each sensor. Locate the three wires going to the Hall switch at the ECU connector (leave the connector plugged into the ECU). Turn the ignition key to the on position, back probe (using a safety pin poked into the back of the connector and connected to the voltmeter) each wire and check for a voltage reading. One wire will be ground (0 volts), another wire will be between 5 and 12 volts DC, and the third wire will change voltage (switch from high to low to high to low) when the engine is rotated. The changing voltage through the third wire is the Hall-effect switching signal.

A logic probe can also be used to check the signal wire. The LED on the probe should flash when the engine is cranking over if a pulse signal is present. If no signal is present at the ECU, check all three wires directly at the Hall-effect switch. There could be a broken wire. If the Hall switch has power and a ground, but it's not producing a signal, it's bad.

AC PICKUP COIL TESTING

An AC pickup coil-type sensor can be tested at the ECU connector with it unplugged from the ECU. The AC pickup coil generates a small alternating current voltage signal when the engine is turning. Locate the two wires from the AC pickup coil at the ECU connector and connect the black and red leads from a voltmeter. Set the voltmeter to read AC volts. It doesn't matter which leads are connected to

what wire from the AC pickup coil. Crank the engine over while watching the voltmeter. If the sensor is working, an AC voltage reading should be displayed. Voltages will be low in the 0.5- to 3-volt range.

If no voltage is present, set the voltmeter to read ohms and check the AC pickup coil's resistance. There may be a specification for ohms in the service manual. If no reading is displayed (reads infinity), check again directly at the sensor. You may have a broken wire.

As an alternative to an AC voltage test, a logic probe can be used to check for a pulse to indicate a signal from the sensor.

The remaining sensors we are going to test will generally not cause a no-start condition. If a non-starting engine is the focus of your diagnosis, skip to the ECU testing section later in this chapter.

THROTTLE POSITION SENSOR TESTING

The throttle position sensor (TPS) is an important input to the ECU, as it relays rider demands for fuel. These sensors use a variable voltage signal to let the ECU know where the throttle plates are positioned—low voltage (around 1 volt) for a closed throttle and high voltage (around 4-plus volts) for wide-open throttle. The TPS will have three wires: power (5 volts), ground, and signal (voltage varies with throttle position).

To test a TPS sensor, locate the signal wire at the ECU connector (leave it plugged into the ECU). Back probe the

The TPS (arrow) on the outboard intake runner of this BMW sends the rider-demand signal for fuel to the ECU. It also provides the ECU with data as to how fast (or slow) the throttle is opening or closing. Some throttle position sensors are adjustable and others are not. See a service manual to know for sure. *Bob's BMW*

signal wire with a DVOM and turn the ignition switch to the on position. The voltage should rise and fall as the throttle is opened and closed. Look for voltage numbers that skip several digits to indicate a bad TPS sensor. In general, a bad TPS will not cause a no-start condition, but it can make the engine run rough, hesitate, or lack power on acceleration.

MAP SENSOR TESTING

The manifold absolute pressure (MAP) sensor provides the ECU with engine load information. It operates like an electronic-vacuum gauge, since it reads intake manifold vacuum. High readings indicate part throttle operation, and low readings indicate that the throttle is opening and the engine is trying to make power. Most MAP sensors send a varying voltage signal to the ECU. MAP sensors will have three wires: power (5 volts), ground, and signal (.1 to 5 volts, depending on engine vacuum).

If the engine starts and runs, you can back probe the MAP sensor signal wire at the ECU (leaving it plugged in, of course). When you rev the engine, the signal voltage should change. If the engine is a no-start, you will have to apply vacuum to the MAP to see if it is operating correctly. Some sensors have vacuum hoses that come from the intake manifold runners, and other sensors are mounted directly to the manifold. Check the service manual for specific vacuum vs. voltage readings at the MAP sensor.

TEMPERATURE SENSOR TESTING

The engine temperature sensor (ETS) sends a voltage signal to the ECU regarding engine-operating temperature. They work the same for both water-cooled and air-cooled engines. ETS sensors have two wires: one is a 5-volt signal from the ECU, and the other is ground from the ECU. The 5-volt signal changes voltage depending on engine temperature, around 4 volts when cold and less than 1 volt when hot.

This MAP sensor on a Yamaha FJR is attached to a common vacuum source for all four cylinders. It operates like an electronic vacuum gauge and provides the ECU with engine-load information. *Twigg Cycles*

These BMW engine-temperature sensors are mounted in the cylinder head. On liquid-cooled bikes, they are located at the radiator or coolant lines. *Bob's BMW*

To test the sensor, find the ETS wires at the ECU connector and back probe the signal return wire. Start the engine when cold and watch the voltage, which should be around 3.5 volts. As the engine warms up, the voltage should drop steadily to less than 1 volt when the engine gets to normal operating temperature.

Another method for ETS testing is to check its resistance with the engine at different temperatures. In general, resistance should be high (thousands of ohms) when cold and lower (below 2,000 ohms) when hot. See a service manual for exact resistance values vs. temperatures for a specific motorcycle.

O_2 SENSOR TESTING

A malfunctioning O_2 sensor will never cause the engine not to start, but it may cause surging or other rough running issues. O_2 sensors may have two or three wires. Three-wire sensors have an internal heater that runs on 12 volts.

To test the O_2 sensor, the engine should be warmed up to normal operating temperature. With the ECU's connector plugged in, back probe the sensor's signal wire with a voltmeter. Start the engine and maintain speed at 2,000 rpm for 60 seconds. If the O_2 voltage starts switching back and forth between 0.2 and 0.8 volts, the EFI system is in closed-loop mode. (For purposes of this test, it doesn't really matter if the system is in closed-loop or open-loop mode) Next, while watching the voltmeter, snap the throttle wide open. The O_2 voltage should immediately go up to 0.9 volts, indicating a rich mixture. Now hold engine speed steady again at 2,000 rpm, and then quickly close the throttle. This time, O_2 voltage should drop to 0.1 volt or less, because the ECU has cut off fuel to the engine, creating a lean mixture.

How fast the O_2 sensor responds to the changes in exhaust gas oxygen, as well as the range of voltage displayed (0.1 to 0.9), indicates whether the sensor is good or bad. A good sensor should be able to make voltage transitions instantly, while a lazy or worn-out O_2 sensor makes voltage transitions slowly, and won't be able to reach 0.9 volts no matter how rich the fuel mixture is.

The oxygen sensor on this BMW is located in the exhaust, close to the cylinder head. It forms part of the closed-loop feedback process in which the ECU keeps the fuel mixture at an ideal air-fuel ratio. *Bob's BMW*

There is no test for this BMW ECU. Even the factory scanner can only take an educated guess as to if it's working or not. We will apply simple logic to determine if the ECU is doing its job. *Bob's BMW*

A DVOM is used to check a voltage input wire at the ECU. A straight pin is used to back probe the wire inside the connector.

ECU TESTING

As stated earlier, there is no specific test for a good or bad ECU. If the ECU has the input that it needs to operate, and it doesn't operate, it needs to go in the trash. We have gone through the procedures for sensor testing, and only two things are left to check, ECU power and ground.

A quick way to check if the ECU has power is to look for the 5-volt signal at the ETC, MAP, or TPS sensors. This voltage is produced by the ECU via an internal voltage regulator. If this voltage is not present at any of the sensors, the ECU is not working and the power and ground sources need to be checked. Wiring diagrams in a service manual will indicate which wires going to the ECU are power and grounds. There may be more than one of each. Usually there is a key-on power wire, and sometimes an engine-cranking power wire (activated when the starter motor is turning).

With the ECU plugged in, and the ignition switched on, use a digital voltmeter to check for 12 volts at all the power inputs at the ECU. If any power input to the ECU is not present, use the wiring diagram to find its source and repair the problem.

To check an ECU ground, connect the black lead of a voltmeter directly to the negative battery terminal. Connect the red lead to the ground input(s) on the ECU. If any of the ECU ground inputs read higher than 0.06 volts, the ECU's connection to the negative battery terminal is poor and should be repaired. This usually involves cleaning terminals or other connectors between the battery and the ECU. If all the power(s) and ground(s) are good, and the cam and crank inputs at the ECU are working, and the ECU is still not pulsing the injectors or firing the spark plugs, it is probably bad. If you feel confident in your diagnosis, replace the ECU.

If there is still doubt as to whether or not the ECU is good or bad, take the motorcycle to the dealer. Pay them whatever diagnostic fee they charge (usually not more than $100). They will swap the ECU with a new one and verify your diagnosis. This is cheap insurance against purchasing an ECU only to find out something else was the problem.

EFI VS. ENGINE MECHANICAL PROBLEMS

Now that we've dealt with engines that won't start, basic sensor testing, and ECU diagnosis, it's time to move on to performance issues. These can include rough idle, hesitation or stumble on acceleration, surging at part throttle, or lack of power. Because EFI systems are not as widely understood as carburetors or stand-alone ignition systems, they are often blamed for these types of problems. Before spending time, and money, on further EFI diagnostics, the EFI system has to be separated from the engine mechanical system. For example, if a cylinder has low compression, no amount of EFI tuning, sensor testing, or code reading will make the engine run any better until any mechanical problems are repaired.

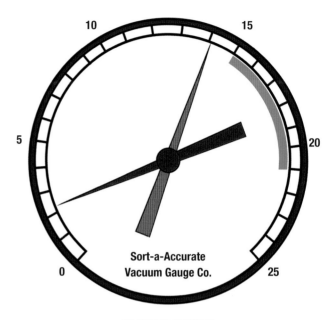

CRANKING VACUUM

FIGURE 3 Using a vacuum gauge to perform a cranking vacuum test will provide information on each cylinder's ability to seal and of the general condition of the engine. Individual cylinders can be tested by connecting the vacuum gauge to the vacuum port in the intake runner. Gauge readings will vary widely between engine types.

ENGINE COMPRESSION— CRANKING VACUUM TEST

We'll start with engine compression, which is directly related to how well an engine seals—specifically piston rings and valves. As with EFI testing, we'll begin with the easiest test that provides the most information.

On many motorcycles, a cranking vacuum test is faster to perform than a compression test and will provide similar results. On three- or four-cylinder engines, cranking vacuum gauge readings can be used as an indication of engine sealing. This test doesn't work on V-twin and single-cylinder engines.

First, remove the ECU or fuel pump fuse so the engine won't start. Connect a vacuum gauge to an intake runner vacuum port and crank the engine over a few times while watching the gauge. Write down the high and low numbers and note how the needle pulses back and forth. The needle movement will vary a great deal between different engine designs and manufacturers. Check each cylinder and compare them to one another. Any cylinder that is substantially different than the others indicates that it is not sealing equally. A compression test of all the cylinders will provide further information and isolate the problem.

ENGINE COMPRESSION TESTING

Overall low compression, or individual cylinders that have low compression, will cause a number of engine-performance problems. Here are the basics of compression testing.

Compression testing has been used to judge engine cylinder sealing since motorcycles have been around. The most difficult part of the test on some bikes is getting to the spark plugs.

First, the engine should be at normal operating temperature. Remove the fuel pump or ECU fuses so the engine won't start. Make sure the battery is charged up or it could affect compression readings (especially those of the last cylinder tested). Remove all the spark plugs and connect a compression gauge to one cylinder, open the throttle all the way, and crank the engine over until the needle on the compression gauge indicates that it has gone through four compression strokes (the needle will pulsate four times). Write down the highest reading for each cylinder. As a general rule, there should be no more than a 10 percent difference between the high and low cylinders. In addition, a service manual should be referenced for specific compression numbers.

For engines with low-compression cylinders there is good news and bad news. The good news is that you can stop diagnosing EFI-related problems, because they're a waste of time at this point. The bad news is that the engine will have to be rebuilt before any EFI issues can be dealt with.

INTAKE LEAKS, IGNITION TESTING, AND TPS ADJUSTMENT

We're almost finished with basic engine testing. The only common things left to check are intake manifold leaks, secondary ignition system testing, and adjustment of the throttle position sensor (the only sensor that is adjustable, though not on all EFI systems).

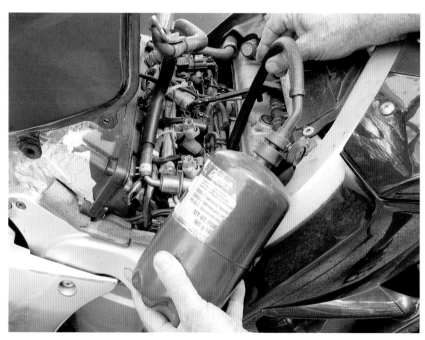

Early in this chapter, propane was used to bypass the EFI system in order to diagnose an engine that won't start. We'll use propane again to determine if there are any intake manifold vacuum leaks. Intake leaks can cause rough idle, surging at part throttle, or a lack of power on acceleration.

LEFT If the engine has an ignition misfire, an inductive timing light can be used as a poor-man's ignition scope to discover which cylinder is having a problem. First, place the timing light's inductive clamp over an ignition wire. With the engine running, point the flashing timing light at your face. The human eye and brain are fast enough to visually register any misfire. Rev the engine several times to try to bring out the misfire. If testing a coil-over-plug system, a temporary ignition wire needs to be installed to provide a place to clamp the timing light's probe.

BOTTOM A test light and spray bottle filled with water is a simple way to find a bad ignition wire or spark plug boot. Spray water on all the secondary ignition wires and start the engine. Ground the alligator clip of the test light and run the pointy end along the wires and around the boots. When the sharp tip of a test light is placed close to an electrically leaking wire, the test light will attract high-voltage spark energy and you will hear the engine misfire. This test also works well in the dark, as leaking ignition wires that are shorting high voltage to the test light can be readily seen. *Battley Cycles*

EFI MAINTENANCE

Unlike carburetors and ignition points that constantly needed cleaning and frequent adjustment, modern EFI systems are well designed and don't require much in the way of maintenance. In fact, because of emissions standards, motorcycle manufacturers don't want owners to alter anything. Therefore, ignition timing, fuel mixture, and idle speed are generally not adjustable on most systems. There are a couple of adjustment exceptions: the throttle position sensor and, on some systems, synchronization of the throttle bodies. Harley-Davidson EFI motorcycles only have one throttle body, so no airflow sync is required. The only real maintenance for EFI consists of inspection or replacement of the air filter, spark plugs, fuel filter (if equipped), and cleaning of throttle bodies.

The rest of this chapter covers what is needed to keep electronic fuel-injection systems performing at their best.

TPS ADJUSTMENT

As mentioned earlier in this chapter, the TPS sensor provides rider demands to the ECU, which in turn will change fuel quantity delivered and ignition timing. On some motorcycles, the TPS sensor is adjustable. This usually involves monitoring the TPS return voltage and rotating the sensor (after loosening the mounting fasteners) at the throttle shaft until a specified voltage is displayed on a digital voltmeter. A service manual will provide the exact voltage or procedure for setting the TPS. A variation of this procedure is using the display to read TPS values from the ECU and making an adjustment based on these values.

A third scenario that is becoming more common is non-adjustable TPS designs. As manufacturers face tighter emission controls, they don't want owners to have the ability to change anything on their EFI systems. Throttle sensors that are not adjustable are found on EFI systems that use what is called "adaptive learning." As the motorcycle is ridden, the ECU learns where the throttle is positioned by the rider under various operating conditions. The ECU's random access memory (RAM) keeps track of this information and uses it as a reference for adjusting fuel and ignition parameters. On some adaptive-learning EFI systems, there is a procedure for setting, or calibrating, the throttle. This gives the ECU a head start on figuring out where the throttle is positioned.

The bottom line is that a service manual must be used to either adjust or calibrate the TPS on any EFI system.

The only electronic adjustment on some EFI systems is the throttle-position sensor, or TPS. The slotted holes on this Yamaha allow the TPS to be rotated for adjustment. On some motorcycles you can do this using a voltmeter as you position the TPS with the throttle closed. Check out a service manual for specific instructions and procedures. Some bikes require the use of a scan tool. Time to visit the dealer.

On this 2005 Yamaha FJR 1300 the TPS percent of opening numbers (arrows) can be displayed on the instrument panel. The number on the left is the TPS closed, and "99" represents wide-open throttle. This display can also be used to diagnose a bad TPS input to the ECU. By observing the numbers counting up as the throttle is slowly opened, a worn TPS will skip several numbers.

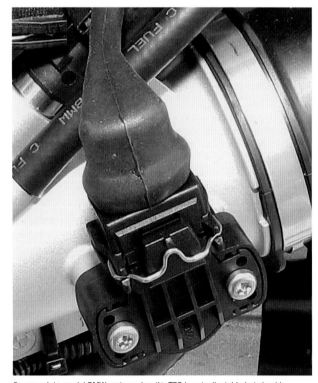

On some late-model BMW motorcycles, the TPS is not adjustable but should be periodically calibrated so that the ECU knows where closed and wide-open throttle positions are. For this BMW 1200 GS, the first step for TPS calibration is to disconnect the battery for 30 seconds (causes the ECU to lose its memory of TPS calibration). Next, the ignition is turned on, but the engine is not started and the throttle is fully opened and shut three times. The next step is to wait 5 seconds, then start the engine. Now the ECU knows where closed- and open-throttle positions are located, and adaptive learning does the rest as the bike is ridden. *Dob's BMW*

THROTTLE BODY SYNCHRONIZATION

Perfect synchronization is important if you ride an EFI-equipped motorcycle that uses more than one throttle body. This common, but sometimes baffling, adjustment ensures that when the throttle is opened each cylinder receives the same amount of air and, consequently, fuel from the fuel injectors. Engine vibration, stretched cables, and throttle-body linkage wear all contribute to uneven airflow between cylinders and lead to the need to synchronize throttle bodies periodically—usually every 5,000 miles. If your bike is starting to exhibit a rough or unsteady idle, sluggish throttle response, uneven running, surging at part throttle, or vibration at certain rpm where none used to exist, it may be time to sync up the airflow going into the engine.

Throttle body synchronization should be the last procedure performed when tuning an EFI system. There are several tasks that should be accomplished before adjusting throttle bodies. Adjusting the valves after syncing the EFI system can and will change the results, because the valves have a direct relation to airflow entering the engine. Check a service manual for procedures for adjusting valves if your bike requires adjustment. Don't overlook engine compression, especially if there are lots of miles on the odometer. If the compression numbers between cylinders vary by more than 10 percent, the sync operation may be difficult to do. Check for intake leaks around the rubber boots that attach the throttle bodies to the cylinder head (intake runners). Cracks in the rubber or loose mounting clamps can cause air to bypass the throttle body, affecting airflow and fuel mixture. The air filter should be cleaned with compressed air or replaced.

Now that the routine maintenance stuff is out of the way, it's time to get to the fun part: synchronizing your engine's airflow. Manufacturers use different methods of adjustment to change the angle of throttle openings in throttle bodies. Some motorcycles use one throttle body that has no adjustment. This non-adjustable throttle body is then used as a reference point to which the others are adjusted. Linkage setups may use two, three, or four adjustment screws. Some BMWs use throttle cables that divide in two, and the adjustment is made via cable length. Take a look at your bike's service manual or visually inspect the throttle body linkage adjustments that your motorcycle uses to determine how to make airflow adjustments and in what order the adjustments should be made.

We're almost ready to start adjusting, but first we need a way to measure airflow into each throttle body and intake runner. In fact, we will not actually measure airflow, but engine vacuum instead. The intake manifold vacuum in the individual cylinders is an indirect way to determine airflow. With the throttle plates closed and the engine at idle, vacuum levels will be high. As the throttle is opened, vacuum will start to decrease.

In theory, a vacuum gauge for each cylinder could be used to balance each cylinder to another, but vacuum gauges are not very accurate. A set of mercury manometers (aka carb sticks) will work, except that they have been banned from sale due to the hazardous nature of liquid mercury. Fortunately there are a couple of electronic vacuum tools and a mechanical one available that work better than the old manometers—the CarbMate, TwinMax, and Morgan Carbtune Pro. All three are high-quality and easy to use.

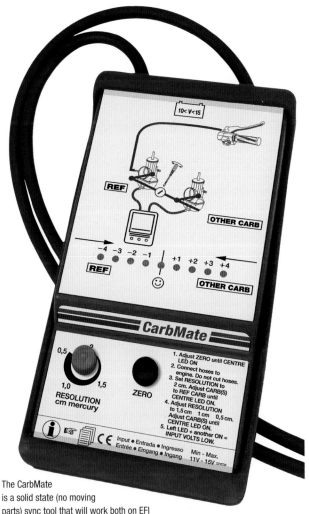

The CarbMate is a solid state (no moving parts) sync tool that will work both on EFI and carbureted motorcycles. A series of horizontal LEDs are used to visually balance two throttle bodies at one time. The tool is powered by the motorcycle's battery via a power cable. The CarbMate is available from TecMate North America Electronic Tools and Chargers and costs around $100 (www.tecmate.com). *TecMate*

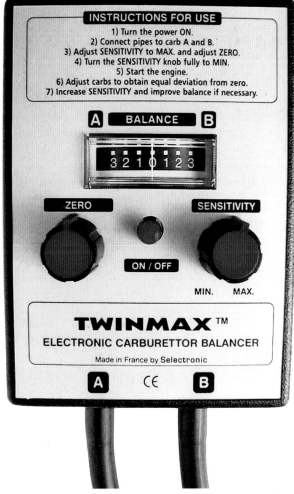

Despite the name, the TwinMax Electronic Carburetor Balancer will work on all EFI systems to balance multiple throttle bodies. The tool uses a needle and scale to indicate when two connected vacuum sources are in balance. An internal 9-volt battery powers the tool. It's available from Frank Cooper's Adventure Motorcycle Gear (www.adventuremotorcyclegear.com), and costs around $100. *Adventure Motorcycle Gear*

The Morgan Carbtune Pro uses no electronics. Instead, stainless-steel rods move up a clear tube to indicate vacuum readings. No calibration or set-up is required, and the unit comes with four 5- and 6-millimeter adapters for connecting to a wide variety of motorcycles. The Carbtune is available from the manufacturer in England (www.carbtune.co.uk) and sells for around $100.
Morgan Carbtune

Both the CarbMate and TwinMax are pressure-differential measurement tools. Using two vacuum sources, the tools indicate the level of balance between them. Both can balance two cylinders with each other. For engines with four cylinders, the throttle bodies are balanced in pairs and then the two pairs are balanced together. This is easily accomplished by swapping the tool's vacuum hoses between the throttle bodies. For three-cylinder engines (can you say Triumph?), a reference throttle body is used to match the other two cylinders.

Because both of these cylinder balance tools have essentially identical operation and use the same controls, they will be referred to as the "sync tool" in this chapter. The Morgan Carbtune Pro can balance up to four cylinders at one time and uses vacuum restrictors inside the connection hoses to damp the movement of the stainless steel rods as they move within the glass tubes.

Note: The throttle body sync procedure discussed in this chapter is very generic. The details for the actual procedures for specific motorcycles are covered in their service manuals and should be used for adjustments. This discussion will give the reader a good general idea of how to balance, or sync, airflow on a motorcycle engine. Many service manuals and manufacturers make a big deal regarding the specific level of vacuum for idle and synchronization. More important is that all the cylinders are the same (vacuum level), or close, than are the actual vacuum readings.

Before we start syncing, the motorcycle should be ridden until the engine is at normal operating temperature. A good idea is to place a large fan in front of the bike, so the engine won't overheat during the adjustment process. The fan will also keep you cool.

In this example of throttle body sync adjustment, a two-cylinder engine will be used. The procedure for a four-cylinder is similar, but with more steps in the adjustment process.

Connect the sync tool to the throttle bodies. On many motorcycles, there is a vacuum port for connecting the sync tool's vacuum hoses. Some bikes use a threaded hole that takes either a 5- or 6-millimeter adapter. Now we're ready for the first step in the process of syncing or balancing airflow into the throttle bodies.

Step 1. Turn the sensitivity, or resolution, knob on the sync tool to its maximum value and adjust the zero knob until the sync tool's gauge or LEDs are at 0 value. Turn the sensitivity back to minimum. The Carbtune does not require this adjustment.

Step 2. If the throttle bodies have idle air bypass screws, turn them all the way in, and then back out two turns (a service manual may be more specific).

Note: If your motorcycle uses an idle speed controller (BMW), it may have to be disconnected so the ECU doesn't change the idle speed as you are trying to make sync adjustments—see your service manual.

Step 3. Start the engine and rev it between idle and 4,000 rpm while watching the sync tool. When the engine is accelerating to 4,000 rpm is when to observe if the throttle bodies are in balance. The vacuum pulses for individual cylinders are more steady when engine rpm is increasing.

Note: Holding the engine at a steady high rpm to sync the throttle bodies is difficult at best and will result in an inaccurate sync adjustment. If you try this method, you will notice that each time you make an adjustment the sync readings will change. Noting sync measurements only when the engine is accelerating will provide you with more consistent measurements and an overall better cylinder balance.

Step 4. If the two cylinders appear to be in balance, increase the sensitivity on the sync tool until a deviation is observed. If the sensitivity is turned all the way up and the tool indicates 0, then the two cylinders are in sync. If they are not, proceed to Step 5.

Step 5. Make a small adjustment on the throttle linkage (or cable, depending on motorcycle) and again accelerate the engine to 4,000 rpm while watching the sync tool. Repeat this step until the pair of cylinders is in balance with each other.

Note: For a four-cylinder engine, sync the other pair of throttle bodies using Step 5. After the two pairs of cylinders are balanced, balance the pairs to each other so that in the end all four cylinders are the same on the sync tool. If you are syncing a three-cylinder engine, use one throttle body as a reference and balance the other two cylinders against it. If the Morgan Carbtune is used, all four cylinders can be balanced at the same time.

Step 6. Let the engine idle. You may have to make an idle adjustment to get the engine to idle at the correct speed (service manual anyone?).

Step 7. Use the individual throttle-body air screws (if equipped) and adjust the sync so that all the cylinders are in balance.

Step 8. Go back and repeat Step 5 to check for sync at high rpm. You may have to repeat this step several times to get the balance right.

Step 9. Repeat Step 7 to adjust the idle sync.

Step 10. Adjust engine idle speed (if adjustable) to the correct setting, and you're done.

The previous 10 steps for throttle body synchronization will take you longer the first time through. After a little practice, this procedure will become faster and more easily accomplished. Here are some tips to make the job go more smoothly:

- Don't be in a hurry to do this, especially the first time.
- Try syncing as a group activity for your riding club or online forum.
- Don't be overly concerned about the actual vacuum level of the cylinders. It's more important that the cylinders are balanced with respect to one another.

- Don't try to get the balance exactly perfect, especially when holding the throttle steady at 3,000 or 4,000 rpm. You'll never get there. Close is good enough.
- Go for a ride to test the results of your sync adjustments. If you did it correctly, the engine should feel smoother at all rpm.

TECHRON FUEL ADDITIVE

Techron Concentrate Plus is a patented fuel additive developed by Chevron. Techron uses two chemical technologies, Polybutene Amine (PBA) and Polyether Amine (PEA), to clean harmful deposits that build up in injectors

The mid-1980s saw the start of widespread use of electronic fuel injection in cars and light trucks. Up until that time, oil companies only had to formulate fuel that worked in carbureted vehicles. But with EFI systems squirting millions of gallons of fuel into U.S. cars, gasoline had to change. As it turns out, it didn't change fast enough and an epidemic of clogged fuel injectors was the result. Our favorite oil companies had to scramble to address the problem, and various fuel additives were introduced to loosen the gummed-up fuel injectors. One of the more effective products is Chevron's Techron.

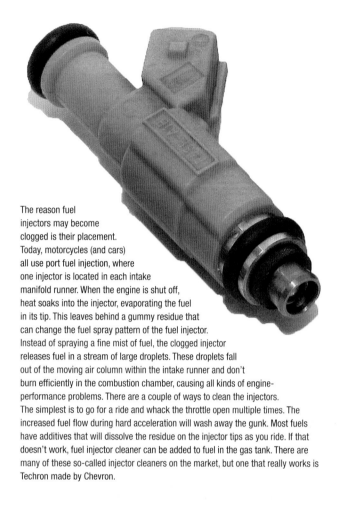

The reason fuel injectors may become clogged is their placement. Today, motorcycles (and cars) all use port fuel injection, where one injector is located in each intake manifold runner. When the engine is shut off, heat soaks into the injector, evaporating the fuel in its tip. This leaves behind a gummy residue that can change the fuel spray pattern of the fuel injector. Instead of spraying a fine mist of fuel, the clogged injector releases fuel in a stream of large droplets. These droplets fall out of the moving air column within the intake runner and don't burn efficiently in the combustion chamber, causing all kinds of engine-performance problems. There are a couple of ways to clean the injectors. The simplest is to go for a ride and whack the throttle open multiple times. The increased fuel flow during hard acceleration will wash away the gunk. Most fuels have additives that will dissolve the residue on the injector tips as you ride. If that doesn't work, fuel injector cleaner can be added to fuel in the gas tank. There are many of these so-called injector cleaners on the market, but one that really works is Techron made by Chevron.

and on intake valves and intake cylinder head ports. Does it work? Well, lots of companies think so. Toyota dealers use a Toyota-branded fuel system cleaner with a unique part number for solving a variety of drivability problems related to clogged fuel injectors and intake valves with excessive carbon buildup. On the label of the can, in fine print, it states "Contains Techron." Mercedes Benz and Volvo also use similar branded products. Chevron and Texaco fuels contain Techron, but in much lower concentrations than the bottle version. Fortunately, Techron in a bottle doesn't have to be purchased at an automotive dealer. It is widely available at auto parts stores, Wal-Mart, Kmart, Price Club, and Costco.

Because motorcycles have very small fuel tanks when compared to automobiles, some caution needs to be exercised when using Techron. A 10-ounce bottle is formulated to be added to at least 15 gallons of fuel. Obviously, a smaller amount should be used for motorcycle applications. For example, if a motorcycle's fuel tank holds 5 gallons, add just 3 ounces of Techron.

Also, don't add Techron and then let the motorcycle sit for days or weeks. There is a possibility that some rubber parts in the fuel system could be damaged. Instead, add several ounces to a tank and go for a long ride—enough to use all the fuel. If your motorcycle was running rough, and the problem was not caused by other EFI-related problems, Techron may smooth things out. Different engine designs, brands of motorcycles, and where you purchase fuel all are factors in how often (if at all) you need to use Techron. Your results may vary.

After racking up mileage, throttle bodies on EFI motorcycles can become gummed up or clogged with fuel deposits that mix with dust and dirt that make it past the air filter. A shot of carb spray and a brush is a good way to restore throttle-body performance to like new. *Battley Cycles*

CLEANING THROTTLE BODIES

Cleaning EFI throttle bodies is a maintenance item of which most owners are unaware. This consists of removing the residue from throttle plates and the insides of the throttle bores with a brush and solvent. This type of cleaning was never required on carbureted motorcycles. Here's why. With the engine running, every time the throttle opened, fuel metered by the carburetor would wash away any deposits inside the carburetor's main body and throttle plate. This built-in cleaning action kept carburetors relatively clean, and with a good quality air filter, dirt was not usually an issue.

When air enters a throttle body on an EFI system, there is no fuel mixed with it, because the fuel is injected downstream into the intake runner. Without a solvent (fuel) to keep the throttle bodies clean, they can become gunked up over time. Making this problem worse, emissions standards require that blow-by from the engine's crankcase be routed into the airbox so that the fumes can be burned by the engine instead of vented into the atmosphere. These fumes condense on the throttle plates and inside the throttle bores, forming a thin film of oil. When the engine is shut off, the plates and bores are heat soaked and the oil in the fumes is baked onto the surfaces. Over time, and many miles, it forms a black-looking crusty build-up and can limit airflow and block off air passages within the throttle body. Periodically cleaning the throttle bodies will keep an EFI system running as it should. Cleaning is easily accomplished with a soft round brush and some solvent—ironically, spray carburetor cleaner works best, and it's available at any auto parts store.

—Tracy Martin

See ya...
Tracy Martin

Appendix

Thanks to the following motorcycle dealerships and companies for help with the images and information contained in this book. Their kind assistance made this a better book both technically as well as artistically. All of these dealers and manufacturers offer great products and services for professional and do-it-your-self technicians alike. Contact information is listed for each company. Check out their websites.

DYNOJET RESEARCH

Dynojet Research supports its customers worldwide through partnerships with industry-leading companies in more than 56 countries. This ensures that local technical support for the customer is always available. This continued commitment to being a world-class supplier means the product is available worldwide and used by OEM manufacturers, importers, exhaust manufacturers, tuners, race teams, dealers, service shops, and motorcycle and ATV magazines.

Established in 1972, Dynojet is a research and development company, employing more than 100 people in Montana, Nevada, Holland, Germany, and England.

Dynojet Research develops aftermarket performance products and diagnostic tools for the motorcycle and automotive industries. Dynojet's extensive product development testing required the use of a dynamometer. Unable to find a dynamometer to meet the needs of the staff, Dynojet went to the drawing boards and pioneered the first single-roller, inertia, chassis dynamometer for motorcycles in 1989. Shortly thereafter, Dynojet developed a computer interface and software package and began selling the first Model 100 Motorcycle Chassis Dynamometer.

The Model 100 is affordable, reliable, accurate, and above all, consistent. This was the case not only from one measurement to the next, but also from one Dynojet dynamometer to another, enabling communication and sharing of test data. The success of the Model 100 led to further developments in chassis dynamometer technology.

www.dynojet.com
www.powercommander.com
800-992-4993

ZIPPER'S PERFORMANCE PRODUCTS

The year 2011 marked the 30th anniversary of Zipper's Performance Products. Zipper's was formed from a deep passion for racing Harley-Davidson motorcycles. The team developed an extensive line of products and services that propelled them to five national titles and many world records. Development of racing parts led to manufacturing new components to improve reliability, performance, and the overall riding experience for the H-D enthusiast.

Today, Zipper's offers hundreds of aftermarket components for most every rider. Zipper's offers high-quality products such as Redshift cams, ThunderMax EFI systems, and complete, pre-engineered engine kits. Zipper's Performance solutions are available through a worldwide network of dealers.

DOBECK PERFORMANCE

Dobeck Performance is a worldwide leader in research and development for electronic fuel injection controllers to increase performance and drivability across a vast assortment of powersports vehicles. Dobeck engineers its products as a tool set for others to easily configure and adjust to achieve improved all-around performance. Dobeck Performance products are designed and developed to provide an affordable solution to increasing the "fun factor" or rideability of powersports vehicles. Power and performance describes not only the industry, but Dobeck Performance as well.

www.dobeckperformance.com
877-764-3337

NONLINEAR ENGINEERING INC.

Nonlinear Engineering's mission is to provide the latest and most innovative technologies at the most affordable price. Nonlinear Engineering was established in 2002 to provide performance measurement electronics for motorcycle enthusiasts. NLE works closely with its customers to continually provide products with the best features, quality, and value. The company manufacturers the Veypor and VR2 Motorcycle Intelligence data-logging system for use on all types of powersports equipment as well as automotive applications.

www.veypor.com

GS-911 HEX CODE

Hex Code is the maker of the GS-911, a diagnostic tool for BMW motorcycles. This specialized tool consisting of an intelligent electronic interface that connects to the motorcycle's diagnostic port and works in combination with Windows software and Blackberry and Windows Mobile based phones. The cell phone interface makes the GS-911 portable for motorcycle travel. The GS-911 is available in enthusiast and professional versions. In addition, both versions use USB connectivity and both have Bluetooth as an option. The difference between the pro and enthusiasts GS-911 units is in the number of motorcycles they can connect to. The enthusiast version is limited to 10 VIN numbers. Pro can connect to an unlimited number of BMW motorcycles.

www.hexcode.co.za

Ted Porter's BeemerShop, U.S. distributor
http://www.gs911usa.com
831-438-1100

BUB ENTERPRISES

BUB Enterprises is all about performance and no one exemplifies this better than Denis "BUB" Manning, who at the age of 22 built his first streamliner. In 1970, Manning built the world record–breaking Harley-Davidson streamliner that was ridden at 265 miles per hour by the late Cal Rayborn. Manning has designed and built streamliners for Harley-Davidson, Triumph and Norton and has owned 6 of the 11 fastest motorcycles in history. In 2004 Manning and daughter-in-law, Delvene, began the International Motorcycle Speed Trials by BUB as an annual event to provide a venue for motorcycle land speed racing. In 2006, at his third annual BUB Speed Trials, Manning and the "Seven" streamliner crew recaptured the elusive title of "World's Fastest Motorcycle" with a world record speed of 350.884 miles per hour. His streamliner, piloted by Chris Carr, was also the first motorcycle to go over 350 miles per hour. Manning, with the support of the industry, has advanced the sport of motorcycle land speed racing and in October 2006,

(Continued)

(Continued)

fresh from his world record run, he was inducted into the AMA Motorcycle Hall of Fame.

BUB Enterprises manufactures high-performance exhaust systems for Harley-Davidson, Honda, Kawasaki, Suzuki, Triumph, and Yamaha in its 15,000-square-foot, state-of-the-art manufacturing facility in California. BUB is the first exhaust manufacture to produce a street legal, high-performance catalyst system for Harley-Davidson FL models. The BUB "Seven" meets California emission requirements and is EPA sound compliant.

www.bub.com
800-934-9739

TWIGG CYCLES INC.

Twigg Cycles celebrated its 75th anniversary in 2006. H. William Twigg sold his first bicycle in 1932 and established Twigg Cycles as an Indian motorcycle franchise in 1936. The family-owned-and-operated dealership has carried 42 brands since that time, including Matchless, ATS, CS, Jawa, Triumph, BSA, Ariel, Zundapp, Ducati, Benelli, American Eagle, Wizzar, and BMW. Today, Twigg sells Yamaha, Suzuki, Kawasaki, and Honda. In addition to motorcycles, Twigg carries watercraft, including Polaris and Sea-Doo.

Twigg Cycles has satisfied thousands of customers in the Maryland, Pennsylvania, and West Virginia area. Twigg Cycles provides every customer with guaranteed satisfaction and creates an environment of friendliness and superior quality for maximum enjoyment of the unique motor sports lifestyle offered by its people, products, and services.

www.twiggcycles.com
301-739-2773

BATTLEY CYCLES/BATTLEY HARLEY-DAVIDSON

Battley Cycles/Battley Harley-Davidson is the Baltimore/Washington, D.C., area's only multiline dealer representing the most storied brands in the motorcycle industry. It is the longest-serving dealer in the area for BMW and Ducati and has been a Harley-Davidson and Yamaha dealer for more than 25 years. Battley Cycles was the first Buell dealer in the world, and it still has the first production Buell RR1000 in our collection of vintage motorcycles.

Battley has been involved in all facets of motorcycle racing since the late 1970s. Battley's sponsored riders have won numerous national championships from the beginning. Its involvement in racing plus factory training has enabled its service department staff to always stay current with state-of-the-art technology in motorcycling. Whether it is building a big-inch H-D motor or blueprinting a Ducati, Battley has the expertise to make it happen. Battley has the most advanced performance tuning center in the area and is equipped with an infrared gas analyzer and Dynojet Dynamometer. The technicians are factory trained to program Dobeck Performance products, like the GEN3 controller, Dynojet's Power Commanders, and Harley-Davidson's Screamin' Eagle Pro Race Tuner.

www.battley.com
301-948-4581

bobsbmw.com

BOB'S BMW

Bob's BMW is one of the most respected BMW motorcycle dealerships in North America and the winner of several awards for overall excellence, customer satisfaction, and community service. From its convenient location near Columbia, Maryland, Bob's serves riders throughout the Washington, DC, Baltimore, and northern Virginia region.

Beyond the local level, though, Bob's is a destination of choice for BMW enthusiasts from far and wide, thanks largely to the thriving mail-order parts business that is nationally renowned as the BMW rider's prime source for parts, accessories, and apparel—and not only to owners of new models, but also to collectors of classic and vintage BMWs. There is even an on-site vintage museum at Bob's featuring rare bikes and artifacts that illustrate the complete history of BMW motorcycling.

Bob's BMW is more than just a full-service dealership in the conventional sense. There's a feeling about the place, where the special camaraderie shared among the many BMW riders who make Bob's their meeting place creates what the company calls the "BMW environment." It's what sets Bob's apart from all other BMW motorcycle dealerships.

Bob's BMW Motorcycles
10720 Guilford Road
Jessup MD 20794-9385
www.bobsbmw.com
301-497-8949

HARLEY-DAVIDSON OF FREDERICK

Harley-Davidson of Frederick is a full-service Harley-Davidson and Buell dealership. The Harley-Davidson–certified service department has services that include Quick bay services while you wait, Maryland state inspections on all brands, Dyno test station for all brands, and the area's most highly trained and certified technicians. In addition, the company offers a full-service, high-performance and customer-fabrication machine shop featuring state-of-the-art equipment and a talented crew of dedicated professionals.

Harley-Davidson of Frederick has a huge selection of MotorClothes and collectibles, as well as parts and accessories to personalize your ride. Harley-Davidson of Frederick has recently started converting two-wheeled motorcycles to trikes and services them as well.

No matter what your motorcycling needs, chances Harley-Davidson of Frederick can help. The team is dedicated not only to exceeding the highest standards of professionalism and technical achievement but to unparalleled customer service as well.

www.hdoffrederick.com
301-694-8177

Motorcycle Consumer NEWS

MOTORCYCLE CONSUMER NEWS

Motorcycle Consumer News is the monthly consumer resource for unbiased reviews of motorcycles and related aftermarket products and services. Combined with in-depth technical features and top-notch investigative reporting, it is considered "The Bible" for serious motorcycle enthusiasts. Unlike other powersports publications, *MCN* has no advertising and relies only on reader subscriptions as its source of income. This allows them unprecedented editorial freedom to write the "truth" regarding how well a product or service really works—or doesn't. If you want to know what brand of jacket, gloves, riding pants, bike cleaning products, electronics, tires, helmets, and a host of other motorcycle-related products are best and how they compare to the competition, this is the magazine that is unafraid to tell it like it is.

(Continued)

(Continued)

In-depth reviews for new motorcycles let readers know before they buy what they're getting for their money. Columns on "Mental Motorcycling" and motorcycle design trends make for interesting and informative reading. A quarterly "Used Bike Value Guide" can make purchasing a second-hand motorcycle a more enjoyable experience. The monthly column "Proficient Motorcycling" provides readers with valuable riding skills tip and techniques. Bulletins regarding factory recalls and letters from manufacturers and readers all add value for motorcyclists.

www.mcnews.com
888-333-0354
Contact: editor@mcnews.com

ROADBIKE

RoadBike is a uniquely positioned magazine that provides street-motorcycle enthusiasts all the news they need to stay informed. It offers the entertainment and enthusiasm that defines an enthusiast's lifestyle. Catering to real-world riders of all brands, every issue of *RoadBike* features reviews of new bikes and products, tech and how-to articles, breaking news, useful information, personality profiles, tours, and event coverage. Its also features stories on riding clubs, motorcycle-based organizations, and custom bikes from mild to wild.

The diverse staff of riders and writers provides a wide range of perspective and experience presented in a practical, user-friendly package featuring top-notch photography and state-of-the-art graphics with sensible copy. This is a real-world magazine for the real-world motorcyclist.

www.roadbikemag.com
877-693-3577

AMERICAN IRON MAGAZINE

American Iron Magazine is a Stamford, Connecticut-based American motorcycle magazine specializing in the coverage of American-made motorcycles, including Harley-Davidson, Indian, and Big Dog. *American Iron Magazine* (or *AIM*) features columns by editor-in-chief Buzz Kanter, editor Chris Maida, and motorcyclists Genevieve Schmitt and Stephanie Feld, as well as standard tech articles by writers Donny Peterson, Tom Johnson, and Tracy Martin. Typical articles include how-to stories on motorcycle repairs and maintenance, classic bikes, custom builds, motorcycle reviews, motorcycle product/accessory reviews, events, the Hog Helpline for tech questions, and recommendations on routes for motorcycle enthusiasts.

www.aimag.com
877-693-3577

VINTAGE JAPANESE MOTORCYCLE CLUB

Founded in 1977, the Vintage Japanese Motorcycle Club (VJMC) is the premier worldwide club dedicated to the preservation, restoration, and enjoyment of vintage Japanese motorcycles (20 years old or older) and the promotion of the sport of motorcycling. Thousands of members enjoy the many benefits offered by the VJMC, including a bi-monthly magazine dedicated to vintage motorcycling. One of the most highly regarded vintage motorcycle publications in the world, the VJMC magazine includes stories related to vintage bikes and the people who ride them, technical and restoration tips, coverage of bike shows, rallies, and local events, and classified ads. The club also offers members-only content on its web site, including recent classifieds, tech tips and articles, free digital back-issues of the magazine, an extensive members' bike photo archive, video clips and slide shows, a VJMC regalia store, and registration information for various VJMC events.

www.vjmc.org

TURBO MOTORCYCLE
INTERNATIONAL OWNERS ASSOCIATION

Though originally founded in 1987 as a Honda CX Turbo owners club and expanded in 1991 to include all factory Turbo bikes, the Turbo Motorcycle International Owners Association is dedicated to the preservation of all turbocharged motorcycles. Since 1987, the association has collected and disseminated information and material of particular interest and assistance to Turbo motorcycle owners through *Turbo News*, a quarterly newsletter.

In 1996 a web site was added. Then in 2002, the web site was completely re-engineered, allowing TMIOA members and enthusiasts the world over to access the latest club information instantly, as well as exchange opinions on the forum. In 2003, *Turbo News* ceased publication after 51 issues, mainly due to the web site's popularity and with it paid membership in the club ceased.

Today, the TMIOA serves as a worldwide resource for Turbo owners by maintaining the web site, hosting Turbo rallies, and offering *Turbo News* back issues and factory Turbo service manuals on CD-rom, action-packed Turbo videos and Turbo troubleshooting guides on DVDs, and club T-shirts. There is no paid staff (there never was), only volunteers giving their time, expertise, and knowledge with the goal of sharing the joys of turbocharged motorcycles.

There are active Turbo clubs in Germany, Holland, Norway, Australia, Japan, and the United Kingdom. The links are on the club's web site.

www.turbomotorcycles.org

ROB'S DYNO SERVICE

Are you curious what you have for horsepower? Don't understand why those new exhaust pipes, cams and/or filters aren't really increasing your performance the way you thought they would? In about half an hour, your motorcycle can be mounted and ready for dyno testing at Rob's Dyno Service. Each run takes less than five minutes to complete and allows plenty of time for between-run engine tuning. "Putting your motorcycle on the dynamometer can give you the baseline stats for your bike and provide direction towards needed adjustments to get all the components of your bike working together," says Robert Swartz, owner/operator of Rob's Dyno Service. Rob uses Dynojet's 250i Dynamometer, a performance diagnostic tool that is used to accurately and simultaneously measure rear wheel horsepower, torque, speed, RPM and air/fuel ratio of any motorcycle. It can accurately test from as little as five horsepower to as much as 500 horsepower. Rob's Dyno Service can dyno-test all brands of motorcycles and is specifically certified for the following manufactures: Victory, Kawasaki, and S&S VFI. Rob's was the first portable load cell dyno Power Commander tune center for Dynojet and S&S VFI tune center in the Northeast. Each year Rob's Dyno Service attends motorcycle and motorsport events in the New England area. Check out the website for a schedule or appearances or for more detailed information about the company's capabilities. Contact Rob for an appointment at one of these events or to schedule his services at your gathering or garage.

Rob's Dyno Service, Gardner, MA
978-895-0441
www.robsdyno.com.

Index